Decolonizing the University, Knowledge Systems and Disciplines in Africa

Recent Titles in the
CAROLINA ACADEMIC PRESS
AFRICAN WORLD SERIES
Toyin Falola, Series Editor

Africa, Empire and Globalization: Essays in Honor of A. G. Hopkins
Edited by Toyin Falola and Emily Brownell

Authority Stealing: Anti-Corruption War and Democratic Politics in Post-Military Nigeria
Wale Adebanwi

The Bukusu of Kenya: Folktales, Culture and Social Identities
Namulundah Florence

Contemporary African Literature: New Approaches
Tanure Ojaide

Contesting Islam in Africa
Abdulai Iddrisu

Converging Identities: Blackness in the Modern African Diaspora
Edited by Julius O. Adekunle and Hettie V. Williams

Decolonizing the University, Knowledge Systems and Disciplines in Africa
Edited by Sabelo J. Ndlovu-Gatsheni and Siphamandla Zondi

Democracy in Africa
Edited by Saliba Sarsar and Julius O. Adekunle

Diaspora and Imagined Nationality
Koleade Odutola

Èṣù: Yoruba God, Power, and the Imaginative Frontiers
Edited by Toyin Falola

Ethnicities, Nationalities, and Cross-Cultural Representations in Africa and the Diaspora
Edited by Gloria Chuku

Gendering African Social Spaces: Women, Power, and Cultural Expressions
Toyin Falola and Wanjala S. Nasong'o

Ghana During the First World War: The Colonial Administration of Sir Hugh Clifford
Elizabeth Wrangham

Globalization and the African Experience
Edited by Emmanuel M. Mbah and Steven J. Salm

Globalization: The Politics of Global Economic Relations and International Business
N. Oluwafemi Mimiko

A History of Class Formation in the Plateau Province of Nigeria, 1902–1960
Monday Yakiban Mangvwat

Horror in Paradise
Edited by Christopher LaMonica and J. Shola Omotola

Ifá in Yorùbá Thought System
Omotade Adegbindin

Imperialism, Economic Development and Social Change in West Africa
Raymond Dumett

In Search of African Diasporas: Testimonies and Encounters
Paul Tiyambe Zeleza

The Indigenous African Criminal Justice System for the Modern World
Olusina Akeredolu

Intercourse and Crosscurrents in the Atlantic World: Calabar-British Experience
David Lishilinimle Imbua

Julius Nyerere, Africa's Titan on a Global Stage: Perspectives from Arusha to Obama
Edited by Ali A. Mazrui and Lindah L. Mhando

Life Not Worth Living
Chima J. Korieh

Local Government in South Africa Since 1994
Alexius Amtaika

The Muse of Anomy: Essays on Literature and the Humanities in Nigeria
Femi Osofisan

Narratives of Struggle
John Ayotunde Bewaji

Pan-Africanism in Ghana: African Socialism, Neoliberalism, and Globalization
Justin Williams

Perspectives on Feminism from Africa
Edited by 'Lai Olurode

Satires of Power in Yoruba Visual Culture
Yomi Ola

The United States' Foreign Policy in Africa in the 21st Century
Edited by Adebayo Oyebade

The Vile Trade: Slavery and the Slave Trade in Africa
Edited by Abi Alabo Derefaka, Wole Ogundele, Akin Alao, and Augustus Babajide

The Women's War of 1929: A History of Anti-Colonial Resistance in Eastern Nigeria
Edited by Toyin Falola and Adam Paddock

The Yoruba Frontier
Aribidesi Usman

Women, Gender, and Sexualities in Africa
Edited by Toyin Falola and Nana Akua Amponsah

Decolonizing the University, Knowledge Systems and Disciplines in Africa

Edited by

Sabelo J. Ndlovu-Gatsheni

Siphamandla Zondi

CAROLINA ACADEMIC PRESS

Durham, North Carolina

Library of Congress Cataloging-in-Publication Data

Names: Ndlovu-Gatsheni, Sabelo J., editor. | Zondi, Siphamandla, editor.
Title: Decolonizing the university, knowledge systems and disciplines in
  Africa / edited by Sabelo J. Ndlovu-Gatsheni and Siphamandla Zondi.
Description: Durham : Carolina Academic Press, 2016. | Series: African World
  Series | Includes bibliographical references and index.
Identifiers: LCCN 2015050802 | ISBN 9781611638332 (alk. paper)
Subjects: LCSH: Education, Higher--Social aspects--Africa. |
  Decolonization--Africa. | Racism in higher education--Africa. | Knowledge,
  Theory of--Africa. | Eurocentrism--Africa.
Classification: LCC LC191.98.A35 D43 2016 | DDC 378.6--dc23
LC record available at http://lccn.loc.gov/2015050802

CAROLINA ACADEMIC PRESS, LLC
700 Kent Street
Durham, North Carolina 27701
Telephone (919) 489-7486
Fax (919) 493-5668
www.cap-press.com

Printed in the United States of America

Contents

Part II
Decoloniality, Disciplines, and Ideology

Part III
Methods, Methodology, and Subjectivity

Series Editor's Foreword

The *Carolina Academic Press African World Series*, inaugurated in 2010, offers significant new works in the field of African and Black World studies. The series provides scholarly and educational texts that can serve both as reference works and as readers in college classes.

Studies in the series are anchored in the existing humanistic and the social scientific traditions. Their goal, however, is the identification and elaboration of the strategic place of Africa and its Diaspora in a shifting global world. More specifically, the studies will address gaps and larger needs in the developing scholarship on Africa and the Black World.

The series intends to fill gaps in areas such as African politics, history, law, religion, culture, sociology, literature, philosophy, visual arts, art history, geography, language, health, and social welfare. Given the complex nature of Africa and its Diaspora, and the constantly shifting perspectives prompted by globalization, the series also meets a vital need for scholarship connecting knowledge with events and practices. Reflecting the fact that life in Africa continues to change, especially in the political arena, the series explores issues emanating from racial and ethnic identities, particularly those connected with the ongoing mobilization of ethnic minorities for inclusion and representation.

Toyin Falola
University of Texas at Austin

Notes on Contributors

Sabelo J. Ndlovu-Gatsheni is Professor and Head of Archie Mafeje Research Institute for Applied Social Policy (AMRI) based at the University of South Africa (UNISA). He is also the founder and coordinator of the Africa Decolonial Research Network (ADERN) based in at the University of South Africa. He is a decolonial theorist who has published extensively in African history, African politics, and development. His major publications include *The Ndebele Nation: Reflections on Hegemony, Memory and Historiography* (Amsterdam & Pretoria: Rosenberg Publishers & UNISA Press, 2009); *Do 'Zimbabweans' Exist? Trajectories of Nationalism, National Identity Formation and Crisis in a Postcolonial State* (Oxford & Bern: Peter Lang International Academic Publishers, 2009); *Redemptive or Grotesque Nationalism? Rethinking Contemporary Politics in Zimbabwe* (Oxford & Bern: Peter Lang International Academic Publishers, 2011); *Empire, Global Coloniality and African Subjectivity* (New York & Oxford: Berghahn Books, June 2013); *Coloniality of Power in Postcolonial Africa: Myths of Decolonization* (Dakar: CODESRIA, 2013); *Nationalism and National Projects in Southern Africa: New Critical Reflections* (Pretoria: Africa Institute of South Africa, 2013); *Bondage of Boundaries and Identity Politics in Postcolonial Africa: The 'Northern Problem' and Ethno-Futures* (Pretoria: Africa Institute of South Africa, 2013); *Mugabeism? History, Politics and Power in Zimbabwe* (New York: Palgrave Macmillan, August 2015); *The Decolonial Mandela: Peace, Justice and Politics of Life* (New York and Oxford: Berghahn Books, forthcoming) He is the Editor-In-Chief of the *Africa Insight* published by Africa Institute of South Africa (AISA) and the Human Sciences Research Council (HSRC) in South Africa and Deputy Editor of the *International Journal of African Renaissance Studies* published by the University of South Africa Press and Francis and Taylor.

Siphamandla Zondi researches Africa's international relations with an interest in promoting African renaissance in a world that must decolonise. His recent publications cover issues of African agency in international diplomacy, peace diplomacy in Madagascar and Zimbabwe, SA's Ubuntu diplomacy and NATO's imperial designs over Libya. He is the executive director of the Institute for Global Dialogue, a Unisa-associated foreign policy think tank based in Pretoria. Zondi teaches African renaissance at Thabo Mbeki African Leadership Institute and Africa and international organisations at University of Johannesburg, while he also guides MA and PhD students at the Universities of North-West and Kwazulu-Natal. He completed his undergraduate studies at University of Durban-Westville in South Africa and his MPhil and PhD at Cambridge University, UK.

Skype: siphamandlazondi. E-mail. s.zondi@icloud.com.

Tendayi Sithole is Associate Professor for African Politics at the University of South Africa. He holds a doctorate in African Politics and his research focused on the political thought of Achille Mbembe. His research interests are black radical thought, decoloniality, Africana existential phenomenology, and Black Consciousness. He is completing a book on the meditations of Steve Biko.

Serges Djoyou Kamga is Associate Professor at the Thabo Mbeki African Leadership Institute (TMALI), UNISA. He is a member of the 'building committee' of the Cross-Cultural Human Rights Centre, a consortium of ten Chinese and four African universities aimed at bringing Southern concepts and ideas in the area of human rights to Northern audiences. His areas of interest include the African renaissance, good governance, the African human rights system, development and human rights, socio-economic rights, disability rights, gender justice as well as well human rights from a cross-cultural perspective. He publishes in these areas. Professor Kamga holds an LLD from the Centre for Human Rights, University of Pretoria.

Teboho J. Lebakeng obtained his doctorate degree from the University of Limpopo, South Africa; MA in Sociology from the University of Dar es Salaam, Tanzania; MS in Human Service Management at Springfield College, USA; and BA in Sociology from the American University in Cairo, Egypt. Dr Lebakeng has published numerous academic and popular articles in journals, newspapers and book chapters. Although currently with the South African Permanent Mission to the United Nations in New York, Dr. Lebakeng continues to contribute scholarly and popular works, especially on the impact of epistemicide and valuecide on education in general and the social sciences and humanities in particular.

Nontyatyambo Pearl Dastile is a Senior Lecturer in the Department of Criminology and Security Sciences at the University of South Africa. Her research interests include female criminality, gender and crime, decolonial school of thought and African centred paradigms.

Fidelis Allen is Associate Professor and Acting Director of University of Port Harcourt Centre for Ethnic and Conflict Studies. He has published fairly well in local and international journals. Allen is the author of Implementation of Oil-Related Environmental Policy in Nigeria: Government Inertia and Conflict in the Niger Delta (Cambridge Scholars Publishing London).

Nokuthula Hlabangane was awarded a PhD in Anthropology in 2012 by the University of the Witwatersrand, South Africa. Her doctoral thesis is titled "The political economy of teenage sexuality in the time of HIV/AIDS: The case of Soweto, South Africa." Her research interests include Knowledge and power, sexuality, gender and reproductive health, religion and ritual, urbanization, violence and transition, and anthropology of community. So far, her research interests have directed her towards home—she chooses to be a student in her own community—the reasons have been both ideological and practical. Her ethics are about redress and restoration and as such she has a vested interest in decolonizing Anthropology by painting pictures of strength and resilience where others have left bleak images of savagery and inferiority. Her research practices shy away from delving into cultural pluralism, a fascination with the thick description of the mundane-made-exotic. Rather, she attempts to interpret micro-practices through macro-systems. She is aware of meditations that speak to "African anthropologies" as her thinking is informed by decolonial meditations that places a responsibility for African(ist) intellectuals to see Africa from within. She also gravitates towards inter/a-disciplinarity in her thinking and research. Hlabangane teaches at the University of South Africa.

Morgan Ndlovu is a lecturer in the Department of Development Studies at the University of South Africa. He holds a PhD in Social Anthropology from Monash University (Australia), an MSc in Social Research Methods from Sussex University (United Kingdom) and an MA from the University of the Witwatersrand (South Africa). He has published a number of journal articles and book chapters on identity, culture and development in Africa. He is currently editing book entitled: "Simulating Identity in the Age of Modernity/Coloniality in South Africa."

Zodwa Radebe holds a BA (Hons) and MA in anthropology, both from Wits University. She is a PhD candidate in the department of anthropology at UNISA, her thesis focusing on informal economy. She teaches at UNISA in the department of Anthropology and Archaeology. She is an artist, an activist and a decolonial scholar that is imagining a different world. Her contributions are through storytelling performances and scholarly work.

William Mpofu holds a Masters in Communication Science. His research interests are in Political Communication, African Literature, Semiotics and Philosophy of Liberation. He is presently a researcher at the Unisa College of Human Sciences, reading for a PhD in the Philosophy of Liberation.

Puleng Segalo is Associate Professor in Social and Community Psychology at University of South Africa. She holds a Masters and PhD in psychology from City University of New York. He areas of specialization include Community Psychology, Social Psychology and Gender and Feminism in Psychology. Her research work and publications cover a wide range of areas including gendered experiences of women in various aspects of life, Critical Participatory Research Practices and Knowledge Production, Power and Decoloniality. Professor Segalo has won several performance awards, the latest being Young Woman Scientist Award won in 2014.

Decolonizing the University, Knowledge Systems and Disciplines in Africa

Chapter 1

Introduction:
The Coloniality of Knowledge:
Between Troubled Histories and
Uncertain Futures

Sabelo J. Ndlovu-Gatsheni and Siphamandla Zondi

If we all agree that we need a reinvigorated humanities and social sciences, we would be remiss in not acknowledging, debating and encouraging critical scholarship on how exactly colonialism, settler colonialism and apartheid have shaped the modern university in Africa—its core concepts, its rituals, its conceptions of autonomy, its disciplines and intellectual traditions, its lingua franca, and the knowledge it produced and continues to produce and transit.

—Suren Pillay (*Supplement to the Mail & Guardian*, 7–13 June 2013)

Introduction

Cognitive justice dominates the current decolonial discourses. At the centre of the demand for cognitive justice is the problem of epistemicides and colonization of the minds. As such, 'decolonizing' the university, epistemology and disciplines becomes part of the longstanding demand and struggle for exorcizing 'the Hitler' inside us.[1] This 'Hitler' is a symbol of racism and genocide. Racism, genocides, epistemicides, and linguicides are a central leitmotif of coloniality. Coloniality is a global power structure that continues to reproduce Eurocentrism in society and academy long after the dismantling of the 'physical empire.'[2]

In South Africa, the student movements rocking the country's universities have attacked coloniality from the vantage point of the 'Rhodes Must Fall' decolonial discourse. Just like Adolf Hitler, Cecil John Rhodes is another symbol of racism and genocide. Racism is at the heart of 'imperial reason' that left black people out in the cold, to use Lewis R. Gordon's terminology.[3] The current Westernized university becomes a legitimate site of decolonial struggles because it continues to reproduce coloniality.

The geopolitical locus of the writing of this book is South Africa — a country that was not only imagined by imperialists and colonialists as the 'little Europe of Africa' but that became the last outpost of the empire, and is today facing student uprisings unprecedented since the Soweto Student Uprising of 1976. The original epicenter of the student uprising has been the University of Cape Town (UCT) — a premier institution of higher education that has been struggling to transform itself from white domination to an inclusive one.[4] The immediate spark to the student uprising has been the presence of the statue of Cecil John Rhodes — an imperial colonial ideologue who wanted to colonize Africa from Cape in the South to Cairo in the North.

It would seem the demands by the students for the removal of the statue was not about the statue per se. Rhodes' stature was correctly interpreted as a symbol of the 'metaphysical empire' that has outlived the 'physical empire.'[5] This correct diagnosis of the neo-apartheid South African problem that is captured in the epigraph by Suren Pillay, produced a student formation known as the Rhodes Must Fall Movement (RMF), which demanded 'decolonization' of UCT. By 'decolonizing' the university, students meant among others structural changes: curriculum change; epistemological paradigm shift from Eurocentric knowledge to Africa-centred knowledge; and a change of university cultures and systems that are alienating as well as increased and affordable access to education in general.

Inevitably, what began as the Rhodes Must Fall Movement grew into such other movements as the Open Stellenbosch Collective (OSC) in the predominantly white Stellenbosch University; Black Student Movement (BSM) at Rhodes University — an institution carrying the name of Rhodes; Transform Wits at the University of the Witwatersrand; Black Thought UJ at the University of Johannesburg and many others. At the University of South Africa (UNISA), Africa Decolonial Research Network (ADERN) has been in existence since 2011 and an Annual International Summer School on Decolonizing Power, Knowledge and Identity has been organized and hosted by UNISA since 2013.[6] The discourse framing and informing the student movements is that of decolonization as an essential pre-requisite for genuine democratization and respect for human rights. This current decolonization movement pushed forward by students is privileging the need for cognitive justice in a continent that has experienced six forms of 'dismemberment' and is demanding 're-membering' to borrow terms from Ngugi wa Thiong'o.[7] These dismemberment processes can be summarized this way:

a. *Foundational dismemberment* involving the questioning of the very humanity of black people so as to push them out of the human family. This foundational dismemberment has been described by Nelson Maldonado-Torres as 'coloniality of being.'[8]

b. *Enslavement,* which resulted not only in commodification of black people but also in fragmentation of African personhood into two halves: continental and Diaspora.[9]

c. *Berlin Conference of 1884–5,* which literally fragmented and reconstituted Africa into British, French, Portuguese, German, Belgian and Spanish Africa.[10]

d. *Denial of African history,* which unfolded in terms of what I term a Hegelian-Conradian-Hugh Trevor-Ropian discourse that emphasized 'darkness' and 'emptiness' of Africa.[11]

e. *Postcolonial dismemberment* taking the form of reproduction of coloniality by African elites who inherited the colonial state and continued to practise primitive accumulation and reducing ordinary people into subjects.[12]

f. *Patriarchy* that continues to dismember women from power, knowledge, being and citizenship.[13]

At the base of all these forms of 'dismemberment' have been the following technologies of 'dismemberment': genocide (killing of colonized peoples), epistemicides (killing and expropriations of knowledges of the colonized) and linguicides (killing of languages and cultures of the colonized).[14] This background is very important for any deep appreciation of the importance and intellectual interventions of this book—a timely contribution that addresses broader question of decolonizing the university, epistemology and disciplines as demanded by the student movements rocking South Africa today.

This book is about the inextricable connections among power, epistemology, methodology and even ideology. These variables are at the centre of the crisis of knowledge in current intellectual thought which is provoking new questions about the role of knowledge in society as well as possibilities of epistemological decolonization. The book is written at a time that Immanuel Wallerstein understood as dominated by 'uncertainties of knowledge';[15] Lewis R. Gordon conceptualized it as characterized by 'disciplinary decadence';[16] and Patrick

Chabal articulated it as marked by 'the end conceit.'[17] It is a time that the celebrated Slovenian philosopher Slavoj Zizek described as 'living in the end times,' symbolized by the worldwide ecological crisis, the global financial crisis, the biogenetic revolution, and exploding social divisions and raptures.[18] This reality led Wallerstein in *The End of the World as We Know It: Social Science for the Twenty-First Century* to argue that:

> I believe we are in the midst of wandering through dark woods and have insufficient clarity about where we should be heading. I believe we need urgently to discuss this together, and that this discussion must be truly worldwide. I believe furthermore that this discussion is not one in which we can separate knowledge, morality, and politics into separate corners. [...] We are engaged in a singular debate, a difficult one. But we shall not resolve the issues by avoiding them.[19]

The crisis is historically and philosophically traceable to the rise of that modern world system which came into being in 1492. At the centre of the unfolding of the modern world system was modernity, which enabled the processes of colonization of time, space, being, knowledge and even nature as Europe engaged in usurpation of world history. During the unfolding of modernity and the rise of the world capitalist system, 'theo-politics of knowledge' became replaced by 'ego-politics of knowledge' following Rene Descartes' introduction of 'cogito.'[20] The rise of the modern world system accompanied by capitalist economic logic resulted in a new conception of the relationship between nature and humanity as well as body and mind.

Under 'theo-politics of knowledge,' nature and humanity were on par and enjoyed mutual respect. But with the rise of capitalist logic, nature became understood as a natural resource available for exploitation and overcoming by human beings. The human mind was understood as the source of scientific thought and producer of universal truths. Geo- and biography were erased as a source of knowledge as the Cartesian subjects (exclusively understood as Western white men specifically) assumed the attributes of the Christian God, as they articulated Europe as the centre of the world and as they engaged in philosophical meditations that claimed universal resonance. This thinking informed the rise of Euro-North American epistemology, 'in which the epistemic subject has no sexuality, gender, ethnicity, race, class, spirituality, language, or epistemic location within power relations, and a subject that produces truth from an interior monologue with himself without anyone outside him.'[21]

Here was born what Ramon Grosfoguel termed 'a deaf philosophy, a philosophy without a face, which feels no gravity. This faceless subject floats through the sky without being determined by anything or anyone.'[22] Here was born the Cartesian subject as an imperial being who combined the ideas of 'cogito ergo sum' (I think, therefore I am) with the earlier notions of 'ergo conquiro' (I conquer, therefore I am) to engage in slave trade, imperialism, colonialism and apartheid.[23] Here was born Eurocentrism and scientism. Wallerstein defined 'scientism' in this way:

> By scientism, I mean the claim that science is disinterested and extra-social, that its truth claims are self-sustaining without reference to more general philosophical assertions, and that science represents the only legitimate mode of knowledge.[24]

This 'scientism' was said to be the preserve of modern subjects (Cartesian subjects). Such modern subjectivity was claimed by Europe and later North America as producers of progressive scientific ideas. Whatever idea they produced was articulated as disembodied, un-situated, objective, truthful and universal.[25] The subject that spoke totally assumed a 'God-eye view' of the world.[26] Indeed a Euro-North American 'conceit' was being constructed which had far reaching consequences for the non-Western world in general and Africa in particular. This conceit gave birth to Eurocentrism, which is well articulated by James M. Blaut in his *The Colonizer's Model of the World: Geographical Diffusionism and Eurocentric History* and by Samir Amin in *Eurocentrism: Modernity, Religion and Democracy: A Critique of Eurocentrism and Culturalism.*[27]

Eurocentrism assumed the form of a theory of world history underpinned by a bundle of prejudices, Euro-North American-ethnocentrism, ignorance and mistrust of non-Western people, chauvinism and xenophobia.[28] Despite the existence of strong archeological evidence that indicated to Africa as the cradle of mankind, Eurocentrism as a discourse continued to articulate a Western-centric idea of human history and progress from the Greek-Roman classical world to Christian feudalism, to the current European-centric global capitalism. It is this Eurocentric narration of history that silenced Africa, which provoked such scholars as Cheikh Anta Diop to write such works as *African Origins of Civilization: Myths and Reality* and *Civilization or Barbarism: An Authentic Anthropology.*[29] Such Africa-centred interventions opened the way for the rise of Afrocentricity and Afrikology as intellectual initiatives that try to restore African people's ontological density and claim their rightful place in world history.[30]

A combination of critiques from epistemologies from the Global South, contradictions reverberating within Euro-American modernity, 'critiques of modernity from within modernity' taking the form of Marxism, postmodernism, and post-structuralism as well as postcolonialism, and exhaustion of Euro-North American epistemologies have resulted in the modern world system falling into a deep epistemological crisis. It is haunted by crisis of epistemology, crisis of methodology, crisis of legitimacy, and crisis of ideology. This is why one finds such philosophers as Francois Chatelet openly railing against methodology: 'Methodology, I have to admit, is starting to bug the shit out of me. The whole enterprise of research and furthering knowledge is ruined by the imperialism of methodology.'[31] This is why one finds such decolonial philosophical thinkers as Lewis R. Gordon working consistently in revealing epistemological colonization 'lurking even at the heart of method.'[32]

Even the leading French theorist Michel Foucault mediated on the coming epistemological crisis, which he articulated in terms of an 'epistemic break.'[33] It refers to a historical rupture which occurs when one epistemic system breaks down and another begins to take its place.[34] As a concept, epistemic break captures a situation that the Italian theoretician Antonio Gramsci termed an interregnum. Gramsci articulated interregnum as arising from crisis of hegemony. This how he put it:

> If the ruling class has lost its consensus, i.e. is no longer 'leading' but only 'dominant,' exercising coercive force alone, this means precisely that the great masses have become detached from their traditional ideologies, and no longer believe, what they use to believe previously [...]. The crisis consists precisely in the fact that the old is dying and the new cannot be born; in this interregnum a great variety of morbid symptoms appear.[35]

Epistemologically speaking, the modern world is at a crossroads, dominating rather than leading in the domain of knowledges. The Euro-North American epistemology that underpinned the imperial and colonial processes of usurpation of world history by Europe and North America and which succeeded in appropriating and displacing other knowledges is now facing its deepest epistemic crisis. The crisis is manifesting itself in modernity producing numerous modern problems to which it is not in a position to provide modern solutions.[36] That Euromodernity was destined to be devoured by its own contradictions was foreseen by leading decolonial thinker Aime Cesaire as far back as 1955 when he wrote that:

> A civilization that proves incapable of solving the problems it creates is a decadent civilization. A civilization that chooses to close its eyes to its most crucial problems is a stricken civilization. A civilization that uses its principles for trickery and deceit is a dying civilization. The fact is that the so-called European civilization—'Western' civilization—as it has been shaped by two centuries of bourgeois rule,

is incapable of solving the two major problems to which its existence has given rise: the problem of the proletariat and the colonial problem; that Europe is unable to justify itself before the bar of 'reason' or before the bar of 'conscience,' and that, increasingly, it takes refuge in a hypocrisy which is all the more odious because it is less likely to deceive. *Europe is indefensible* […]. What is serious is that 'Europe' is morally, spiritually indefensible. And today the indictment is brought against it not by the European masses alone, but on a world scale, by tens and tens of millions of men [and women] who, from the depth of slavery, set themselves up as judges.[37]

The crisis is compounded by the fact that the exhausted Euro-North American epistemology is refusing to open up for other intellectual traditions and epistemologies. The current book is specifically about the global epistemic crisis which has been deepening in Africa in particular since the time of colonial encounters. The colonial encounters that date back to the fifteenth century inaugurated what Grosfoguel has described as the racially hierarchized, patriarchal, hetero-normative, Christian-centric, Euro-North-American-centric, capitalist, imperial, colonial, and modern world system.[38]

The decolonial school of thinkers involves many who are actively seeking an alternative to decadent civilization and the poverty and violence-generating world system it created, alternatives that cannot be found within Eurocentrism. They are pursuing what the Puerto Rican critic Ramon Grosfoguel calls 'a horizontal, liberatory dialogue as opposed to a vertical, Western monologue,' which 'requires the decolonization of global power relations.'[39] Such a liberatory dialogue is premised on imagination of a new world system and a new international order that is beyond the dilemma of current Euro-North American as well as third world fundamentalisms. It calls for what the Asian scholar Kuan-Hsing Chen called 'decolonization, deimperialization and de-cold war.'[40] Decolonization has to deal with impositions of cultures, psyches and epistemologies, whereas deimperialization addresses Euro-American 'imperialist histories and the harmful impact those histories have had on the world.'[41] Deimperialization is further elaborated on by Stephen Ellis in his inaugural lecture accepting the position of VU University Amsterdam Desmond Tutu Chair on Youth, Sports and Reconciliation, entitled 'South Africa and the Decolonization of the Mind':

> By the same token, we Europeans must do something similar for ourselves. We too still live with a myth that was generated by the experience of world domination, namely that every society must sooner or later follow the Western path of development if it is truly to reach

the modern age. The rise of Asia, including by its acceptance of intellectual cosmopolitanism, implies that ideas of Asia and African
provenance not only have their own validity, but also have the potential to become relevant to Europe. […]. If we Europeans are to understand the world now emerging, it is in our own interest to accept
that not all of the ideas that we have distilled from a reading of our
own history are signboards to be passed by all mankind on its journey
into the future. We will have to judge the histories of countries outside
Europe partly by criteria derived from their own readings of their past.
Further, we may even have to review aspects of our own history in
that light. […]. In the case of South Africa, we will be able to con-
ceive of its current state and future prospects in ways that are not determined by a failure to be like us. […]. This is not a call for us to
abandon our most cherished ideas in a spirit of despair, for example
in regard to human rights and basic liberties, but rather to reinvigorate
them by paying far more attention to data drawn from outside Europe
than we have done, and by respecting the authority of thinkers in other
traditions. Increasingly, we have to appreciate the ways others see the
world, not only for purposes of comparison and insight, but simply
to understand how the world has become what it is. We should cease
believing almost instinctively that ideas emanating from Africa must
be wrong, since our underlying assumption is that they are destined
to be replaced with ideas made in Europe. This will break the habit
of decades, even centuries. *We Europeans, too, have to decolonize
our minds* [emphasis is mine].[42]

Deimperialization is therefore a process through which Europeans decolonize
their minds. It must happen simultaneously with the decolonization of African
minds. Taken together, these simultaneous processes provide a way of navigating and dealing with troubled histories and uncertain futures. Decolonization
of African minds should not be taken to mean rejection of the troubled past
but, as suggested by Suren Pillay, 'acknowledging, debating and encouraging
critical scholarship on how exactly colonialism, settler colonialism and
apartheid have shaped the modern university in Africa—its core concepts, its
rituals, its conceptions of autonomy, its disciplines and intellectual traditions,
its lingua franca, and the knowledge it has produced and continues to produce
and transmit.'[43] In short, the beginning of decolonization of African minds is
the understanding of coloniality and its invisible colonial matrices of power.
Decolonization cannot work without deimperialization. Without deimperialization, decolonization becomes a myth.[44] Deimperialization becomes a form

of voluntary 'disclosures' that were called for by Albert Memmi in 1957 when he wrote that:

> The disclosures having been made, the cruelty of the truth having been admitted, the relationship of Europe with her former colonies must be reconsidered. Having abandoned the colonial framework, it is important for all of us to discover a new way of living with that relationship.[45]

While decolonization entailed abandonment of epistemological colonization, deimperialization gestures towards abandonment of the colonial framework as well as Europeans learning to be 'humble about [their] knowledge claims' as part of deimperialization of theory, methodology and epistemology.[46] As emphasized by Chen:

> Dialectical interactions between these two processes [decolonization and deimperialization] is a precondition for reconciliation between the colonizer and the colonised, and only after such a reconciliation has been accomplished will it be possible for both groups to move together towards global democracy.[47]

Nowhere is the need for decolonization and deimperialization more urgent than in Africa.[48] Africa's need for decolonization of the territory, the body, the mind and the epistemology has been articulated at length elsewhere.[49] The stark reality is that despite achievement of political independence, Africa continues to suffer from 'imperiality of knowledge' taking the form of 'interweaving of geopolitical power, knowledge and subordinating representations of the other.'[50] This means that since the time of colonial encounters Africa and its people have been struggling to navigate their troubled histories and negotiate the complex realities of the murky present as it gestures towards uncertain and mysterious futures.

African struggles for liberation have involved protracted engagements in the domains of political power and epistemology, in the process revealing the limits of Eurocentrism and the poverty of epistemologies informed by alterity. The African struggles have now entered a phase of serious epistemological battles in which epistemologies of the Global South in general and Africa in particular are locking horns with previously hegemonic Euro-North American epistemologies. This reality is well captured by Jean Comaroff and John L. Comaroff in their book entitled *Theory from the South or How Euro-America is Evolving Towards Africa*. This is how they put the challenge:

> Western Enlightenment thought has, from the first, posited itself as the wellspring of universal learning, of Science and Philosophy, uppercase; concomitantly, it has regarded the non-West — variously

known as the ancient world, the orient, the primitive, the third world, the underdeveloped world, the developing world, and now the global south—primarily as a place of parochial wisdom, of antiquarian traditions, of exotic ways and means. […] But what if, and here is the idea in interrogative form, we invert that order of things? What if we subvert the epistemic scaffolding on which it is erected? What if we posit that, in the present moment, it is the global south that affords privileged insight into the workings of the world at large? […]. That, in probing what is at stake in it, we might move beyond the north-south binary, to lay bare the larger dialectical processes that have produced and sustained it […]. Each is a reflection on the contemporary order of things approached from a primarily Africa vantage, one, as it turns out, that is full of surprises and counter-intuitives, one that invites us to see familiar things in different ways.[51]

Patrick Chabal in *The End of Conceit: Western Rationality after Postcolonialism* concludes that 'The end of conceit is upon us: Western rationality must be rethought.'[52] If Chabal is only realizing the limits of Western rationality in recent years and that as instruments of understanding the world 'the social sciences we employ to explain what is happening domestically and overseas—are both historically and conceptually out of date,'[53] then he has to seek salvation in the African archive, which since the time of colonial encounters has been exposing the limits as well as dangers of Eurocentric knowledge. Dani Wadada Nabudere's *Afrikology, Philosophy and Wholeness: An Epistemology* and *Afrikology and Transdisciplinarity: A Restorative Epistemology* not only privilege Africa as the cradle of humanity but also make a strong case for holistic and integrated knowledge that transcends the current crisis of disciplinary decadence. According to Nabudere, 'Afrikology as an all-inclusive epistemology based on the cosmologies emanating from the Cradle of Humankind, can play a role in rejuvenating the Universal Knowledge.'[54]

The current book challenges those who take refuge in ideological denial and those who are trying to normalize the abnormal—the abnormality of the Euro-Americans thinking for and writing for the rest of the world and elevating their parochial ideas into universal truths and universal knowledge.[55] South Africa as the last African state to achieve freedom from the notorious apartheid colonial system that had far reaching consequences on the minds of black people is today engulfed by animated debates on 'colonization,' 'decolonization' and 're-colonization' of the humanities and social sciences. These debates are taking place within a context in which three fundamental questions continue to cry out for resolution: What kind of post-apartheid social order is being constituted?

What figure of freedom is being promoted? What mode of the 'human' is under construction? These questions were partly dealt with in Heather Jacklin and Peter Vale's *Re-imagining the Social in South Africa: Critique, Theory and Post-Apartheid Society*, where some refreshing questions about power, epistemology, the role of the university, the role of the humanities in liberation as well as those about belonging and citizenship were raised.[56] But the question which this important volume avoided was raised by Suren Pillay: 'Why do we speak of deracialization, and not of decolonization, in the dominant discourses of knowledge transformation in post-apartheid South Africa?'[57]

While in the South African context the multifaceted question of decolonization is often reduced by liberal white scholars to a resolution of a national question of class rather than race, which the Marxist-oriented liberals dismiss as false consciousness, the current book opens a wider canvas to touch on disciplines, methodology and pan-Africanism. When race is taken into account within the South African academy, deracialization is often decoupled from decolonization to the extent that the preferred solution becomes that of increasing black representation in specific disciplines and academic positions. But as pointed out by Jacques Depelchin in his groundbreaking book *Silences in African History: Between the Syndromes of Discovery and Abolition*:

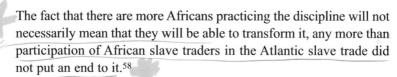

> The fact that there are more Africans practicing the discipline will not necessarily mean that they will be able to transform it, any more than participation of African slave traders in the Atlantic slave trade did not put an end to it.[58]

Deracializing knowledge is different from decolonizing knowledge. It starts off with subverting the colonial archive and colonial library. It culminates in epistemological disobedience, which includes challenging even the existing methodologies. Grappling with the pertinent question of decolonizing knowledge in South Africa, Pillay posed penetrating questions:

> How do we think of apartheid, as more than the combined legacy of race and class as the defining constituent logics of a system of domination that creates apparatuses of repression, that sets in motion modes of thought and counter-thought that deny the limits of their hegemonic status? In other words, how do we bring into question the power relations that have shaped the concepts, objects and discourses through which we make sense of 'South Africa' as an object of study, and that continue to shape how we think the South Africa present after apartheid? This would be one of the challenges that a post-apartheid conception of the humanities would need to attend to when it thinks

beyond deracialization, and towards the substantive challenge presented by the decolonization of knowledge production.[59]

To Pillay, while the predicament of the humanities and social sciences in South Africa has to do with some problems that are common across the world — such as forces of marketization and commodification of knowledge, invasion of consultancy cultures together with external and private funding that impose themselves on research agendas, massification of education as part of universalizing access for excluded and subaltern groups, and many others — there are South Africa-specific challenges emanating from particular histories that need to be confronted head on.[60] These are debates that the rest of Africa has been grappling with for decades since independence, pointing to the imperiality of Western social sciences,[61] the need for unthinking in order to rethink alienated knowledge[62] and opening spaces for alternative ways of knowing, including those that re-center Africa.[63] These raging debates foreground the problem of coloniality of knowledge as the elephant in the room.

This book grapples with the question of coloniality of knowledge from various vantage points such as methodology, African research subjects, the decadence of disciplines, and disciplines as carriers of coloniality.

Organization and Scope of the Book

The essays in this book — organized broadly under part 1, 'Modernity, Knowledge and Power'; part II, 'Decoloniality, Disciplines, and Ideology'; and part III, 'Methods, Methodology and Subjectivity' — capture and interrogate the topical issues of decolonizing the university, epistemology, disciplines and methodology.

The first part brings together chapters that engage with questions of modernity, power and knowledge, offering perspectives on how obfuscated ideas of university, law and sovereignty, and geopolitics might be responded to through the decoloniality lens of enunciation. The section begins with a chapter by Sabelo J. Ndlovu-Gatsheni that locates the modern university within the centre of the modern world system in order to explain the conundrum facing the desire to transform knowledge in African settings like South Africa. It traces the trajectories of the modern university from the time of the European Renaissance to the current phase of market colonization of the academy. This open canvas enables Ndlovu-Gatsheni to deal effectively with the broader question of politics and sociology of knowledge and its role in the emergence of the empire and the colonization of the non-Western world. Consequently, the chapter yields a rich repertoire and tapestry of the shifting configuration and articulation of the modern university from the Renaissance university, Enlighten-ment university, Humboldtian-Kantian and post-colonial 'developmental uni-versity' to the current corporate university. What emerges poignantly in this chapter is that just like the modern world system, the modern university—within which the current African university was born—has been resistant to decolonization, choosing instead to perpetuate the modern world system and its shifting international orders. African nationalist attempts to transform the Westernized university into a 'developmental university' in service of African humanity within a context in which the world system itself remained un-de-colonized became a waste of time. What existed were universities in Africa rather than African universities, hence the need for a more fundamental process of transformation designed to comprehensively decolonize their mission, iden-tity, epistemology, archive and curriculum.

The following chapter by Teboho Lebakeng contends that the impact of colonialism on African demography may be characterized as genocidal; its ef-fect on the African pool of knowledge and Africa's ability to evolve its own forms of knowledge in the modern era can be described as epistemicidal. This killing of African epistemology facilitated the imposition of Eurocentric par-adigms of thought that have become pervasive even after independence. A sur-vey of the general approaches in the social sciences and humanities leads him to evidence of this epistemic tyranny and its ability to foreclose African inge-nuity and agency. On this basis, the chapter calls for the Africanization of social sciences, especially as they are presented in African universities that have yet to be transformed. The final part of the chapter is a critical look at the African university and its deep-seated distortions owing to its origin from within the Western university, and offers concrete proposals on how the uni-versity could be Africanized in a manner that would enable the decolonization of social and human sciences.

The last chapter in part 1 is by Serges Kamga and it looks critically at the normative question of international law and sovereignty as the basis of the contested idea of an international community in which states are supposed to cooperate on the basis of equality, justice and fairness. He employs the Third World Approaches to International Law (TWAIL), as a decolonial epistemic option, to critique the role of international law in subverting the cause of de-colonization of the principle of "sovereign equality of states" by excising it from within the dominant narrative and hegemonic intents of the Global North that ingrain power asymmetry between the core-states and peripheral areas in the world system. In this sense, he shows that the concept is denied its decol-onizing potential due to its use as rhetoric rather than a commitment. Thus, equality is not reality in the current international system, both in the dominant interpretations of the United Nations (UN) Treaty and in the prosecution of the UN mandate, especially in the UN Security Council. Thus this law-making body, the Security Council, translates the national interests and imperial designs of the Global North into de facto international law, regimes and norms. The chapter suggests in response decolonial epistemological options in the analysis of international law and practice, options that make possible an alternative narrative that does not only unmask the coloniality of the current interpretations of international law and the so-called international community, but also support declarations of global injustice by the subalterns or the marginalized and inspire imaginative thinking about a truly just, fair and equal world.

In part II of the book, the focus is on the deconstruction of the coloniality of knowledge, especially as it presents itself through the tyranny of disciplined thought. Part II is constituted by four chapters, which, taken together, provide a rich tapestry of ways of critiquing disciplinary decadence that epitomize the knowledge presented through academic disciplines. Part II opens with William Mpofu's chapter in which he presents the outcome of a decolonial 'rereading' of Ngugi wa Thiong'o's novel *Devil on the Cross* to amplify its skilful unmasking of the resurrected devil of coloniality and his satanic machinations on African politics, economy and social life in the form of poverty, environmental pollution, political violence, class exploitation, muzzled voices, ubiquitous inequalities, divide and rule and so forth long after the dismantling of colonial administrations. Read through decolonial Afrocentric lenses, African literature ceases to be a province of Western literature, a literature without traditions, models and norms of its own. Mpofu opens vistas of opportunities for decolonial reading of African artistic works, especially fiction, such that their Afrocentric loci of enunciation and authentic combat with the coloniality narrative is made visible, thus positioning African literature as a site of epistemic subversion, disobedience and break with Eurocentric fundamentalism and coloniality.

The next chapter is by Tendayi Sithole and it uncovers the absolutism of disciplinarity as stubbornly embedded and abetted through the nebulous idea of Multi-Inter-Transdisciplinary (MIT) approaches to knowledge production. Sithole moves from the well-established premise that disciplinarity with its echoes of the order of prison and the culture of the military is constitutive and foundational to coloniality, being also an epitome of the very construction of Eurocentric epistemicide by which knowledges falling outside disciplines are de-legitimized, denigrated and forestalled. He shows that the construction of knowledge around disciplines is in the very logic of Western modernity that is implicated in this colonization of thought and acts of erasure designed to leave many things unsaid. This has the implication of excluding ways of knowing and knowledges from below and by the other, and thus it constitutes a decapacitation of African imaginaries needed for imagining futures and horizons beyond the Eurocentric lenses. By building on ("enriching") rather than rebelling against disciplinarity, Sithole shows, MIT fails to offer truly decolonial epistemological and methodological options for perspectives from below, for the excluded and denigrated ways of knowing, and for the undisciplined knowledges. In this sense, MIT does not avoid disciplinary decadence, the inability of disciplined thought to offer true plurality of thought and diverse ways of knowing. Instead, it rescues disciplines from being exposed for their dark underside, thus helping to perpetuate Eurocentric negations and the coloniality of modern knowledge in general. Sithole suggests that instead of MIT, there is a need for a complete break with disciplined thought in all its mutations towards undisciplined and freed ways of knowing, using the concept of ecologies of knowledge rather than disciplined thought. On this basis, he contends, a better relationship between ontologies and epistemologies would be achieved, thus enabling border thinking or epistemological pluralism. This is crucial for excluded and silenced voices in scholarship and knowledge.

In 'A Decolonial Analysis of Coloniality in the Discipline of Anthropology' Nokuthula Hlabangane and Zodwa Radebe demonstrate the epistemological locatedness of the discipline of anthropology. They show how its curiosity about people thought of as different, if not inferior and conquered, entrench Western modernity and Eurocentric lenses of analysis. The impulse to discover gives rise to the tendency to cement differences in notions of cultural difference in bifurcated lines of inferiority and superiority. In this sense, the authors show, anthropology occupies a pride of place within the coloniality of knowledge, most obvious in its remaining a Western episteme dedicated to the study of natives in the Global South, generating knowledge used for the prosecution of the coloniality of being (such as in racism) and coloniality of power (as in colonial rule). In this context, the much-praised focus on collecting raw data from the field masks the tendency to collect African data in order to validate concepts and assumptions conceived elsewhere, what Hountondji calls 'extroversion.'[64] On this basis, African subjects and sites of research remain a research laboratory for the Western academy. The authors also grapple with the resultant dilemma facing subaltern anthropologists attempting epistemic disobedience within the discipline because of the ingrained double-bind where the anthropologist continues to be both the creator of a homogenous world and a creature in the same and the tensions between the mantra of objective study and the reality of an objectifying approach to knowledge. Thus, they open the way for unthinking the anthropology fashioned within the coloniality of knowledge in order to make possible de-linked analysis, located in epistemic pluralism.

Also writing on the theme of disciplinarity but with a specific focus on the discipline of tourism studies, Morgan Ndlovu makes telling connections between the underlying epistemological tenets of the discipline and the colonial type of relations between the core and the periphery in the modern world system. He suggests that in this case, there is a strong correlation between the manner in which knowledge is produced in tourism studies and the tendencies in actual tourism in the Global South and in Africa in particular. Ndlovu contends that this area of study's tendency to draw from various disciplines — including anthropology, geography, history, arts and business studies, among others — does not make it an epitome of post-disciplinary knowledge claimed by some. A wide-ranging discussion of underlying assumptions about the subject, subjectivity and loci of enunciation, as well as the debate between perspectives in favour of its disciplinarity and those arguing for de-disciplining shows the extent to which, and ways in which, tourism studies is entrapped within Western logo-centrism. The willingness to ignore and forget the voices and ways of knowing of the 'Other' in pursuit of the universalist pretensions of Western knowledge implicates the discipline in the subjugation, silence, and destruction of knowledges. In its acceptance of the notion of profiting from the difference of the other, freezing them in a world of statues to be viewed as museums, and its furtherance of the assumption that the Other has culture where the West has knowledge, the discipline becomes complicit in imperial designs intended to perpetuate the coloniality of the world. Ndlovu concludes with an argument for a decolonial turn within tourism studies through epistemic disobedience and shifting the geography of reason such that cognitive justice and epistemic plurality are possible.

The last chapter in this section, by Puleng Segalo, explores questions of coloniality and ideology of knowledge as they manifest themselves in the discipline of psychology. The tendency to import theories, concepts, categories and methods of study from Western knowledge results in the importation of alienated ways of knowing and discourses. In doing this, psychology is implicated in mimicry and epistemicide by which other knowledges are erased and silenced. Segalo suggests that this lies at the heart of the long-standing concerns about the tendency of the discipline to understand and present social phenomena, people's lived realities and experiences, as pathologies to be diagnosed and treated. Segalo traces these tendencies to the evolution of the discipline over a century from its Freudian roots to the phenomenology phase, showing that it has throughout developed practices of symbolizing and understanding human behaviour that is not unrelated to the structure of the world system and the historical and cultural environments. This has thus enabled the discipline to dice around the questions of power and domination, and therefore the constitution of questions of social injustice that continue to haunt the subjects that psychologists study and assist. For Segalo, failure to engage with knowledges in their context and to allow the voices from below to percolate has made the discipline party to epistemic and ontological oppression through the universalization of knowledge under the invisible banner of Eurocentrism. Efforts to expand the curriculum and thus allow more content in the discipline is found to have changed little because it has avoided changing the very terms on which knowledge continues to be constructed within the discipline. She draws inspiration from the emergence of "alternative" paradigms that challenge the coloniality of psychology, thus opening opportunities for a decolonial turn in this area of knowledges that make possible epistemic pluralism and new ecologies of knowledge related to matter that psychologies are preoccupied with.

Part II of this book deals with possibilities for decolonial theorizing on subjectivity, methods and methodology. They are thus forward looking, offering broad methodological options that give effect to a decolonial turn in the study of African phenomena. The section opens with Fidelis Allen's chapter, examining the state of political science as taught and practiced in Africa, the so-called African political science, against the backdrop of the evolution of mainstream political science as a discipline of Western modernity. The chapter provides rich insights into how this political science continues to conform to what Claude Ake once called social science as imperialism, in that writings in political science use the Western political experiences, political values and interests as a locus of their enunciation, thus positioning themselves as tools in the civilizing mission to transform Africa in the image of the West. As a result, political science has acted as a conduit for transmitting to Africa ideas within Western modernity, especially neoliberal ideology. African political science, Allen shows, has failed to challenge the Western narrative about African political geography and the future of the continent's politics. As a result, this political science has been alien to African realities and has alienated African thought and experiences. The chapter then suggests ways in which the discipline could build upon a growing number of African political scientists that have not conformed to the imperiality of the discipline in order to decolonize and indigenize it for the benefit of the African continent and its peoples.

In 'Telling Our Own Stories: Narratology as Decolonial Methodology,' Nontyatyambo Dastile proposes narratology as a combative methodological and epistemological tool for enabling Africans to speak for themselves, represent their lived experiences and thus challenge current distortions and erasures. This, she argues, is made necessary by the tendency of the current Eurocentric epistemological and methodological prescriptions to negate, silence and erase African people from the narrative about them and their lived experiences. This produces cognitive, testimonial and hermeneutical injustices, and enables epistemicides and ontological murder. She then proposes narratology—which is the recording and engagement with oral testimonies of the subjects of study—as a form of decolonial option, underpinned by decolonial mediations as an epistemological and methodological tool for both unmasking the epistemicides that take place and for foregrounding the voices and choices of the subalterns, the silenced and excluded in the story about their lives and circumstances. This allows the theorization of experiences from below, especially when they seem to contradict conventional wisdom, thus shifting the geography of reason from the Eurocentric knower to the African subjects under study. The chapter demonstrates how this could redefine the packaging of knowledge and lead to serious rethinking of the ways of knowing and how we have known what we thought we knew.

Tendayi Sithole's chapter casts the spotlight on the foundations and central questions of the discipline of African politics as an afterthought and sub-discipline of Western political science, uncovering the imperial reason that positions the African subject as an object central to discourses in this field of study. In this sense, African people are a problematic people whose appearance brings the problem of existence, the existential enigma that produces alienation and debasement for the African subject. On this account, African politics is deemed to have become mere representation and presentation of African subjects outside their ontological landscape and therefore causing them to appear as deformed and debased, an epitome of problems. They are thus excluded by presentation and representation in this void, and an Africa that is defined by deficiency or nothingness is thus naturalized as a norm to be resolved by those positioned as agents of life, the saviours. Sithole then zooms in on the question of method as a central tool in the production of an Africa of deficiency and Africans of ontological voids. He draws from the works of subaltern thinkers to establish the point that the mainstream method is contaminated with ideological, cultural and other biases of Westernized social science, a provincial science that backs its claims to universality via epistemicides. Sithole then marshals an argument for a decolonial turn in African thought generally and African politics more specifically to enable Africans to think from where they are, what he calls a method against method.

This book closes with a chapter by Siphamandla Zondi, which contends that African continental politics coined in terms of the pursuit of unity and integration has been warped in alienated discourses premised on imported theoretical models having very little to do with the African experience of the coloniality of being, power and knowledge. As a result, the sub-discipline has been pre-occupied with subliminal questions about how far down the road towards a European model of integration Africa has gone rather than understanding Africa as an agent in its own right and not a copycat of Europe. This, he argues, is produced by the tendency to think about Africa from outside Africa, a common ailment in international relations, diplomatic history and African political science. Moving from the premise that we have not adequately understood why this age-old dream of unity and integration remains elusive because of the contaminated epistemic lenses we have used, it contends that we are unlikely to understand this because of the tendency to mimic Eurocentric epistemic prescriptions and European experiences. The chapter goes on to outline how Afrocentric decolonial options might offer located and situated insights into the problems and foresights into the future. The chapter links this to the question of African agency, arguing that it is impossible to see and understand Africans as agents in their geopolitics without applying Afrocentric decolonial methodologies, which the chapter demonstrates. On this basis, the chapter suggests that African unity is born out of the desire to transform Africa's relations with the world from a subservient, dependent and attached Africa to one that works to transform the world system by freeing itself from the peripheralising tendencies of the system. Zondi, therefore, demonstrates an important methodological option of a decolonial and Afrocentric nature for our understanding of African agency to enable the students of African integration to rethink Africa's role in the fashioning of an equal, just and fairer world order.

Conclusion

The volume is intended to be a platform for opening debates about the questions raised by Pillay in the quotation at the beginning of this chapter: that transforming the social sciences and humanities entails understanding their entanglement in the global matrices of power that manifest as colonialism, imperialism, neo-colonialism and apartheid on African soil. If we accept, as we should, that independence did not mark the destruction or collapse of this model of power we call coloniality, then it is obvious that the colonial underpinnings of the Westernized social sciences and humanities still being taught in Westernized universities physically in Africa and occupied mostly by Africans remain in place. This calls for understanding a deeper meaning of the concept of transformation of higher education in Africa in pursuit of an elusive African university or multiversity than is generally assumed. This debate must link the body-politics, theo-politics and geopolitics of knowledge in order to make possible new global liberatory discourses about the future of the humanities and social sciences.

Therefore, the book does not claim a final word on the subject of decolonizing the university, epistemology and disciplines, but does establish a basis for further work on a decolonial turn in the debate. It should encourage further debates on the specificities of the curriculum, pedagogy, and administration of higher education, and enable life stories to be told by those who experience this deep-seated alienation and damnation in the Westernized university in Africa. The book should also stimulate a greater engagement with the Global South and African decolonial mediations about knowledge, power and being that remain hidden away and ignored in discourses. It is a timely work, written within a context in which students are refusing to be taught a 'white curriculum' and are actively redefining teaching to be a negotiated activity in which issues of context and relevance matter.

Notes and References

1. Cesaire, A. *Discourse on colonialism*. New York: Monthly Review Press, [1955] 2000.

2. Quijano, A. Coloniality of power and social classification.' *Journal of World Systems*, 6(2), 2000, pp. 342–386.

3. Gordon, L. R. *Fanon and the crisis of European man; An Essay on philosophy of the human sciences*. New York & London: Routledge, 1995.

4. Ndlovu-Gatsheni, S. J. Decoloniality in Africa: A continuing search for a new world order. *Australasian Review if African Studies*, 36(2), December 2015, pp. 22–50.

5. Ndlovu-Gatsheni, S. J. Decoloniality as the Future of Africa. *History Compass*, 13(10), September 2015, pp. 485–496.

6. Each year the summer school has continued to increase its intake and exposed the participants to the complexities of imperialism, colonialism and coloniality not as a past but as a present that continues to shape what is taught at universities as well as subjectivity.

7. Ngugi wa Thiong'o. *Remembering Africa*. Nairobi/Kampala/Dar es Salaam: East African Educational Publishers Ltd, 2009.

8. Maldonado-Torres, N. On coloniality of being: Contributions to the development of a concept.' *Cultural Studies*, 21(2–3), 2007, pp. 240–270.

9. Ngugi wa Thiong'o. *Something torn and new An African renaissance*. New York: Basic Civitas Books, 2009.

10. Ngugi wa Thiong'o, *Something torn*, p. 5.

11. Ndlovu-Gatsheni, Decoloniality in Africa, pp. 25–26.

12. Ndlovu-Gatsheni, S. J. *Coloniality of Power in Postcolonial Africa: Myths of Decolonization*. Dakar: CODESRIA Books, 2013.

13. Ndlovu-Gatsheni, S. J. 'Aluta continua or end of liberation? Rethinking colonialism, nationalism and decolonization in Southern Africa.' Keynote address delivered at the international conference on the theme: *A Luta continua, 40 years later: Entangled histories and legacies of Empire in Southern Africa, organised by the French Institute of South Africa, Johannesburg, South Africa, 5–6 November 2015*.

14. Ngugi wa Thiong'o. *Something torn*, pp. 5–15.

15. Wallerstein, I. (2004). *The uncertainties of knowledge*. Philadelphia, PA: Temple University Press.

16. Gordon, L. R. (2006). *Disciplinary decadence: Living thought in trying times.* Boulder, CO: Paradigm Publishers.

17. Chabal, P. (2012). *The end of conceit: Western rationality after postcolonialism.* London, England: Zed Books.

18. Zizek, S. (2010). *Living in the end times.* London, England: Verso.

19. Wallerstein, I. (1999). *The end of the world as we know it: Social science for the twenty-first century.* Minneapolis, MN: University of Minnesota press, p. ix.

20. Grosfoguel, R. (2012). Decolonizing Western uni-versalisms: Decolonial pluri-versalism from Aime Cesaire to the Zapatistas. *Transmodernity: Journal of Peripheral Cultural Production of the Luso-Hispanic World,* 1(3), p. 88.

21. Grosfoguel, Decolonizing Western uni-versalisms, p. 89.

22. Grosfoguel, Decolonizing Western uni-versalisms, p. 89.

23. Grosfoguel, Decolonizing Western uni-versalisms, p. 89.

24. Wallerstein, *The uncertainties of knowledge,* p. 13.

25. Grosfoguel, The epistemic decolonial turn, pp. 211–223.

26. Grosfoguel, The epistemic decolonial turn, pp. 211–223.

27. Blaut, J. M. (1993). *The coloniser's model of the world: Geographical diffusionism and Eurocentric history.* New York, NY: Guilford Press; and Amin, S. (2009). *Eurocentrism: Modernity, religion, and democracy: A critique of Eurocentrism and culturalism.* New York, NY: Monthly Review Press.

28. Amin, *Eurocentrism,* p. 178.

29. Diop, C. A. (1974). *African origins of civilization: Myths and reality.* Chicago, IL: Lawrence Hill Books; and Diop, C. A. (1980). *Civilization or barbarism: An authentic anthropology.* Chicago, IL: Lawrence Hill Books.

30. Asante, M. K. (1988). *Afrocentricity.* Trenton, NJ: Africa World Press; Nabudere, D. W. (2011). *Afrikology, philosophy and wholeness: An epistemology.* Pretoria, South Africa: Africa Institute of South Africa; and Nabudere, D. W. (2012). *Afrikology and transdisciplinarity: A restorative epistemology.* Pretoria, South Africa: Africa Institute of South Africa.

31. Quoted in Deluze, G. (2004). *Desert islands and other texts.* Cambridge, MA: MIT Press, p. 54.

32. Gordon, *Disciplinary Decadence,* p. 88.

33. Foucault, M. (1970). *The order of discourse: Archaeology of the human sciences.* London, England: Tavistock.

34. Mills, S. (1997). *Discourse.* London, England: Routledge.

35. Gramsci, A. (1971). *Selections from prison notebooks.* New York, NY: International Publishers, p. 68.

36. Escobar, A. (2004). Beyond the Third World: Imperial globality, global coloniality and anti-globalization social movements. *Third World Quarterly,* 25(1), pp. 207–230.

37. Cesaire, A. (1955). *Discourse on colonialism.* New York, NY: Monthly Review Press, p. 23.

38. Grosfoguel, R. (2007). The epistemic decolonial turn: Beyond political-economy paradigms. *Cultural Studies,* 21(2–3), March/May, pp. 211–223.

39. Grosfoguel, R. (2012). Decolonizing Western uni-versalisms: Decolonial pluri-versalism from Aime Cesaire to the Zapatistas. *Transmodernity: Journal of Peripheral Cultural Production of the Luso-Hispanic World,* 1(3), p.96.

40. Chen, K-H. (2010). *Asia as method: Toward deimperialization.* Durham, NC: Duke University Press, p. xii.

41. Chen, *Asia as method*, p. vii.

42. Ellis, S. D. K. (2009). South Africa and the decolonization of the mind. (Unpublished Inaugural Lecture Delivered Upon Accepting the Position of VU University Amsterdam Desmond Tutu Chair Holder in Areas of Youth, Sports and Reconciliation, Faculty of Social Sciences, VU University Amsterdam, 23 September, pp. 15–16).

43. Pillay, S. (2013). Institutional autonomy a myth? *Supplement to the Mail & Guardian,* June 7 to 13, p. 8.

44. Ndlovu-Gatsheni, S. J. (2013). *Coloniality of power in postcolonial Africa: Myths of decolonization.* Dakar, Senegal: CODESRIA Book Series.

45. Memmi, A. (1991). *The coloniser and the colonised.* Boston, MA: Beacon Press, p. 146. (Original work published 1957).

46. Chen, *Asia as Method*, p. 3.

47. Chen, *Asia as Method*, p. vii.

48. Fanon, F. (1952). *Black skin, white masks.* New York, NY: Grove Press; Fanon, F. (1967). *The wretched of the earth.* New York: Grove Press; and Memmi, A. (1957). *The coloniser and the colonised.* London, England: Earthscan Publications.

49. Ngugi wa Thiong'o, (1986). *Decolonizing the mind: The politics of language in African literature.* Nairobi, Kenya: Heinemann Education Publishing Ltd; Chinweizu, (1987). *Decolonizing the African mind.* Lagos, Nigeria: Pero Press; Ake, C. (1979). *Social science as imperialism: The theory of political development.* Ibadan, Nigeria: Ibadan University Press.

50. Slater, D. (2004). *Geopolitics and the post-colonial: Rethinking North-South relations.* Victoria, South Africa: Blackwell Publishing, p. 223.

51. Comaroff, J., & Comaroff, J. L. (2012). *Theory from the south or how Euro-America is evolving towards Africa.* New York, NY: Paradigm Publishers, pp. 1–2.

52. Chabal, *The End of Conceit*, p. 335.

53. Chabal, *The End of Conceit*, p. viii.

54. Nabudere, 2011, *Afrikology*, p. 2.

55. Ndlovu-Gatsheni, S. J. (2013). *Empire, global coloniality and African subjectivity.* New York, NY: Berghahn Books.

56. Jacklin, H., & Vale, P. (Eds.). (2009). *Re-imagining the social in South Africa: Critique, theory and post-apartheid society.* Scottsville, South African: University of KwaZulu-Natal Press.

57. Pillay, S. (2009). Translating 'South Africa': Race, colonialism and challenges of critical thought after apartheid. In H. Jacklin & P. Vale (Eds.), *Re-imagining the social in South Africa* (p. 235).

58. Depelchin, J. (2005). *Silences in African history: Between the syndromes of discovery and abolition.* Dar Es Salaam, Tanzania: Mkuki na Nyota Publishers, p. 109.

59. Pillay, Translating 'South Africa', p. 263.

60. Pillay, Institutional autonomy a myth? p. 8.

61. Ake, *Social science.*

62. wa Thiong'o, (1986). *Decolonizing the mind;* Chinweizu, *Decolonizing the African mind.*

63. Devisch, R., & Nyamnjoh, F. (2011). *The postcolonial turn,* Bameda: Langaa Research and Publishing.

64. Hountondji, P. (1997). *Endogenous knowledge: Research trails.* Dakar, Senegal: CODESRIA Books.

Part I

Modernity, Knowledge, and Power

Chapter 2

The Imperative of Decolonizing the Modern Westernized University

Sabelo J. Ndlovu-Gatsheni

Introduction

We need to emancipate the educational system in the Congo from the Western model by going back to the Authenticity while paying due attention to scientific knowledge: I have always thought it inappropriate for us to train our youth as if they were Westerners. It would be more desirable to have an educational system which shapes the youth according to our requirements. That would make them authentically Congolese. Their ideas, reasoning and actions would be Congolese, and they would see the future in Congolese terms.[1]

The rise of the academic managerial class has been, perhaps, the most catastrophic development in the modern university. [...] What is clear is that the academic managerial class, unlike past scholars who so happened also to administrate, no longer has knowledge as part of its telos. That class has folded onto itself as the object of its own preservation, and the result is its own proliferation. Faculties are up in arms at many universities at which administrators are now outnumbering them, and the avalanche continues as the phenomenon of graduate students pursuing doctorates without an aim of producing knowledge but going directly to administration. The joined forces of academic administrators consisting of failed academics and scholars whose credentials do not extend beyond earning their doctorates led to a sociology of revenge and entrenched resentment towards productive and influential scholars.[2]

27

The modern African institutions of higher learning exist as part of the glob-alised, 'Westernized' university international order. This means that they are deeply imbricated in reproduction of Euro-American-centric modernity and hegemony. While located in Africa, they do not produce or inculcate indige-nous and endogenous knowledge. Inevitably, their graduates emerge as alien-ated beings that are consistently trying to abandon the Africa that produced them and gesturing towards Europe and America, which selectively accom-modate those considered to be the brightest of Africans. What is more troubling in postcolonial Africa is what Reiland Rabaka has termed 'epistemic apartheid' that is compounded by 'disciplinary decadence' and 'intellectual historical am-nesia.'[3]

The enormity of this crisis can be understood deeply if one approaches it from a world systems perspective in combination with decolonial analysis that enable delving deeper into the sociology and politics of the coloniality of knowledge. According to Immanuel Wallerstein, world-systems analysis priv-ileges world systems rather than nation-states and considers historical processes as they unfold over long periods of time, while combining within a single an-alytical framework bodies of knowledge usually viewed as distinct from one another, such as history, politics, economics, philosophy and sociology.[4] What emerges from this innovative approach is that Africa has since the time of colonial encounters gradually and accumulatively been pulled into the nexus and snares of what David Slater terms 'imperiality of knowledge.'[5] Imperiality of knowledge speaks to the 'interweaving of geopolitical power, knowledge and subordinating representations of the other.'[6] Its genealogy is traceable to the birth of the modern world system in 1492. What distinguished the modern world system is a particular modernity which not only unleashed colonization of time, space, being, and even nature but promised to use science to overcome all challenges to human progress. Knowledges which were not considered as science became targets of epistemicides. At a broader level, this imperial-colo-nial modernity unfolded in terms of usurpation of world history as Europe claimed to be the centre of the modern world.[7]

The usurpation of world history by Europe and North America had far reaching implications for knowledge, being and power. Europeans and Amer-icans emerged as leading producers of universal knowledge. Euro-American knowledge producers managed to hide their local and particular perspective under universal pretensions.[8] In the domain of being, Europeans and white Americans claimed superiority over all other races of the world. Here was born the problem of racially hierarchized conceptions of being and social clas-sification of people in accordance with race. These notions of being impinged on configurations of power. This is why in the realm of power, the modern world system emerged as a racially hierarchized, patriarchal, Christian-centric, Western-Centric, Euro-North American-centric, hetero-normative, capitalist, colonial, and modern formation.[9] This modern world system has remained resistant to decolonization. Its global orders are impervious to deimperialization. Since 1492, the world system has enabled and authorized various epochal international orders such as the post-1648 Westphalian order and the post-1945 United Nations sovereignty order. Africans have found themselves struggling to fit into these orders. Where they have been invited into the power structures, Africans still occupy the lowest echelons. Once accommodated, Africans then reproduce Western-centric normative values.

Inevitably, at the political symbolic level, the post-1945 African political sovereignty as a subtext of the global United Nations international order materialised in the following manner: adoption of a new vernacular name for the state, composition of a new national anthem and raising of a new flag, adoption of a new currency, having a new university, and the appearance of a black face at the state house and black faces in parliament. Having a national university became a sign of being sovereign. This national university was commonly inherited from colonialism for most of the 'postcolonial' states. Even where new ones were created, the model followed was that of a 'Westernized' university, making it a university in Africa rather than an authentic African university.

The major point is that one cannot fully understand the history of the modern Westernized university and its role in coloniality outside a clear comprehension of the political constitution of the modern world system together with its shifting world orders. The modern university emerged as a global structure of Euro-North American-centric modernity. Its models have been shifting in accordance with the changing world orders. For example, a shifting world order from the Westphalian order that commenced in 1648 to the current post-1945 United Nations sovereignty order, and a shifting model of the university from the Renaissance to the Enlightenment, to the Kantian-Humboldtian, to the current corporate university, must not be taken to mean that the world system and the Euro-American-centric epistemology, respectively, have finally succumbed to decolonization and deimperialization.

The struggle for decolonization of the world system and the modern Westernized university must be intensified now that modernity has thrown up modern problems to which it has no modern solutions; now that disciplines are experiencing decadence and Western rationality's claim to overcome all human problems is failing; and now that an epistemic rupture is in the air. An epistemic rupture is similar to an interregnum, whereby a previously dominant epistemic order becomes exhausted, opening the way for a new one. In this instance, the Euro-American epistemology that has assumed global status is in crisis, provoking even some Western scholars like Patrick Chabal (being one of the latest comers to this debate) to write of 'the end of conceit' and admitting that 'the instruments we use are no longer fit for the job. [...] [T]he social sciences we employ to explain what is happening domestically and overseas—are both historically and conceptually out of date.'[10]

But historically speaking, when the post-1945 United Nations sovereignty system replaced the Westphalian order, enabling decolonization to gain momentum and to produce African 'postcolonial states,' there was some optimism and certainty about the possibility of a postcolonial world order. However, what became celebrated as decolonization took the form of admission of 'ex-colonies' into the lower echelons of a racially hierarchized, patriarchal, Western-centric, Euro-American-centric, Christian-centric, hetero-normative and modern world system that has been in place since 1492.[11] The United Nations is part of this system and its role has been to accommodate anti-systemic movements and forces, as it gives the Euro-American-centric world system a new spin and new lease of life.[12] What was introduced by the United Nations was a new world order, which must not be confused with the notion of a new world system.

The world system maintains and protects itself from anti-systemic movements and forces through epochal authorizing of new world orders. This is why even though the African 'postcolonial' states were enabled by the United Nations sovereignty system, they would still hark back to the Westphalian nation-state template as they tried to project their sovereignty. Basil Davidson termed this process of the replication of the Westphalian nation-state template the 'black man's burden' and described it as a 'curse.'[13] What this revealed was that Africa was simply being shifted from the order of 'global colonialism' (direct colonial administration) to 'global coloniality' (indirect colonial administration on a world scale).[14] This shift has culminated in neo-liberal rationality and the coloniality of market relations, which in turn gave birth to the Westernized corporate university. It is an epoch characterized by a people worshipping at the altar of wealth accumulation and consumptionist cultures rather than knowledge production. It is an epoch of the commodification and marketization of education and knowledge.

But the greatest irony of Africa is that even those people who fought heroically against imperialism and colonialism tend to develop a very complacent view towards the imperialism of knowledge, which is more dangerous than physical political domination. The imperialism of knowledge works on the minds of African people whereas religious colonialism works on the soul. These dangerous forces operate in the form of soft power informed by long-standing colonial matrices of power. These colonial matrices of power operate as a set of technologies of subjectivation, consisting of four types that were clearly distilled by the Peruvian sociologist Anibal Quijano as: *control of economy*, which manifested itself through dispossession, land expropriations, exploitation of labour and control of African natural resources; *control of authority*, which includes the maintenance of military superiority through stockpiling of weapons of mass destruction by Western powers and monopolization of means of violence; *control of gender and sexuality*, which involves the re-imagination of the family in Western-Christian-bourgeois terms and universalization of one-wife-one-husband; and *control of subjectivity and knowledge*, which includes epistemological colonization and re-articulation of the African being as inferior and constituted by a series of 'deficits' and a catalogue of 'lacks.'[15]

It is important to emphasize that while some ex-colonized people have developed a complacent view that colonialism is over and summon others to forget about it, coloniality is not complacent or tired of acting on the so-called 'postcolonial subjects.' The reality is therefore that while some Africans could be tired of talking about colonialism, coloniality is not yet tired of dominating, exploiting, and oppressing Africans. It is African complacency which made it hard to decolonize the inherited Westernized university. Perhaps it was this complacency that provoked Frantz Fanon to pray: 'O my body, always make me a man who questions!'[16] For Africans, being a man or woman who questions entails consistently raising critical questions about colonialism and coloniality, about received Euro-American knowledges and inherited institutions, while at the same time inventing ways of creating African futures unencumbered by coloniality.

The decolonial message is that African people must wake up from the dangerous habit of normalizing coloniality and rise up to embrace decoloniality, which enables them to unmask the constitution of Euro-America-centric modernity and to pass critical judgments on the enduring impact of the slavery, imperialism, colonialism, apartheid, neo-colonialism, and neo-liberalism that constitute coloniality.[17] Africans must open their eyes and see that the European diaspora living in Africa is justifiably right to be frantically opposed to decoloniality because they never experienced the dark side of modernity. Colonialism and apartheid actually empowered the European diaspora resident in Africa both economically and epistemologically. Coloniality enables them to maintain their loot while decoloniality threatens their ill-gotten wealth and racially constructed notions of superiority.

Coloniality is very dangerous because it causes mental confusion among Africans, to the extent that one finds some Africans who are socially located on the oppressed side of the colonial difference, thinking epistemically like the ones in the dominant positions.[18] The worst cases are those of Africans who are lobbied to be angry on behalf of coloniality, that is, on behalf of those who benefited from colonialism and who are today shielded by coloniality from accounting for their loot. Such people try to even take drastic measures to ban decoloniality as critical social theory.[19] Those who espouse decoloniality are put under extreme pressure to explain its value whereas those who espouse some nameless equilibrium-oriented discourses are allowed to speak freely without anyone asking them to explain the value of their discourses. Decolonial thinkers become endangered academic species within the context of the un-decolonized Westernized university.

Decolonial thinkers are called such names as dogmatic, ideological, polemic, and reverse-racists for the simple reason that they have chosen to continue the long-standing decolonization agenda that was disciplined by coloniality into reformism and emancipatory processes away from their original formulation as liberatory processes.[20] Decolonial thinkers have chosen to take a position and refuse to remain neutral in a world that is not neutral. On the question of neutrality, Ngugi wa Thiong'o emphasized that African thinkers have a very clear choice to make: either on 'the side of the people or the side of the social forces and classes that try to keep the people down. What he or she cannot do is to remain neutral. Every writer is a writer in politics. The only question is what and whose politics?'[21] But only people with decolonized minds can be on the side of the people rather than that of the oppressing classes, and such people need to be knowledgeable about colonialism and coloniality as well as the essence of the world system and its world orders.

Africa in the Present World Order

The present world system is a socio-political construction that took shape during the expansion of Europe to the Americas, Asia, Caribbean, and Africa. The year 1492, when Christopher Columbus reached the Americas, is identified as the commencement of the making of the modern world system. The year 1648, when the Treaty of Westphalia was signed, marking the end of the Thirty Years War, also signaled the institutionalization and 'norming' of a particular modern world order as a juridical political formation.[22]

The dominant European states—namely Germany, Spain, France, Sweden and the Netherlands—agreed to recognize and respect each other's sovereignty in the wake of the Thirty Years War. At the same time, they continued to intensify expansion beyond Europe in violation of other non-European people's dignity and freedom. While the institutionalization of the slave trade became the first manifestation of the dark side of modernity, the Berlin Conference of

1884–5 enabled colonialism and laid a firm basis for global coloniality.[23] The scramble for and partition of Africa among European powers amounted to an open disregard and disdain for the African people's dignity, rights and freedoms.[24]

What is emerging clearly is that a combination of the use of naked brute force and the advantages of technology, particularly the gun and fruits of science, were deployed in the process of the creation of the current world order and the production of the present social reality along with the subjectivities that animate it. The rhetoric of modernity operating at the centre of the construction of the present world order actualized itself through colonization of time, colonization of space, colonization of people, and colonization of nature.[25] A particular epistemology that broadly cascaded from Euro-American experience was effectively used to put Europe on a new pedestal as the centre of the world. Particularistic and contextual European knowledge was universalized. This is why Western thinkers from Descartes to Zizek always articulated their knowledge as disembodied, universal, neutral, objective, truthful, and un-situated. Santiago Castro-Gomez termed this claim by Western thinkers the 'point zero' perspective.[26] No other knowledge prior to theirs. No other knowledge except theirs. No other knowledge after theirs.

This is why those who worship at the altar of modernity and who are quick to credit it for all positive things tend to be silent on the 'dark side' of modernity that stifled innovation and invention in Africa. They are silent on coloniality as the underside of modernity. They don't understand that as modernity deposited its positive fruits of industrialization and liberal democracy in Europe, it was simultaneously unleashing the slave trade, imperialism, colonialism and apartheid in Africa that crippled endogenous innovation. They are silent on its role in the re-production of African subjectivity as that of deficient and lacking beings—lacking souls, lacking history, lacking civilization, lacking development, lacking democracy, lacking human rights and lacking knowledge. This imperial and colonial attitude enabled the use of race and scientific racism to organise and classify human beings into primitive and modern, civilized and uncivilised, Western and non-Western, colonizer and colonized, superior and inferior.[27]

The decoloniality agenda is therefore very important, not only because it enables Africans to unmask Euro-American deceit but because African people continue to manifest the disease of mental colonization, which makes them assist in the reproduction of a racially hierarchized world system. The implications and consequences of mental colonization are long-standing and terrible. In the first place, a people suffering from mental colonization cannot innovate and have no potential or agency for pace-setting. Such a people develop a very low self-esteem and consistently manifest inferiority complexes. They suffer from dependency syndromes which make them very timid.[28] They tend to hate themselves and wish to be white. This is why Albert Memmi portrayed a colonized person as someone whose 'first ambition' 'is to become equal to that splendid model [white colonizer] to resemble him to the point of disappearing in him.'[29]

In the second place, mentally colonized people fail to challenge existing Euro-American epistemologies, mainly because while they live in Africa they were made to think as though they were in Europe and America. This is why Ngugi wa Thiong'o in his analysis of what he termed 'the education of the colonial bondsman' noted that beyond colonialism's deployment of coercive physical force, it also unleashed 'an even more coercive element of mental force [that] may compel a distorted consciousness of the reality of their actual relationship. The fact is, the master is in control of both coercive forces: the physical and the mental. He has the monopoly of education, the content, the form, the space, and the order of its delivery.'[30]

Ngugi wa Thiong'o elaborated that the colonial process dislocated the African mind 'from the place he or she already knows to a foreign starting point even with the body still remaining in his or her homeland. It is a process of continuous alienation from the base, a continuous process of looking at oneself from the outside of self or with the lenses of a stranger. One may end up identifying with the foreign base as the starting point toward self, that is from another self towards one self, rather than the local being the starting point, from self to other selves.'[31]

Consequently people whose mentalities remain colonized consistently manifest what William Du Bois described as a 'double-consciousness' that reveals the worst form of alienation.[32] This is why a people suffering mental colonization exhibit an identity crisis as they continue to think in a restrictive and programmatic way informed by textbook knowledge. What also distinguishes a people suffering from an invisible colonial mentality is the excessive fear of critically judging European history, civilization and epistemology. Instead they live to mimic whatever Europeans do and say.[33] Such a people's critical thinking is compromised as they live through adaptation to what exists. They tend to be afraid of radical change, including one that is beneficial to them. As aptly described by Jean-Paul Sartre, people who are mentally colonized exist as 'living lies' without any clear locus of enunciation.[34]

Africa continues to be inhabited by a people suffering from mental colonization to the extent that a majority of them are comfortable with being judged by Europeans and always striving to get validation of whatever they do from Europeans and Americans. In Zimbabwe, one finds a group of people who call themselves veterans of the liberation struggle who have constructed a state that is used to create what Kizito Muchemwa termed a 'Chimurenga aristocracy' while silencing and disciplining everyone who dares to question this reproduction of coloniality. In countries like South Africa, where administrative apartheid existed longer than anywhere in Africa, one finds a people that have so deeply internalized racism to the extent of hating blackness while they are black themselves. The consequences have been the challenges of Afrophobia and xenophobia.[35]

The cancer of colonial mentalities forces Africans to often gesture towards Europe and America for solutions to African problems. Universities in Africa become nothing more than centres for testing European- and American-generated theories on African realities. A majority of African scholars find no problem in importing methods, paradigms and theories from Europe into Africa. Consequently, they consistently reproduce knowledges and advance epistemologies and methodologies of equilibrium.[36] This is why there is an urgent need to understand the genealogy and trajectories of the Westernized university before one can delve into the pertinent question of decolonizing the university in Africa.

The Trajectory of the Modern Westernized University

Tracking the trajectory of the university, one identifies the following shifts, informed by the mutating imperatives of modernist Western thought: the Renaissance university, Enlightenment university, Kantian-Humboldtian university, and the current corporate university.[37] The Renaissance university was the centre for theological and rhetorical studies. Knowledge was organized into the *trivium* (in the service of the church) and *quadrivium* (in the service of the monarchy/crown).[38] Just like the Euro-American constituted international system, the university and its episteme is resistant to radical decolonial change. What only occasionally happens across history is what Foucault terms 'epistemic breaks,' which do not interfere with the Euro-American epistemic but signify epochal changes in the world order.

The Renaissance university was the home for humanistic learning. The Enlightenment university was the centre of secular knowledge and the triumphalism of science over theology. The Kantian-Humboldtian university was organized around philosophy and sciences in the service of emerging nation-states and colonialism.[39] The corporate university began to replace the Kantian-Humboldtian university in the 1970s. It was imposed on Africa in the 1980s during the heydays of structural adjustment programmes and triumphalism of neo-liberalism.[40]

What must be emphasized is that the Kantian-Humboldtian university became part of the colonial project, playing a leading role in the introduction of Western knowledge and displacement of existing forms of knowledges that were labeled 'native,' 'traditional,' 'primitive' and considered repugnant to modernity. Ironically, it was also the Kantian-Humboldtian university that produced the African educated elite that spearheaded the decolonization project as nothing but another stage within the modernity process. Social sciences became very important during the age of the Kantian-Humboldtian university because they were required to enable the organization of modern governments and civil society as well as management of a capitalist political economy.

This is why Immanuel Wallerstein made it clear that social sciences were never a bounded and autonomous arena of social action; rather, they have always been an important segment of larger structures of knowledge of the modern world.[41] Analyzing the role of Western social sciences from Africa, Claude Ake clearly associated them with imperialism, noting that they played an important role in keeping Africans subordinated and underdeveloped, and inhibiting African understanding of the problem of the modern world system. He elaborated that they continue to feed Africans 'noxious values and/false hopes; to make us pursue policies which undermine our competitive strength and guarantee our permanent underdevelopment and dependence.'[42]

At the time of decolonization and attainment of political independence, the African nationalist governments with their obsession with development promoted the idea of the 'developmentalist university,' which was not totally decoupled from the global Westernized university. The nationalist governments struggled to 'indigenize' the colonially inherited universities that had for years operated as colleges of metropolitan universities such as the University of London. To the African nationalist governments, a national university was not simply a symbol of sovereignty, but was also expected to play a supportive role to the nation-state-building project. But as noted by Mahmood Mamdani:

> Indeed, the university occupied a contradictory location, for the university was an incubator of not only critical thought but also a political counter-elite. Critique could and did mask ambition. The more professors acted like ministers-in-waiting and, in some cases, like presidents-in-waiting, the more their critique sounded self-serving. In a single-party context, the university took on the character of an opposition party.[43]

The inherited universities used the discourse of maintaining international standards in their resistance to be decoupled from the Westernized university order. They also resisted interference of government through claims of protecting academic freedom. This behaviour of the university set it on a collision course with such leaders as Kwame Nkrumah, who railed against the university in these words:

> We do not intend to sit idly by and see these institutions which are supported by millions of pounds produced out of the sweat and toil of common people continue to be centres of anti-government activities. We want the university college to cease being an alien institution and to take on the character of a Ghanaian University, loyally serving the interests of the nation and the well-being of our people. If reforms do not come from within, we intend to impose them from outside, and no resort to the cry of academic freedom (for academic freedom does not mean irresponsibility) is going to restrain us from seeing that our university is a healthy university devoted to Ghanaian interest.[44]

While the state-university relationship was deteriorating another problem emerged. The developmental university underwent corporatization as the postcolonial state lost its little autonomy to global multi-lateral financial institutions, particularly the International Monetary Fund (IMF) and the World Bank (WB). The rise of the corporate university in the 1970s did not help. It worsened the situation. It brought in the coloniality of market forces within a neoliberal global political-economic framework.

The corporate university privileged the rule of technologically-oriented social sciences such as economics and accounting. The humanities and interpretive social sciences such as history and cultural anthropology lost their previous standing. Corporate values invaded the university together with new quality controls over the faculty, departments and degree programmes. Professors became under pressure to account for their research and publications in terms of quantity rather than quality. Education and knowledge underwent commodification and marketization. Knowledge became conceived in terms of 'technicism' and 'innovation.'[45] Universities introduced such portfolios as Research and Innovation as drivers of research. Peter Stewart commented that knowledge in a corporate university became reduced to the 'polytechnic/technikon and industry mode of know-how' (brick and mortar terms).[46] Intellectual thought was measured in terms of its instrumentalism.

Research in the present phase of the corporate university has shifted from being a long-range diagnostic enterprise to a quick prescriptive exercise. Mahmood Mamdani described this as the invasion of the university by consultancy cultures.[47] The emphasis is on training in descriptive and quantitative data collection methods. The penchant for quantification of complex human phenomena greatly reinforced the conservatism of Western social science. Fundamental issues which were not easily amenable to quantification became sidelined. Claude Ake provides the example of the complex problem of democracy, which was reduced to the abstractions of political participation—which was itself 'reduced to voting and voting studies and attitude surveys.' [48]

The major point here is that the privileging of quantification of complex human phenomena cascaded from the belief that 'major problems of social life have been solved and that all that remains is a few minor problems of adjustment which do not call the foundations of the society into question, but rather require merely technical solutions.' [49] Within this type of a university the knowledges produced are for equilibrium. Large-scale and radical changes of a revolutionary nature are not envisioned or tolerated. Ake noted that 'there is bias against change as is evident in the use of concepts with negative connotations to describe elements of change—e.g., disequilibrium, deviance, crisis, stress, conflict, instability, etc.' [50]

Consultancy reports rather than scholarly books dominate research in a corporatized university. The university becomes viewed as similar to other corporate entities whose efficiency and value is measured in monetary terms. Leadership which is based on vision is substituted by rigid managerialism.

As this process is consolidating itself in universities across the world, those academics pursuing knowledge become endangered species. Their ideas are ridiculed, distorted and deliberately misrepresented. Critical thinking is no longer valued. Intellectual timidity is tolerated. One finds full professors for whom a Google search does not even turn up any publications.

At the centre of the corporate university is what Lewis R. Gordon terms disciplinary decadence. [51] This decadence takes the form of failure by disciplinary-based knowledge to produce solutions to pressing social problems. Gordon noted that the decadence manifests itself in the form of scientists criticizing the humanities for not being scientific, and literary scholars criticizing scientists for not being literary. [52] In the process, disciplines fail dismally to deal with or confront those pertinent questions 'greater than the discipline itself.' [53] Attempts to resolve the crisis of disciplinary decadence is by way of MIT (multi-, inter-, and transdisciplinary approaches). The assumption here is that disciplines are free from coloniality. Research methods are free from coloniality. The reality is that such disciplines as anthropology carried coloniality. All disciplines as packaged from the West carry coloniality. If we accept this, then how can multiplying them, inter-breeding them and cross-breeding them resolve the problem of coloniality? Is MIT not therefore reinforcement of coloniality?

MIT is nothing less than a mere sugarcoating of the coloniality of knowledge and concealment of the continuing subordination of other knowledges to Euro-North American-centric knowledges. In decolonial thinking, the solution is not MIT but ecologies of knowledges.[54] European, African, Asian and Latin American knowledges must be allowed equal space in the academy. The crisis of disciplinary decadence is rooted in European fundamentalism, which unfolded in terms of displacement and appropriation of other knowledges. Human ontology and experience is plural and only a plurality of knowledges can deal effectively with multiple human challenges. An African university as opposed to a university in Africa must be a centre of ecologies of knowledges. It must have a distinct identity and mission.

The African University

There is something disappointing about the current initiatives in decolonization of the university in Africa. The initiatives involve cosmetic changes of names of the universities from colonial names to local vernacular ones, including naming them after those heroes who actively fought for the liberation of Africa from colonialism. These cosmetic changes also involve high-sounding missions like an 'African University in the Service of Humanity.' It would seem that some Africans think that by merely changing the names and re-writing the vision statements and mission statements the inherited universities would begin the journey of decolonization. The reality is that those in charge of universities in Africa simply change names and mission statements without full commitment to real structural changes and going deeper into epistemological and disciplinary transformations to reflect African identities and other imperatives.

This is why there is still urgent need for universities in Africa to be radically transformed into African universities through thorough decolonization of curriculum and institutional frameworks as well as faculty members. The process must include careful and deep thinking on what values should distinguish and underpin an African university; what competencies and critical skills must distinguish its products; what psychologies, ideologies, visions, and worldviews an African university should nurture and inculcate on its students; and what teaching methodologies should an African university develop in its endeavor to produce pan-African students able to creatively, innovatively and originally respond to African development challenges.

An ideal starting point is to embrace Kwasi Wiredu's point that 'conceptually speaking, then, the maxim of the moment should be: 'African, know thyself.'[55] The African university must be founded on a critical Africa-centred epistemology that is focused on a deep understanding of politics of knowledge generation, involving reanalyzing the claims of received sciences for the benefit of Africa and its people. An African university must not be a centre of intellectual complacency but one where evaluation of the risks contained in received methodologies, epistemologies and disciplines takes the centre-stage.[56]

This starting point is ideal as the African university must always be sensitive to its location within a Euro-American world that is working hard to remain dominant. Its mission must always be cognizant of the fact that existing Western social science was not meant to solve African problems and instead was used to keep Africa and its people in a subordinate and underdeveloped state.[57] Following this logic one can argue that there would be no point in establishing an African university if it won't be different from existing Westernized universities in Africa. In an African university Africa must be privileged as a legitimate epistemic site of research, and African people should not be treated as objects of knowledge but must be enabled to regain their lost epistemic virtue as repositories of knowledge. An African university must be deeply aware of where Africa is coming from epistemologically speaking and build from there. Up to today, colonization of the mind has remained the worst form of colonization, as it affects and shapes African people's consciousness and identity. An African university must work flat out to reverse this colonial thinking. But the process of decolonizing the minds of Africans has proven to be a very difficult task to achieve, because it must take the form of restoration of displaced knowledges and realisation that Euro-American epistemology is just one among other modes of knowing and knowledges. It is this challenge that an African university needs to confront directly, and pan-African students and their professors must brace themselves to directly confront present day 'coloniality' that has been naturalised, universalised and normalised.

The first thing to address is the identity of an African university. This crisis of identity is linked to other crises such as the 'crisis of legitimacy,' 'crisis of relevance,' 'crisis of appropriate epistemology,' 'crisis of historical representation' and 'crisis of student identity.'[58] These visible and invisible crises are linked to a bigger crisis — 'the crisis of the mission of the African university against the backdrop of that university being in Africa but not being an African one by characterisation.'[59]

The second challenge is that as the African university searches for alternatives to domination and oppression, it must be careful in distinguishing 'between alternatives to the system of domination and oppression and alternatives within the same system.'[60] The persistent challenge since the dawn of political independence has been how do Africans fight against Euro-American epistemological hegemony using the conceptual and political instruments given by the same epistemology and world system?

The time has come for Africans to realise that decolonization of being can only begin with decolonizing epistemology — that is, decolonizing ways of knowing and knowledge production itself. The time has also come for Africans to realise that the ongoing struggles for social justice are inseparable from the struggles for cognitive justice. The African university must be ready to carry forward this burden.

The mission of the African university must be that of facilitating the crystallization of an African collective vision for attaining pan-African unity and being a driver for social, political, and economic development of the continent through fostering high-quality basic and applied research in areas critical to African technical, economic, political, and social development. The African university must be a strategic and distinctive site for higher education teaching and research excellence capable of producing students capable of generating original and home-grown solutions to African problems while also drawing from global human experiences. By and large, it must be a centre for the production of African-centred knowledge that contributes to the global knowledge economy while solving African problems and having global appeal and reach. It must not lose sight of its agenda of being a site of questioning of existing Euro-American epistemology, old models, curricula and research paradigms that constrain innovation, creativity, originality, and the spirit of invention.

The African university must reflect carefully on the problem of disciplinary decadence and avoid organising knowledge in narrow terms of rigid disciplines organised into inflexible academic 'tribes' and 'silos' of mono-disciplines. Knowledge must be organised into broad fields such as African Studies that embrace various disciplines. This means that the African university must be distinguishable by innovative fields of study and a research agenda that are directly informed by the desire to solve pressing African problems and challenges. This means that it is home-grown and it promotes endogenous knowledge production that has been pushed to the margins of society by Euro-American epistemology.

The African university must pride itself as a generator of knowledge rather than a mere consumer of global knowledge. It must produce original thinkers in the mould of Frantz Fanon who are capable of theorising complex issues while at the same time engaged in artisational empirical research. Such a university must be distinguishable by the epistemological position from which its faculty and students speak, which we describe as the locus of enunciation. The locus of enunciation must be clearly African, including the African diaspora. It means that its faculty and students must display the values of speaking from the vantage point of 'colonial difference,' and this will enable them to appreciate the reality that Africa and other parts of the ex-colonized world experienced the 'darker side' of modernity—such as mercantilism, the slave trade, imperialism, colonialism, apartheid, and neo-colonialism—which led to underdevelopment rather than development.

A clear locus of enunciation also reveals that all knowledges are partial and this reality questions the practice of Euro-American epistemology always concealing the locus of the subject, which speaks only to claim universality and to hide dangerous imperial global designs embedded within it. In short, through their clear locus of enunciation, pan-African students will think *from* Africa and the Global South, taking full account of the voices of African subaltern groups as knowledge producers, thinking *with them,* learning *from them,* rather than *thinking about them* and *for them*—collaborating with them in the long process of becoming free human beings and agents of African development.

Finally, the African university must consider fully embracing a decolonial epistemic perspective as a form of critical social theory informing its teaching and research, as this is in tandem with the agenda of liberation and charting sustainable development alternatives. A decolonial epistemic perspective is rooted in African resistance to such oppressive processes as the slave trade, imperialism, colonialism, apartheid and neo-colonialism as well as the disempowering effects of the globalization process. A decolonial epistemic perspective privileges insights and knowledges cascading from African societies within the continent and in the diaspora without necessarily throwing away progressive aspects of Euro-American epistemology and the best of modernity.

Conclusion

The decolonization that is called for today must not be confused with the Africanization and deracialization initiatives that were undertaken by the founding fathers and mothers of postcolonial states in the 1960s and 1970s. Those initiatives were heavily criticised by Frantz Fanon as spearheaded by a lazy, unscrupulous and parasitic national bourgeoisie that had totally assimilated colonial thought in its most corrupt forms. Africanization and nationalization under this national bourgeoisie became interpreted in narrow terms of a simple transfer of colonial loot into the hands of the black national elites that had inherited the colonial state.

It is with this hindsight that the African university must be careful in its recruitment of its professors because most of the African academics and intellectuals are products of Euro-American institutions where they were fully exposed to Euro-American epistemology as the only objective, universal, truthful, neutral and disembodied way of knowing. They themselves require decolonization of the mind and introduction to decolonial epistemic perspectives before they can be entrusted with the challenge and task of producing decolonized and fully pan-African students capable of implementing the pan-African vision.

Decoloniality seeks not only to rescue the university from corporatization but is also pushing for restoration of African knowledges and languages. It is premised on questions of power, being, and knowledge as central constituent elements in the making of the modern world order and production of subjectivities that are mediated by race. Decoloniality invites Africans to think from where they are as the first step towards decolonization of the mind. It strongly advocates for mental decolonization as an important step towards unleashing African people's research and innovative potential. Decoloniality is a redemptive epistemology, a liberatory force and an ethical-humanistic project gesturing towards pluriversalism in which different worlds fit.

As articulated by Achille Mbembe, the decolonization of the university we are fighting for is one that should culminate in 'self-ownership' as 'a precondition, a necessary step towards the creation of new forms of life that could genuinely be characterized as fully human.'[61] What such decolonization entails is advancement from imitations and mimicry of Euro-North American-centric games of domination.

Notes and References

1. Quoted in Mkandawire, T. (2005). African intellectual and nationalism. In T. Mkandawire (Ed.), *African intellectuals: Rethinking politics, language, gender and development.* Dakar, Senegal: CODESRIA and Zed Books, pp. 22–23.

2. Gordon, L. R. (2006). *Disciplinary decadence: Living thought in trying times.* Boulder, CO: Paradigm Publishers, p. 10.

3. Rabaka, R. (2010). *Against epistemic apartheid: W.E. B. Du Bois and the disciplinary decadence of sociology.* Lanham, MD: Lexington Books.

4. Wallerstein, I. (2004). *World-systems analysis: An introduction.* Durham, NC: Duke University Press.

5. Slater, D. (2004). *Geopolitics and the post-colonial: Rethinking North-South relations.* Malden, MA: Blackwell Publishing, pp. 223–233.

6. Slater, 2004, p. 223.

7. Depelchin, J. (2005). *Silences in African history: Between the syndromes of discovery and abolition.* Dar Es Salaam, Tanzania: Mkuki na Nyota Publishers.

8. Grosfoguel, R. (2012). Decolonizing Western uni-versalisms: Decolonial pluri-versalism from Aime Cesaire to the Zapatistas. *Transmodernity, Journal of Peripheral Cultural Production of the Luso-Hispanic World, 1*(3), 88–104.

9. Grosfoguel, R. (2007, March/May). The epistemic decolonial turn: Beyond political-economy paradigms. *Cultural Studies, 21*(2–3), 211–223.

10. Chabal, P. (2012). *The end of conceit: Western rationality after postcolonialism.* London, England: Zed Books, p. viii.

11. Wallerstein, I. (2011). *The modern world-system 1: Capitalist agriculture and the origins of the European world economy in the sixteenth century: With a new prologue.* Berkeley, CA: University of California Press; Dussel, E. (1995). *The invention of the Amer-*

icas: Eclipse of 'the Other' and the myth of modernity. New York, NY: Continuum; Grosfoguel, R. (2007, March/May). The epistemic decolonial turn: Beyond political-economy paradigms. *Cultural Studies, 21*(2–3), 211–223; and Quijano, A. (2007). Coloniality and modernity/rationality. *Cultural Studies, 21*(2–3), 168–178.

12. Grosfoguel, R., & Cervantes-Rodriguez, A. M. (Eds.). (2002). *The modern/colonial/capitalist world-system in the twentieth century: Global processes, antisystematic movements, and the geopolitics of knowledge.* Westport, CT: Praeger Publishers.

13. Davidson, B. (1992). *The black man's burden: Africa and the curse of the nation-state.* Oxford, England: James Currey.

14. Grosfoguel, R. (2007, March/May). The epistemic decolonial turn: Beyond political-economy paradigms. *Cultural Studies, 21*(2–3), 211–223.

15. Quijano, A. (2007, March/May). Coloniality and modernity/rationality. *Cultural Studies, 21*(2–3), 168–178; and Ndlovu-Gatsheni, S. J. (2012, Dec). Coloniality of power in development studies and the impact of global imperial designs on Africa. *The Australasia Review of African Studies, XXXIII* (II), 49.

16. Fanon, F. (1952). *Black skin, white masks.* New York, NY: Grove Press, p. 206.

17. Grosfoguel, R. (2007), p. 213; Ndlovu-Gatsheni, S. J. (2013). *Coloniality of power in postcolonial Africa: Myths of decolonization.* Dakar, Senegal: CODESRIA Book Series.

18. Grosfoguel, 2007, p. 213.

19. Ndlovu-Gatsheni, S. J. (2013, May). Decolonizing the university in Africa. *The Thinker, 51*, 46–51.

20. For differences between liberation and emancipation see Ndlovu-Gatsheni, S. J. (2012). Fiftieth anniversary of decolonization in Africa: A moment of celebration or critical reflections. *Third World Quarterly, 33*(1), 71–89.

21. Ngugi wa Thiong'o. (1981). *Writers in politics.* London, England: Heinemann, p. 4.

22. Hardt, M., & Negri, A. (2000). *Empire.* Cambridge, MA: Harvard University Press, p. 3.

23. Ndlovu-Gatsheni, S. J. (2013). *Empire, global coloniality and African subjectivity.* New York, NY: Berghahn Books.

24. Mazrui, A. A. (2010). Preface: Black berlin and the curse of fragmentation: From Bismarck to Barack. In Adebajo, A. (2010). *The Curse of Berlin: Africa after the Cold War.* Scottsville, South Africa: University of KwaZulu-Natal Press, p. xi.

25. Chinweizu. (1987). *The West and the rest of us: White predators, black slavers and the African elite.* Lagos, Nigeria: Pero Press.

26. Castro-Gomez cited in Grosfoguel, 2007, p. 214.

27. Ndlovu-Gatsheni, 2013, pp. 100–118.

28. Chinweizu. (1987). *Decolonizing the African Mind.* Lagos, Nigeria: Pero Press.

29. Memmi, *The colonizer and the colonized*, p. 164.

30. Ngugi wa Thiong'o. (2012). *Globalectics: Theory and the politics of knowing.* New York, NY: Columbia University Press, p. 28.

31. Ngugi wa Thiong'o, *Globalectics*, p. 39.

32. Du Bois, W. E. B. (1903). *The souls of black folk: Essays and sketches.* Chicago, IL: A.C. McClurg & CO.

33. Bhabha, H. (1994). *The location of culture.* London, England: Routledge.

34. Satre, J. P. (1962). *Black orpheus.* Paris, France: Presence Africaine.

35. Neocosmos, M. (2010). *From 'foreign natives' to 'native foreigners': Explaining*

xenophobia in post-apartheid South Africa: Citizenship and nationalism, identity and politics. Dakar, Senegal: CODESRIA Books.

36. Ake, *Social science as imperialism*, pp. 58–67.

37. Tlostanova, M. V., & Mignolo, W. D. (2012). *Learning to unlearn: Decolonial reflections from Eurasia and the Americas*. Columbus, OH: Ohio State University Press, pp. 196–216.

38. Tlostanova and Mignolo, 2012, p. 201.

39. Tlostanova and Mignolo, 2012, p. 201.

40. Tlostanova and Mignolo, 2012, p. 202.

41. Wallerstein, I. (2004). *The uncertainties of knowledge*. Philadelphia, PA: Temple University Press, p. 16.

42. Ake, C. (1979). *Social science as imperialism: The theory of political development* (2nd ed.). Ibadan, Nigeria: Ibadan University Press, p. xiv.

43. Mamdani, M. (2013). *Define and rule: Native as political identity*. Johannesburg, South Africa: Wits University, pp. 87–88.

44. Quoted in Mkandawire, T. (2005). African intellectuals and nationalism. In T. Mkandawire (Ed.), *African intellectuals: Rethinking politics, language, gender and development*. Dakar, Senegal: CODESRIA and Zed Books, p. 22.

45. Ndlovu-Gatsheni, S. J. (2012). Coloniality of power in development studies and the impact of global imperial designs on Africa. *The Australasian Review of African Studies*, XXXIII (II), December, pp. 58–59.

46. Stewart, P. (2007). Re-envisioning the academic profession in the shadow of corporate managerialism. *Journal of Higher Education*, 5(1), 141.

47. Mamdani, M. (2011, April 21). The importance of research in a university. In *Pambazuka News 526*.

48. Ake, 1979, p. 133.

49. Ake, 1979. p. 133.

50. Ake, 1979. p. 132.

51. Gordon, 2006, p. 33.

52. Gordon, 2006, p. 33.

53. Gordon, 2006, p. 34.

54. Santos, B. de S. (2007). Beyond abyssal thinking: From global lines to ecologies of knowledges. *Review*, XXX (1), 45–89.

55. Wiredu, K. (1992). Formulating modern thoughts in African languages: Some theoretical considerations. In Valentine Y. Mudimbe (Ed.), *The surreptitious speech: Presence Africaine and the politics of otherness, 1947–1987*, Chicago, IL: University of Chicago Press, pp. 301–332.

56. Diawara, M. (1990). Reading Africa through Foucault: V. Y. Mudimbe's reaffirmation of the subject. In *October*, 55, Winter, pp. 65–96.

57. Ake, 1979, p. ii.

58. Teboho et al, p. 75.

59. Teboho et al. p. 75.

60. Santos, 2007, p. 78.

61. Mbembe, A. (2015). Decolonizing knowledge and the question of the archive. (Unpublished Paper Presented at WISER, University of Witwatersrand, Johannesburg, South Africa, April).

Chapter 3

Reversing Epistemicide and the Quest for Relevant Social Sciences and Humanities

Teboho J. Lebakeng

Historical Precedents

I plead guilty to obsessing over historical precedents. This is because I have previously argued that historically, European colonisation was justified on the basis of two vacuous mythical claims, whose centrality and essence was that when Europeans first came to Africa the continent was both *terra nullius* and *terra incognita*.[1] The former literally and technically meaning the land belonged to no one. The latter essentially implying that the continent was an unknown territory which was an unexplored region. Following from the above preposterous claims, the colonialists proceeded to argue that such territory invited the attention of terrestrial explorers who wanted to explore, know and finally own it. For instance, in justifying British colonisation of a continent which Conrad[2] characterised as a "heart of darkness", Lugard[3] argues that the continent "lay wasted and ungarnered [...] because the natives did not know their use and value. Millions of tons of oil-nuts, for instance, grew wild without the labour of man, and lay rotting in the forests. Who can deny the right of the hungry people of Europe to utilise the wasted bounties of nature, or that the task of developing these resources was, as Mr. Chamberlain expressed it, a 'trust for civilisation' and for the benefit of mankind?"[4]

In doubting, if not completely dismissing, the existence of African reality prior to colonisation, another apologist of colonisation in the person of Van Binsbergen[5] states: "What is more, on theoretical, epistemological and comparative grounds we are to suspect that the Southern African village and the social and normative patterns that governed it, instead of continuing a perennial lived reality, have to some extent been a creation of colonial administration, missionary activities, industrial relations based on labour migration, and social anthropological aggregate description." Historiography is replete with colonial discourse that sought to fix and frame the African continent as a region of complete savagery and intellectual darkness which represented a negative Other without self-consciousness and devoid of an underpinning philosophy of life.[6] Over the years myths represented only the humanity of those who borrow them. This is neither a small matter nor a moot point since, in contrast, Eurocentrism was understood as the implicit view that societies, knowledge, languages and cultural values of colonial origin constitute the 'natural' normative paradigm for the rest of the world to emulate. Babu[7] defines similar dualism as 'the philosophical concept which defines human nature by two opposing sets of qualities such as good versus evil, egotism versus altruism and virtue versus vice.' In essence such negative attributes were ascribed to Africa and the Africans and all righteous and positive ones to Europeans.

The essence of ascribing barbarism to Africans was the primordial justification for the scramble for the continent and the expressed purpose of dehumanising the presumed negative Other with the primary objective of calling into question their humanity. It was a narrative used to dispossess, to destroy and to loot the African continent of its rich and diverse natural and human resources. Given its impact, the concept of dehumanisation has received extensive empirical attention[8] and it is clear that apart from undermining one's individuality, it prevents those dehumanising others from showing compassion towards them. No wonder the naked brutality of the colonialists and the unfathomable sickness of their mind. In practice, dehumanisation occurred discursively, as in idiomatic and metaphorical language that equates certain human beings to animals, specifically to reptiles such as snakes, mammals such as dogs, pigs and donkeys and rodents such as rats, or symbolically, as in imagery, or physically, in the form of chattel slavery. The colonisers, both at the time of making inroads into Africa and during the period of consolidating colonialism, presented Africans as child-like and incapable of managing their own affairs and their way of life as barbaric.[9] It is in this respect that colonisation is a form of dehumanisation[10] and the logic of colonialism was the systematic negation of the humanity of Africans.[11] In sustaining the most pernicious system of derision of Africans, colonialists were essentially devious, evil and cruel as they displayed the highest form of barbarism.

They justified the colonial cause and were prepared to do anything in pursuit of the colonial project, especially in trying to universalise the world by projecting their values. Serequeberhan writes that, in the name of the universality of values, European colonialism violently universalised its own singular particularity and annihilated the historicality of the colonised. In this context, Western philosophy—in the guise of a disinterested universalistic, transcendental, speculative discourse—served the indispensable function of being the ultimate veracious buttress of European conquest.[12] This overlooked the fact that instead of being an abstract activity totally liberated from the contingencies of physical survival, philosophy was developed in response to the predicament of human beings in a precarious world. Such epistemology of alterity,[13] based on juxtaposing and dualising the colonialists and the colonial victims, could not be sustained and advanced without galvanising pseudo-science.

This meant misrepresenting the biblical text in order to dehumanise Africans, as illustrated by a report showing the relationship between colonial apartheid and the church in colonial-apartheid South Africa.[14] As in other parts of colonised Africa, religion was implicated in colonisation. Missionaries came to Africa as the 'self-proclaimed avant-garde representatives of Christian civilisation and their self-perception was that of chosen ones owing to their assumed and claimed racial, moral and technological superiority', on the one hand, and the depravity of African institutions, on the other.[15] This also meant providing racist education and distorted history as part of the mis-education of Africans, especially the intellectual elite, who were the main beneficiaries of colonial education.

What colonialists invented and projected were unmistakably their deepest prejudices as they did not hesitate to abuse (social) science to formulate misconceived, flawed and distorted racist theories about Africans as barbaric subhumans who (1) had no history and therefore could not claim to know themselves and had to be told who they were by Europeans, (2) were cultural children shaped by depraved sexual lust, immorality and degeneration, (3) could not rule themselves because of their primitive irresponsibility and, therefore, needed enlightened masters to show them the ways of superior civilisation and deliver them from ignorance, (4) could not claim ownership of Africa, or even of their lands, since they were incapable of cultivating and managing them, (5) had no right to human justice since they were sub-human and (6) had no religion and therefore needed the light of Christianity if they were to be freed from their chaotic state and animism.[16] In this respect, the colonial encounter led to what Mudimbe calls the 'invention of Africa' and reorganising the continent in both structures and minds.[17]

Sufficient data and persuasive evidence exist proving the fact that before the European conquest of Africa, Africans had built up a pool of knowledge and technology which they used to sustain agriculture, human and animal health, industrial production involving food processing, metallurgy, leather tanning, timber seasoning, fermentation of beverages, making of dyes, mining and architectural engineering.[18] But political subjugation by European colonisers traumatised Africans to the extent that many lost confidence in and looked down upon their own material culture and non-material culture such as traditions, values and norms, thus forcing them to view and embrace Westernisation as the only progressive move. Ironically, fundamental to the justification of colonisation was the presentation of the colonial project as essentially a mission of civilising and humanising non-rational African sub-beings. The irony is that clearly, instead of salvaging Africans, the colonial enterprise savaged them and denied them self-consciousness and self-reflection. Rather than being benevolent and enlightening for Africa and Africans, colonisation pushed Africa and Africans towards darkness through plunder. A roundhouse punch at the essential premise of the colonising mission reveals that rather than encountering a continent that was essentially *tabula rasa*, colonialists imposed different systems of thought, educational practices and philosophising. Therefore, there was clearly a disjuncture between mythological colonial rhetoric and the reality of the African situation.

Premised on the foregoing exposition, colonialism committed epistemicide[19] and technocide, i.e., the killing of the grounds for indigenous African knowledge and its embodiment in the form of their know-how. The ensuing violent destruction, in the physical sense and in the form of epistemicide, facilitated the imposition of Western colonial epistemological paradigms in the form of moral values, traditions, philosophical outlooks, aesthetical preferences and economic fundamentals. These were to constitute universal/golden standards and intellectual code. Thus, epistemicide was comprehensive and totalising as it extended to all spheres of life, including religion, politics, law, education, history and the economy. By this we do not mean that Africans totally lost their old cosmology or basic beliefs,[20] as indigenous African knowledge systems survived and continue to retain their potential as key ingredients for sustainable socio-economic development.[21]

The State of the Art in the Social Sciences and Humanities

The foregoing historical context points to three critical issues. First, it points to how deeply the social sciences and humanities were implicated in the colonial encounter and in further consolidating the colonial project. Second, it points to the need to reverse epistemicide and end the state of decoloniality following the promises of the transition from colonialism to independence and the critical role reoriented social sciences and humanities should play in this intellectual trajectory. Third, the reversal of epistemicide should be fore-grounded across the social sciences and humanities so as to ensure comprehensive freeing of such disciplines from Western epistemological boundaries. Part of the reason is that these disciplines have not covered themselves in glory since the decolonization of Africa, hence the state of decoloniality in knowledge as the archives and canons of the disciplines remain disproportionately Western. After all, even the original colonial university was so unashamedly foreign in an African context and was transplanted with negligible concessions that its core postulates, key concepts, basic methodologies, underpinning theories and competing models were drawn from and essentially represented extrapolates of discrete European and American socio-historical experiences and cultural specificity.[22]

Although anthropology has received a lion's share of the devastating critique,[23] it is self-evident that sociology, criminology, philosophy, religion, history, political science, jurisprudence, psychology, social work, education, ethics, literature, administration and management were effective justificatory instruments of colonisation.[24] With the introduction of Western education in Africa, the educational institutions were modeled after the European ones. The content of education in the social sciences and humanities reflected that of institutions in the colonies. Indigenous African education, which was central to African development during the pre-colonial era, was undermined and destroyed. For the purpose of this paper, what is essential is the question: What is the state of the art in the social sciences and humanities under conditions of post-coloniality? Although there is no moral, pedagogical and epistemic reason to retain colonial education in Africa, as a former lecturer and student of the social sciences and humanities who studied at three universities in Africa, I can attest that despite protestation, both loud and muted, these disciplines are still condemned to paradigmatic dependency and epistemic mimicry. It is noteworthy that this assertion is not meant to underplay the Africanisation project, which continues to seek ways and means of reversing epistemicide, but aims at underlining the remaining daunting challenge.

Scholarship in the social sciences and humanities is still fundamentally derivative and contrived, as it is characterised by the dependency syndrome. Since the inauguration of Western education in the colonies reflected cultural parochialism[25] and knowledge production was steeped in Western intellectual traditions, it is extroverted[26] and has destructive effect on African learners and African societies. In other words, they are not relevant to the social conditions of Africa because they are still encapsulated in ethnocentric (Western) assumptions that are dangerously taken to be universal. By imposing the particular as the universal, the West ensured that conceptualising social relations and social problems and strategising policy options from indigenous African perspectives has a marginal place in the social sciences and humanities. Solutions to African problems are imported from the West with very devastating consequences. For instance, relations between economic ideas and policy making in Africa points to these problems.

In this regard, the dominant curriculum in the disciplines continues to be a source of alienation. Often the curriculum does not speak to the experiences of learners since it does not reflect the philosophical, social and technological realities of their environment. As Mathews recalled in *Freedom for My People*: "Our history as we had absorbed it bore no resemblance to South African history as it had been written by European scholars, or as it is taught in South African schools, and as it was taught to us at Fort Hare. The European insisted that we accept his version of the past [...] if we want to get ahead educationally, even to pass examinations in the subject as he presents it".[27] This example might be from South Africa (and for some a bit dated) but other Africans throughout the continent find resonance as they have the same experiences.

Because intellectuality is decoupled from the existential socio-cultural reality of students and academics, the learning process is still mimetic and there is lack of cognitive justice. This academic mimetism is a function of the failure to cut the intellectual umbilical cord from the Western epistemological paradigm imposed during the colonial conquest and perpetuated in the post-colonial era.[28] The result is an uncritical approach to ideas and concepts from the West,[29] the inability to be creative and raise original problems, the inability to devise original analytical methods, alienation from the main issues of indigenous African society[30] and failure to tap indigenous resources such as indigenous languages.[31] In practical terms, epistemicide closed the African cultural space, hence African cultural traditions as a heritage were never allowed to develop to inform and be informed by African imperatives and sensibilities. Rather, such cultural traditions were presented as a baggage to be despised and thrown away.

Western epistemological tyranny still functions in the academy to undermine efforts to inscribe indigenous African knowledge systems and alternative knowledge production in the curriculum. At the same time, numerous individuals engaged in research and education—especially from dominant cultural backgrounds—continue to dismiss the importance of indigenous knowledge in academic work and pedagogy. Hence, translators, editors, peer-reviewers and language instructors sometimes deliberately and at times inadvertently undermine efforts at reversing epistemicide in the social sciences and humanities, thus effectively ensuring the perpetuation and dominance of Western epistemological paradigms at the expense of all others. Through epistemological xenophobia and being wedded to Eurocentrism, alternative scholarship, narratives and knowledge can easily be dismissed as politicised and polemical.[32] I personally know of a 'reviewer' who disqualifies and dismisses articles by merely looking at the reference section. In the case of South Africa, the general call for Africanisation has caused as much anguish and anger as it has enthusiasm, with those opposed to it seeing it as an insolent provocation[33] and a development that could lead to the lowering of academic standards and sacrificing of excellence and meritocracy.

The logic of monoculture of scientific knowledge has been a subject of contestation by African intellectual luminaries like Claude Ake, Archie Mafeje, Dani Nabudere, Peter Magubane and Joseph Ki-Zerbo, among others, who sought to decolonise the knowledge of and about Africa that the academy produced. Despite their seriously encouraging efforts to rethink the social sciences and humanities, the state of decoloniality still prevails. Hence a requiem for colonial social sciences and humanities in Africa cannot be concluded. The common denominator and probably depressing aspect about all the personalities mentioned is that they have all departed. However, despite variations in their varied intellectual grounding and scholastic enterprises, collectively they produced and left behind a legacy of works spanning theoretical, empirical, historical, epistemological and methodological concerns. These works should provide instructive points of departure in the attempt to reverse epistemicide and assert the right to be an African university. They have helped in arriving at a different examination of the history and dynamics of Africa and provided insight into the forces that influenced and shaped the continent in terms of history and knowledge.

Informed by their tremendous work and insight in reframing the African narrative, in 2001, I made a plea relating to South Africa that the social sciences and humanities should not be sacrificed at the expense of the natural sciences. What had become clear was that in a democratising South Africa these disciplines were in a crisis of relevance to society and to students. The plea was made because it had become evident that the democratising state in South Africa was committing a costly strategic blunder as it was focusing less on such disciplines. This was partly as a reaction to the history and politics of the colonial-apartheid regime policy of making the natural sciences a domain of white people, and partly owing to the imperatives and pressures of globalisation and its academic extremism.[34] At the time globalisation was tying education to the apron strings of the market and higher education was increasingly becoming a site of academic commercialization and marketization.[35] I pointed out that although these disciplines were uncritical conduits and consumers of outmoded and anachronistic theories, the way out was to Africanise rather than to sacrifice them, given their potential added value to society. This was hardly a new call as scholars such as Herbert Vilakazi and Ramose Mogobe had raised these concerns in education in general. For them it was not debatable as the social sciences and humanities in Africa in general and South Africa in particular were in crisis of relevance.

Observing this academic extremism and limitations of binary approaches to knowledge, Makgoba had earlier pointed out that 'Africa has faced some of the great social changes in this century in terms of race, ethnicity, politics, violence, labour relations and industrialization. Graduates in the social sciences and humanities are going to be a critical component of the success of African democracies as they struggle to emerge from the mess in which they have been thrust. Universities are not only essential for the training and nurturing of highly-skilled scholars in the cultural, social, economic and psychological realm, but are poised to make a unique contribution to the overall development of post-colonial Africa'.[36]

As recently as 2011, two reports by the Academy of Science of South Africa (ASSAf) and the Charter for the Humanities and Social Sciences (CHCC) were released on the declining standing of the social sciences and humanities in South Africa.[37] These reports pointed to a crisis in the disciplines and alarming declining rates of student numbers in these subjects. In essence, the ASSAf report expressed concern about the worrying 'intellectual stagnation' in the social sciences and humanities over the last fifteen years, posing the single most important threat to the growth of vibrant intellectual scholarship in the social sciences and humanities. It also noted that the social sciences and humanities are facing increasingly declining student enrolment, declining graduation rates and decreased funding. The CHCC report noted extremely worrying signs of decline that need to be arrested and reversed as a matter of urgency, given the important role the social sciences and humanities have to play in South African society. Importantly, it recognizes the impact of linguicide and the need to revive African languages for educational purposes.

After reading both reports, I could only say: Amen. After all, these disciplines did not deserve praise but pillory for their morbid disservice to a democratising society which is facing a multitude of social problems. These disciplines, as taught in the South African universities, had long become liabilities rather than assets. The proposed six catalytic projects on improving the status and standing of and energising the social sciences and humanities are critical as they demonstrate a renewed interest in and recognition of indigenous African knowledge and the need to centre Africa as a source of inspiration. They fundamentally question the nature and epistemic status of such disciplines. They speak to the question of what kind of sociology, psychology, anthropology, social work, economics and history should be taught? However, it might be interesting to delineate short-term, intermediate and long-term interventions lest—like academic development projects which were aimed at assisting students to adjust and cope with higher education—they become industries in their own right.

I posit that the disciplines need to be Africanised and not just reformed. Advocates of reforming the social sciences and humanities are nothing but protectionists who seek to maintain the status quo by tinkering with a serious epistemic crisis. Reforming the social sciences and humanities is antithetical to substantive Africanisation of these disciplines. Moreover, reforming the social sciences and humanities cannot close the cultural gap between these disciplines and African societies. What emerges, therefore, is that unless the social sciences and humanities are Africanised, these disciplines will always be in crisis as informers of social/public policy and retain diminished relevance. Clearly, the academic landscape in the social sciences and humanities needs an infusion of socio-cultural relevance, conceived as a function of how these disciplines respond to national concerns and global imperatives. As such, the crisis in the disciplines presents an opportunity to engage with broader burning issues in the academy. But the crisis also challenges new intellectual cadres to take forward the intellectual battles so gallantly fought by, among others, the intellectual icons already mentioned above.

Asserting the Right to Be an African University

The history of epistemicide in the social sciences and humanities in Africa raises fundamental questions of cognitive and epistemic justice. This is because subordination of the social sciences and humanities to Western epistemological paradigms dehistoricises and decontextualises the African experience. As such, the call for Africanisation, i.e., indigenisation in the African context, of the social sciences and humanities is a clear reflection of the long-held dissatisfaction with the state of the art in these disciplines. More importantly, it is an attempt to privilege African scholarship in terms of research, teaching and publication in order for such scholarship to assume a respectable position in world scholarship. This will only be possible if these disciplines are grounded in African experiences, sensibilities and aspirations and reflect/articulate African hopes, wishes, dilemmas and predicaments. Moreover, this will confirm the contested position that theories, concepts and methodologies can be derived from and nourished by African historical conditions and socio-cultural practices and imperatives. Clearly the issue is not just about including a few African academics in the academy but one that is fundamentally epistemological in nature.

By this it is meant that all the social sciences and humanities disciplines need to be Africanised. This in itself speaks to the necessity to assert the right to be an African university through the reversal of epistemicide.

Given that cultural imperialism and epistemicide are part of the historical trajectory of Western modernity, it is crucial that the intellectual reclamation project should address issues of justice, including cognitive and epistemic ones. The need is to cultivate a critical intellectual tradition that does not require that others should be less so that indigenous Africans could be better. For many scholars, navigating this problematic poses serious challenges of the dialectic of deconstruction and reconstruction in clearly articulating African political, intellectual and philosophical representations.[38] In this sense, such an intellectual project should negotiate knowledge legacies that Africa has inherited with the fundamental objective of local embeddedness.

It is against this background that contemporary African philosophical rationalisations and political representations should be understood. Not as essentially a negation, but profoundly an affirmation, of indigenous African knowledge systems through reversal of epistemicide. Hence the need for a project that speaks to and engages African authenticity: one that is not just combative but more importantly liberatory. Bewaji, who is a credit to the process of reversing epistemicide, has observed insightfully that, in many cases, the combative nature of the discourses African scholars have engaged in is determined by existential internalities and externalities of a group existence that is defined from perspectives not so clemently disposed to the neutrality of intellectual engagement of problems and issues.[39]

In light of this abiding problematic and as part of my contribution to the raging struggle towards reversing epistemicide and trying to ensure that the social sciences and humanities heritage is of relevance to Africa, I have advocated[40] for the need to look seriously at six areas relevant to the Africanisation of the social sciences and humanities, namely, meta-theoretical, theoretical, methodological, pedagogical, empirical and that of applied knowledge. I posit that these six areas will address the present challenges facing the social sciences and humanities by ensuring that the African experience is central in the design of education and policy options.

The meta-theoretical level: This level of Africanisation entails interrogation of four types of meta-theoretical assumptions with the purpose of underpinning what is taught, learned and researched in the African university. This will make African scholars and learners appreciate the ideographic nature of Western science and thought rather than uncritically embrace them as either 'nomothetic' or 'universal'. At the same time they would take Africa as their point of departure in any research, analysis and teaching and correct the fact that African histories, epistemologies and ontology were not factored in the construction and design of the educational curriculum.[41]

- Ontology: assumptions about existence such as the nature of the human identity and how we relate to the world around us.
- Epistemology: assumptions about knowledge such as what it means to know something, how we know/grounds for knowledge and how knowledge claims to be proven.
- Praxeology: assumptions about the practice of theory such as how a theory should be structured and presented.
- Axiology: assumptions about the values that determine the worth of a theory, how a theory should contribute to society.

The theoretical level: Refers to the generation of concepts and indicators and how they relate to African socio-historical experiences and socio-cultural practices. This is not just about theory but theoretical orientation, as the social sciences and humanities should illuminate the African condition as a guide to political action. It is noteworthy that here the problem is not that of lack/poverty of theories, as indigenous African theories on life, existence and the future are plenty. Rather, it is a question of not theorising or under-theorising as a result of the silencing and marginalisation of African approaches and ways of knowing. Until such time that Africans theorise and adopt appropriate orientations in so doing, Africa will continue to lose the control of its development agenda and Western social science will continue to foist Western values and preferences through development initiatives.

The methodological level: Speaks to methodological approaches adopted and the assumptions underlying them. This level should not be conflated with that of methods and techniques (which is not discussed here). Rather, the two should be subsumed as part of methodology to include philosophical, ideological and politico-ethical issues. In the social sciences and humanities, methodology is not a formula but a set of practices informed by and informing the researcher. Currently social sciences and humanities in Africa are steeped and trapped in positivistic social sciences, thus affecting African scholars' orientation to data.

The pedagogical level: This level is also implicated in that the African university should devote more effort to evolving and sharpening teaching methods that are responsive to or consistent with the socio-cultural background and educational needs of African learners. Currently curricula and text books are similar to and teaching methods are imitative of those from the colonial era. More critically, pedagogical experience, competencies and skills are critical since teaching is a normative activity in which teachers take a stand and decide what to teach. The pedagogical level should deal with the kinds of competencies, experiences and skills required because reversing epistemicide hinges on the ability to transcend the distortions and extroversions that constitute the hallmark of colonial pedagogy. It also hinges on the ability of African intellectuals and academics to break down the fundamental disjuncture between social experience and intellectual pronouncements in the social sciences and humanities. Failure to action culturally responsive pedagogy and make the learning experience truly unique will perpetuate cognitive injustice and violence.

The empirical level: Points to a strict focus on relevance to African existential realities. Most problems raised are not an organic outgrowth of the African environment but are akin to those emanating from the Northern Hemisphere. Addressing the empirical level should ensure the existential context of Africa is taken seriously and observed evidence on it informs appropriateness and relevance in addressing challenges to the African condition. Therefore, rather than being guided by theory, which as things stand (limp?) would come from Western wisdom, the solutions will be guided by practical and observed experience as manifest in Africa. This level intertwines immediately with the following one.

The level of applied knowledge: Is about the specification of remedies, plans and policies. Most remedies, plans and policies have been imposed by aid donors and foreign project funders. Thus new modalities of intervention are required so that policy-oriented research and development projects are informed by the needs and aspirations of everyday African social reality, such as street children, squatter camps, abuse of children and women, displacement, landlessness, HIV/AIDS and other social scourges. Otherwise the social sciences and humanities will remain inconsequential to policy options. The colonial notion of Africa as a sociological and philosophical nonentity implies that no solutions can come out of Africa. Therefore, having determined an African outlook about the past, present and future based on the interrogation of the four meta-theoretical assumptions, this level can provide a methodical search for solutions to practical problems in Africa.

Africanisation should not be equated with a call for a cocoon land wherein African intellectuals and academics fear to pit their intellectual pronouncements against their counterparts elsewhere in the global village. Nor should it be equated with intellectual fads, that is, modish ideas that rise for a time to boast intellectual egos but are destined to disappear. Africanising the social sciences and humanities is trying to establish intellectual traditions, scholarship and research culture that are rooted in and are strongly nourished by (and, in turn, nurture) contemporary African development imperatives and democratic pressures. It is also about intellectual liberation from enforced dependence and mimesis. Only then can these disciplines produce truly African responses to the daunting challenges and social problems crippling the continent. This is possible as long as the social sciences and humanities are not extra-societal or supra-societal, but are objective affirmations of the social reality within which they are embedded. They should, therefore, not be discordant, but adapted to and integrated within African communities. In other words, given the history of the development, growth and nature of universities in Africa, they need to enter into an open and dynamic debate on the dialectical relationship between education, training and development appropriate for the changing techno-scientific environment and ever pressing socio-political and cultural challenges.[42]

Conclusion

The social sciences and humanities are supposed to be torchbearers of African values, systems of power, production, mediation and distribution. However, this has not been the case because, as they are currently constituted, they recycle the values, systems of production, mediation and distribution of the mainly former colonies. Even in this period of the quest for an African renaissance, they still diffuse and disseminate Western culture and literally scorn and denigrate African culture as un-progressive at best and anti-progressive at worse. The social sciences and humanities could benefit a great deal from this repositioning of universities. They would be inspired by and be rooted in the sensibilities, consciousness, aspirations and core values of the indigenous African people.

Any viable transformation of the social sciences and humanities should take the African experience in its totality as an inescapable point of departure for the critique and construction of new knowledge and praxis. Africanisation should be treated as the cornerstone of transformation of the social sciences and humanities. The production and reproduction of social knowledge will have to be consistent with the core requirements of African society. In other words, there is a need for a radical and critical questioning of the dominant Western epistemological paradigm from an African perspective. Such a radical and critical questioning should ignite an epistemological break that would result in an epistemological breakthrough inspired by an African ontology. On whatever grounds, it is no longer acceptable, as it is no longer justifiable, for the Western epistemological paradigm, characterised as it is by ethnocentric proclivities, to retain primacy and dominance in post-colonial Africa. Western epistemological paradigms, derived as they are from their unique ontology, cannot be transplanted and be relevant to Africa.

Having advocated for the reversal of epistemicide and asserting the right to be an African university through Africanising the social sciences and humanities, one is not oblivious to the prospects and problems of such an under-taking. Factors such as globalisation have both hindered and, ironically, in-spired this move. Moreover, many have been cowed or convinced to believe that the academic status quo in the social sciences and humanities need not be tempered with lest intellectual, academic and managerial standards be lowered. Apart from the lowering of standards, some among us hold the view that the disciplines will be incongruent to globalization as indigenous knowledge sys-tems are not compatible with progress, modernisation and development. In other words, they have bought into the argument of the protectionist and apol-ogists that 'things as they stand are good'. On the other hand, we are inspired by the deconstructive intellectual activities of the older generation of African scholars who were not wedded to perpetuating the myth of the African conti-nent as a philosophical, sociological and historical nonentity. The task ahead is to nurture a new social sciences and humanities generation that is able and willing to take forward the intellectual struggle from deconstruction to recon-struction so as to turn universities in Africa into African universities.[43]

Notes and References

1. 1 Lebakeng, T. J. (2004). Towards a relevant higher education epistemology. In Seepe, S. (Ed.), *Towards an African identity of higher education* (pp. 109–119). Pretoria, South Africa: Vista University & Skotaville Media; Lebakeng, T.J. (2008). The imperative of Africanising universities in South Africa. *CODESRIA Bulletin*, (3–4), 43–45; Lebakeng, T.J. (2011). Dis-course on colonial epistemicide and contemporary attempts to re-affirm indigenous knowledge systems, with particular reference to South Africa. *Caribbean Journal of Philosophy, 3*(1), 1–11. Available at: http://ojs.mona.uwi.edu/index.php/cjp/article/view/2507 (accessed 7 March 2013).

2. Conrad, J. (1995). Heart of darkness. In Lyon, J. (Ed.), *Joseph Conrad: Youth, Heart of Darkness, The End of the Tether*. London, England: Penguin, p. 45. (Original work pub-lished 1899).

3. Lugard, F. D. (1965). *The dual mandate in tropical Africa*. London, England: Frank Cass.

4. Quoted in Lugard, 1965.

5. Van Binsbergen, W. M .J. (2001). Ubuntu and the globalisation of Southern African thought and society. *Quest—An African Journal of Philosophy, 15*(1–2).

6. Memmi, A. (1963). *The coloniser and the colonised*. Boston, MA: Beacon Press; Ramose, 1999; Itandala, A. B. (2001). European images of Africa from early times to the eighteenth century. In D. M. Mengara (Ed.), *Images of Africa: Stereotypes and realities* (pp. 61–81). Trenton, NJ: Africa World Press.

7. Babu, A. R. M. (1981). *African socialism or socialist Africa?* Harare, Zimbabwe: Zimbabwe Publishing House.

8. Moller, A. C., & Deci, E. L. (2010). Interpersonal control, dehumanisation, and vi-olence: A self-determination theory perspective. *Group Processes & Intergroup Relations*,

(13), 41–53; Haslam, N., et al., (2008). Sub-human, inhuman, and superhuman: Contrasting humans with non-humans in three cultures. *Social Cognition, 26*(2), 248–258.

9. Cornevin, M. (1980). *Apartheid: Power and historical falsification*. Paris, France: UNESCO.

10. Cesaire, A. (2000). *Discourse on colonialism*. New York, NY: Monthly Review Press.

11. Ramose, M. B. (2003). Transforming education in South Africa: Paradigm shift or change? *South African Journal of Higher Education, 17*(3), 137–143; Lebakeng, 2004.

12. Serequeberhan, T. (1991). African philosophy: The point in question. In Serequeberhan (Ed.), *African philosophy: The essential readings*. New York, NY: Paragon.

13. Essentially the epistemology of alterity refers to the othering of Africa and Africans with the purpose of dehumanising and decentring them in all spheres of life and denying them authentic interlocution.

14. Randall, P. (Ed.). (1972). *Apartheid and the church: Report of the church commission of the study project on Christianity in apartheid society*. Johannesburg, South Africa: SPROCAS.

15. Groves, C. P (1969). Missionary and humanitarian aspects of imperialism from 1870–1914. In L. H. Gann & P. Duignan (Eds.), *Colonialism in Africa 1870–1960* (Vol. 1). Cambridge: Cambridge University Press. p. 488.

16. Mengara, D. M. (Ed.). (2001). *Images of Africa: Stereotypes and realities*. Trenton, NJ: Africa World Press.

17. Mudimbe, V. Y. (1988). *The invention of Africa: Gnosis, philosophy, and the order of knowledge*. Indiana: Indiana University Press.

18. Rodney, W. (1972). *How Europe underdeveloped Africa*. Dar-es-Salaam, Tanzania: Tanzania Publishers House.

19. The term 'epistemicide' was coined by the sociologist Boaventura de Sousa Santos to describe the systematic eradication of Third World knowledges and grounds for knowledge by "Western" science.

20. Veriri, A., & Mungwini, P. (2010). African cosmology and the duality of Western hegemony: The search for African identity. *The Journal of Pan African Studies, 3*(6), 27–42.

21. Payle, K. D., & Lebakeng, T. J. (2006). The relevance of indigenous knowledge systems in socio-economic development: Is globalization a threat? *Africa Insight, 36*(1), 40–45; Lebakeng, T. J. (2010). Discourse on indigenous knowledge systems, sustainable socio-economic development and the challenge of the academy in Africa. *CODESRIA Bulletin,* (1–2), 24–29.

22. Lebakeng, T. J. (2000). Africanisation of the social sciences and humanities in South Africa. In L. A. Kasanga (Ed.), *Challenges and changes at historically disadvantaged universities* (pp. 93–109). Sovenga, South Africa: University of the North Press.

23. Mafeje, A. (2001). Anthropology in post-independence Africa: End of an era and the problem of self-redefinition. In A. Mafeje (Ed.), *African social scientists reflections: Part 1*. Nairobi, Kenya: Heinrich Boll Foundation; Asad, T. (Ed.). (1973). *Anthropology and the colonial encounter*. London, England: Ithaca Press.

24. Mafeje, A. (1976). The problem of anthropology in historical perspective: An inquiry into the growth of the social sciences. *Canadian Journal of African Studies, 10*(2), 307–333; Ake, C. (1982). *Social science as imperialism: The theory of political development*. Ibadan, Nigeria: Ibadan University Press.

25. Ashby, E. (1964). *African universities and western tradition*. London, England: Oxford University Press.

26. Houtondji, P. (1997). *Endogenous knowledge: Research trials.* Dakar, Senegal: CODESRIA.

27. Mathews, Z. K. (1981, published posthumously). *Freedom for my people: The autobiography of ZK Matthews: Southern Africa 1901–1968.* Cape Town, South Africa: David Philip.

28. Lebakeng, T. J., Phalane, M. M., & Nase, D. (2006). Epistemicide, institutional cultures and the imperative for Africanisation of universities in South Africa. *Alternation, 13*(1), 70–87.

29. Myrdal, G. (1957). *The economic theory and underdeveloped regions.* New York, NY: Harper & Row. Bondy, A. S. (1969). The meaning and problem of Hispanic American thought. Reprinted in Gracia, J. J. E. (1986). *Latin American Philosophy* (pp. 233–244); Alatas, S. H. (1972). The captive mind in development studies. *International Social Science Journal, 34*(1), 9–25.

30. Bondy, 1969; Alatas, S. H. (1974). The captive mind and creative development. *International Social Science Journal, 36*(4), 691–699.

31. Thiong'o, Ngugi wa. (1987). *Decolonising the mind: The politics of language in African literature.* Harare, Zimbabwe: Zimbabwe Printing Press; Wiredu, K. (1995). Conceptual decolonisation in African philosophy. In O. Oladipo (selections and introduction), *Conceptual decolonisation in African Philosophy: Four essays.* Ibadan, Nigeria: Hope Publications.

32. For an extensive engagement with this issue, see Sithole, M. P. (2009). *Unequal peers: The politics of discourse management in the social sciences.* Pretoria, South Africa: Africa Institute of South Africa.

33. Seepe, S. (1998). Towards an Afrocentric understanding. In Seepe, S. (Ed.), *Black Perspective(s) on Tertiary Institutional Transformation.* Florida: Vivlia Publishers & The University of Venda, pp. 63–68.

34. Lebakeng, T. J. (2001). Africanise rather than sacrifice the social sciences and humanities: A challenge for educational transformation at South African universities. A paper presented at the Joint Centre for Political and Economic Studies, Centurion Lake Hotel, Centurion, Pretoria. Retrieved from www.unisa.za/contents/colleges/col … /africanisesacrifice.doc.

35. Chachage, S. L. (1999). Transformation and programmes: Some reflections. Department of Sociology: University of Cape Town. Unpublished paper.

36. Makgoba, M. W. (1997). *MOKOKO: the Makgoba affair: A reflection on transformation.* Florida Hills: Vivlia Publishers & Books, p. 180.

37. State of Humanities in South Africa and Charter for Humanities and Social Sciences: Final Report—30 June 2011. Retrieved from www.assaf.org.za/wp-content/upload/2011/08/25-July-final.pdf and httw://charterforhumanities.co.za/final.charter-report-released.

38. For instance, these views have been expressed in Mafeje, A. (1992). *African Philosophical Projections and Prospects for the Indigenisation of Political and Intellectual Discourse.* Seminar Paper Series No. 7, Harare, Zimbabwe: SAPES Books; Outlaw, L. (1991). Deconstruction and reconstruction challenges. In Oruka, O. H. *Sage philosophy: Indigenous thinkers and modern debates in African philosophy.* Nairobi, Kenya: ACTS Press.

39. Bewaji, J. A. I. (2006). Discoursing philosophy through cultures—Challenges, opportunities and dangers. Retrieved from http//www.cavehill.uwi.edu/fhe/histphil/Philosphy/CHiPS/2006/Paper.

40. Lebakeng, 2000.

41. Ramose, M. B. (2004). In search of an African philosophy of education. *South African Journal of Education, 18*(3), 138–160.

42. Lebakeng, T. J. (1997, July–August). Africanisation and higher education. *Southern African Political and Economic Monthly, 10*(10), 4–7.

43. The problem of academic mimicry and other associated challenges facing the academy is not uniquely South African. Although the focus of this piece is on South Africa, it is clear that it is an African problem despite years of independence in African countries. South Africa can, however, learn a number of lessons from processes which have taken place in other African countries, and these have been with uneven success.

Chapter 4

Sovereignty, Equality of States and International Law: A Critique

Serges Djoyou Kamga

Introduction

Coloniality is a term used to describe how colonial masters keep colonialism going in the postcolonial era. It operates as a "structuring process within global imperial designs, sustaining the superiority of the Global North [or Western powers] and ensuring the perpetual subalternity of the Global South using colonial matrices of power".[1] The tools used for this process include humanitarian intervention, development,[2] modernity, civilisation, globalisation and international law. The latter plays a vital role in legitimizing and perpetuating the hegemony of the Global North or Western powers.[3] Because international law is a broad subject, this chapter will specifically investigate the imperial role of the international law concept of "sovereign equality of states" as it plays out in global organisations.

In this investigation, the chapter uses the Third World Approaches to International Law (TWAIL) method. This method is informed by an international law discourse that seeks global justice, and it is defined as:

> [A]n alternative narrative of international law that has developed in op-
> position to the realities of domination and subordination prevalent in
> the international legal apparatus. A fundamentally counter-hegemonic
> movement, TWAIL is united in its rejection of what its champions regard
> as an unjust relationship between the Third World and international law.[4]

Put differently, TWAIL focuses on putting forward an international law discourse that responds to the needs and desires of the population of the Third

World.[5] In this perspective, as much as the chapter rejects the hegemonic feature of the current "sovereign equality of states", it does not call for the full dismantlement of this concept. It calls for its revision so as to ensure that it accommodates the needs of developing countries, particularly African countries. In this way, the chapter neither paints a pessimistic concept of sovereign equality, nor a totally optimistic concept, but seeks an alternative narrative to sovereign equality that militates for a just global order. Indeed, the chapter seeks solutions to the coloniality of power through the international law principle of sovereign equality. In doing so, it offers a critique of this principle and suggests mechanisms to turn international law into a platform for global justice.

In terms of structure, this chapter is divided into five parts, including this introduction. The second part presents an overview of the concept of "sovereign equality of states". The third part critiques the concept and shows how it serves the hegemonic goals of the Global North. The fourth part proposes mechanisms to ensure the decoloniality of power by suggesting approaches to equalise states through reconceptualisation of the principle of "sovereign equality", and the final part offers concluding remarks.

The Concept of Sovereign Equality: An Overview

Inspired by the natural law theory, which posits that all men are equal by nature, the so-called international community transferred the same notion of equality to states at a global level.[6] In this vein, just like human beings, states are inherently equal by nature, "as it occurs with men by virtue of natural law".[7] This logic informed the Treaty of Westphalia,[8] also known as Peace of Westphalia, which followed thirty years of wars between Europe's Catholic and Protestant monarchs. Though the treaty does not mention "sovereign states" explicitly, it clearly highlights the liberty of religion of each European state, thus laying an important basis for the concept of sovereign equality of states. Similarly, it recognised the power of a monarch over its territory without external interference. As a result of the treaty of Westphalia, European states embarked on respecting each other's sovereignty.[9] In this sense, the concept is therefore constitutive of the Euro-American world system described in Chapter Two and as argued in that chapter, it also evolved as this system validated a succession of epochal world orders, especially after the Peace of Westphalia.

Following the basis established through the Peace of Westphalia, sovereign equality of states developed into a significant element of international law which regulates interstate relations. But it would be in the world order that emerged after the Second World War that the concept would take full hold. Article 2(1) of the United Nations Charter proclaims that the UN is "based on the principle of the sovereign equality of all its Members". Accordingly, all states in the international community are equal. This means that notwithstanding economic, social, political, cultural, religious and other differences, no state is more sovereign than others. In 1979 the UN General Assembly reinforced the idea by passing a resolution entitled "Inadmissibility of the Policy of Hegemonism in International Relations".[10] Similarly, the Friendly Relations Declaration,[11] known as a reliable interpretation of the UN Charter, also emphasises the principle of sovereign equality. Unequivocally, it proclaims that "each State enjoys the rights inherent in full sovereignty", that States are juridically equal, that they have "the duty to respect the personality of other States", and that "each State has the right freely to choose and develop its political, social, economic and cultural system".[12]

As a result of the international recognition of sovereign equality, powerful states are supposed to be unable to rule over weak ones, to impose their laws on others.[13] In this perspective, as Westlake argues, the sovereign equality of a state is at the heart of its independence.[14] This view is also echoed by Oppenheim,[15] who classifies the implications of legal equality in three categories: Firstly, at the concert of nations the principle of one state, one vote applies. Secondly, in spite of the political or military power or weakness of states, all votes in the UN system have the same weight. To use Kokott's words, "the vote of the weakest and smallest State has as much weight as the vote of the largest and most powerful".[16] And finally, based on the rule *par in parem non habet imperium*, no state can claim jurisdiction over another wholly sovereign State.[17] Furthermore, the application of a universal international legal norm to all states, or to all parties to a treaty, is another attribute of state sovereignty.[18]

Overall, state sovereignty is an empowering concept which advocates for equality, democracy, equity, dignity, and global justice and well-being for all on the international plane. Kokott summarises as follows: "In entering the Family of Nations a State comes as an equal to equals; it demands a certain consideration to be paid to its dignity, the retention of its independence, of its territorial and its personal supremacy. […] The equality of States before international law is a quality derived from their International Personality."[19]

However, accepting that the concept of sovereign equality really equalises states at the global level would be refusing to critically analyse interstate relations at that level. It would be an admission that the end of colonialism brought equality between the master and the slave. It would be claiming that international law is not included in various tools of coloniality without exploring the perilous colonial matrices rooted in it. It would be ignoring the geopolitical context in which international law is made, interpreted and implemented.

Sovereign Equality of States and Western Hegemony

The sovereign equality of states is limited by the power of the UN Security Council and the law-making processes at the global level, which are mechanisms designed to ensure the domination of the Global North.

Notwithstanding the clarity of Article 2(1) of the UN Charter, which equalises states in the international community, the same Charter sets up an international system composed of a weak General Assembly and a mighty Security Council. Accordingly, the UN system is characterised by a Security Council with five permanent members (only one of which is non-Western) equipped with the right to dictate, called "veto", and ten temporary members[20] that have little influence on proceedings. This arrangement, tailored to ensure the domination of a few states, destroys the so-called principle of sovereign equality, which after all remains very formal. It is formal for not providing measures to empower the weakest in the international community. In fact, this principle would have been meaningful only if the UN General Assembly was erected as the strongest body, where the community of equal states take concerted decisions on world matters.

In this perspective, the UN Charter through articles 55 and 56 clearly calls on states to work together through international cooperation to improve the standard of living for all.[21] This led to the comment that

> Arts 55 (a) and (b) and 56 UN Charter could be seen as an expression of an international law which promotes the economic and social development of all States, thereby furthering material justice. Moreover, the modern international law of co-operation implies working together with and helping other States.[22]

International decisions made through the UN General Assembly and in line with articles 55 and 56 of the UN Charter mentioned above would provide a bridge to move from the formal equality of states, or empty "sovereign equality", to substantive equality whereby measures are taken collectively to empower the weak and poor states by affording them a better standard of living. The provision for substantive equality between states is clearly addressed by the Charter of Economic Rights and Duties of States[23] in these terms:

> All States are juridically equal and, as equal members of the international community, have *the right to participate fully and effectively in the international decision-making process* in the solution of world economic, financial and monetary problems, *inter alia*, through the appropriate international organizations in accordance with their existing and evolving rules, and to share in the benefits resulting therefrom.

This led Gorelick to argue that "the founding fathers of the UN envisaged an international organisation, whose primary strength will be to act collectively and in the spirit of cooperation in solving international problems."[24] Therefore, the refusal by the designers of the world system on which the UN world order is based to implement the provision mentioned above shows how the UN, the most important world institution, is used for coloniality purposes.

As mentioned above, in its hegemonic endeavour, the Global North confide extraordinary powers to the five permanent members of "its" Security Council. In fact, refusing to comply with the view of the Security Council is a violation of international law and should be punished by another decision of the same council acting as judge and party. In this context, sovereignty is equivalent to "direct subordination" to the Council.[25]

Given that the first signs of sovereignty of states first appeared after the Westphalia treaty, it could be argued that the concept of sovereignty was designed for and applies only to the Global North,[26] which pulls the strings at the Council and to whose advantage the entire world system works. It follows that the application of the rule of law in the international sphere does not have the same meaning for developed and developing countries alike. In fact, the significance of rule of law varies depending on whether you are a totally sovereign state from the Northern hemisphere, or a state from the Southern hemisphere that had lost a part of its sovereignty to colonialism.[27] The historian Anthony Pagden echoes Grotius (master of current international law) as follows: "[s]overeignty beyond Europe, unlike sovereignty within Europe, was [...] very much a divisible notion and was to remain so within all subsequent conceptions" of relationship with the non-Western world.[28] This is a testimony that originally the concept of sovereignty was Eurocentric for the benefit of European states only and this remains the reality. Anghie explains clearly in arguing that Third World sovereignty is simply different from the West's.[29] He also argues that in fact:

> [C]olonialism was central to the constitution of international law in that many of the basic doctrines of international law — including, most importantly, sovereignty doctrine — were forged out of the attempt to create a legal system that could account for relations between the European and non-European worlds in the colonial confrontation.[30]

This explains the virulent resistance of Western powers to reforming the Security Council to include at least one country of the Global South as a permanent member.[31] This shows that the dominant powers have often designed concepts that apply to themselves and ensure their control over others. In this vein, even the postcolonial emphasis on sovereignty and self-determination is just rhetoric for the coloniality of power. China Mieville writes, "The post war drive to self determination is not merely a change in the structure or content of international law, but the culmination of the universalizing and abstracting tendencies in international legal-capitalism."[32]

In other words, the coloniality of power goes beyond the global broadening of an international legal order with capitalism; "it means that the power dynamics of political imperialism are embedded within the very juridical equality of sovereignty".[33]

Overall, the concept of equal sovereignty of states is designed to show formal equality, whereas in reality the Global North exercises full power and domination over the Global South. This is also observed at the level of the law-making process under the so-called sovereign equality of states.

Sovereign Equality of States and Law-Making Processes in Global Organisations

This section focuses on the law making process at the UN level and in other international organisations. At the outset, it is important to keep in mind that at the global level, law making is done through, among others, international agreements and international customary law.[34] Though we refer to customary law, the analysis in this section will have a strong focus on treaties or international conventions, which are the primary sources of international law. The Vienna Convention on the Law of Treaties[35] does not define an international agreement, but this expression is understood as a treaty between states in a written form and governed by international law, whether embodied in a single instrument or in two or more related instruments and whatever its particular designation.[36] From this standpoint, it can be argued that a treaty is just one type of international agreement.[37]

However, the distinction between a treaty and other forms of international agreements is acknowledged by the UN Charter, which refers to both treaties and international agreements.[38] This distinction is important because, on the one hand, treaties or conventions between two states (bilateral treaties) or between many states (multilateral treaties) are legally binding on the parties and are known as "hard law";[39] on the other hand, other forms of international agreements, or "informal agreements",[40] are known as "soft law"[41] are non-binding, in spite of their moral force and the possibility of becoming customary law.[42]

The super power of the UN Security Council observed earlier is more visible in law making. Security Council resolutions are legally binding on other states.[43] In this perspective, the Council is able to impose economic sanctions on other states or use force for the sake of peace. Interestingly enough, permanent members of the Council are able to use their veto to stop resolutions[44] which are likely to threaten their interest.[45] In this context, the Council becomes the world's parliament that adopts the law of nations. In fact, the decision of 15 nations to the total satisfaction of five of them (the permanent members) overrules the view of the 191 nations of the UN General Assembly. In this set up, while the Security Council controls the world, the UN General Assembly, which is the "plenary body"[46] of the UN, can only issue weak or non-binding resolutions with very little effect.[47] This is not an accident, but a well-thought move by the designers of the world system to keep the Global North at the highest level of the ladder. Chimni argues that the distinctive feature of current international law "has served to sustain the *status quo* and prevent the substantive transformation of the content of international law in favour of Third World states".[48] Moreover, in keeping the status quo, the binding decisions of the Security Council are the expression of the rules of the powerful and the legalisation of their supremacy.[49]

Current international law is the triumph of coloniality of international politics, hence its incapacity to change to be progressive. In today's international relations, power politics is central and law secondary. There is a need to develop an international law where instead of thinking in terms of interest, lawmakers think of the conformity of actions with fair legal rules that can benefit all states in the international community. The livelihood of Global South populations shall not become the victim of Western domestic interests. In this perspective, as correctly argued by Umozorike, the world system shall "provide the legal framework within which the new international economic order can be achieved"[50] for the benefit of all.

Besides the pseudo-function of the Security Council to act as the world's parliament, it also behaves like the judiciary. In this regard, the UN Charter urges the Security Council that while acting under Chapter VI to "as a general rule" refer legal disputes to the International Court of Justice (ICJ). This gives the Council executive powers and enables it put the ICJ at the service of its interests in regard to individual Council members or collective interests regarding the world. Nevertheless, the Council often disregards this provision, and opts for political settlement of conflicts[51] or sets up its own jurisdiction. This often leads to the violation of a state's "domestic jurisdiction" covered by the principle of sovereignty. For instance, although international law prohibits the commission of genocide and crimes against humanity, which amount to the violation of *jus cogens*,[52] no states or group of states, or even the Security Council for that matter, can establish a tribunal to try such issues without the consent of the state where the crime was committed. Nevertheless, the Security Council adopted Resolution 955 establishing the International Criminal Tribunal for Rwanda to try crimes committed during the Rwandan genocide. This is a violation of the right to sovereign equality of Rwanda, which had no say on the Council. A similar violation happened in the establishment of the Special Tribunal for Yugoslavia. This is not to condone genocide, but to call for the involvement or meaningful participation of the states that are guilty of the offence to decisions establishing an ad hoc tribunal to deal with the matter.

Even outside the Security Council, some countries from the Global North would not hesitate to violate the principle of sovereignty to assert their domination on their former colonies. For example, on 11 April 2000, in total disregard of the principle of diplomatic immunity, Belgium issued an arrest warrant for Mr Yerodia (then the sitting Minister of Foreign Affairs in DR Congo) if he entered its territory.[53] In reaction to Belgium's arrest warrant, Congo filed an application to the International Court of Justice (ICJ) claiming that Belgium's warrant violated the principle of sovereign equality, the principle that a state may not exercise jurisdiction over another state, and principles of diplomatic immunity. The ICJ's found for the applicant.[54] This attempt by Belgium demonstrates how the Global North disregards international law and the sovereignty of a developing state whenever it is convenient to assert their authority and domination without serious consequences for doing so.

Platforms that form part of global economic governance, there has been an erosion of the principle of sovereign equality to the benefit of the Global North include Western-dominated organisations such as the International Monetary Fund (IMF), the World Bank and World Trade Organisation (WTO), to name just a few. In these financial institutions, voting rights are proportional to the financial power of member states.[55] The ability to contribute financially to the objectives of the organisation is vital for voting rights. The WTO is supposed to be the only truly global international organisation dealing with the rules of trade between (equal) nations.[56] But here as well, the rules of the game ignore the principles of equality of states. Keet writes that the WTO is a complex platform where

> [r]uthless hard bargaining is driven by powerful corporate and national vested interests, not the polite diplomatic positioning or posturing of Heads of State. And, with the WTO Secretariat clearly biased towards the interests and demands of the most powerful member states, and the expansion of the liberalised global trade regime, the WTO is not a neutral open forum or assembly of nations where world leaders gather to debate and "influence" each other's positions.[57]

These hegemonic policies anchored in international financial institutions and WTO regimes disenfranchised Third World countries that have been plundered for centuries and cannot afford the financial demands and bargaining methods established for their exclusion from these organisations.

The disturbing factor is that at the end of the day, Third World states that are forced to sign all kinds of instruments are said to have consented under international law where all states are equal. Chimni correctly argues that global international law, or rather "bourgeois international law", is "the means through which the rights of transnational capital are being safeguarded, among other things, by prescribing uniform global standards—ignoring the phenomenon of uneven development—in key areas such as technology and foreign investment".[58] Sharing this view, Hardt and Negri explain the situation in these terms:[59]

> The position of the newly sovereign nation-states cannot be understood when it is viewed in the rosy UN imaginary of a harmonious concert of equal and autonomous national subjects. The post colonial nation-state functions as an essential and subordinate element in the global organisation of the capitalist market [...]. National liberation and national sovereignty are not just powerless against this global capitalist hierarchy, but themselves contribute to its organisation and functioning.

Overall, in order to keep colonialism alive, the current world system uses international law in which all states are said to be equal to ensure the hegemony of the Global North. In fact, imperialism has some legitimacy when it is applied through international law, and more importantly through an international law underpinned by the principle of equality of states. China Melville explains as follows:

> A historically meaningful imperialism is not only or essentially military and maritime panoply, not only economic and financial prosperity; it is also this ability to determine in and of itself the content of political and legal concepts. This side of imperialism (I speak here not only of American imperialism) is [...] perhaps more dangerous than military oppression and economic exploitation. A people is first conquered when it acquiesces to a foreign vocabulary, a foreign conception of what is law, especially international law.[60]

This was further explained by Chimni, who argues that international law has been vital in subduing the Third World because it is used to legitimise "dominant ideas for its discourse tends to be associated with rationality, neutrality, objectivity and justice".[61] In this vein, it is contended that classical imperialism was underpinned by the work of missionaries and explorers, while contemporary imperialism, in the form of coloniality, is implemented through the concept of sovereign equality of states where states are unequal in reality.

In spite of the hegemonic feature of the world system exposed above, it is important to reflect and work towards the decoloniality of power through international law. This will be the focus of the next section.

Reflections on How to Give the Principle of Sovereign Equality a True Meaning

In order to address the coloniality of power of the principle of equality, it is important to look at how this principle can really equalise states on the international plane. The aim is not to destroy Western hegemony only to install a Global South hegemony, but to open the possibility of true sovereign equality on the basis of a just world system, to open the possibility to have a just world where all states and all people are equal, a world characterised by mutual respect and a world where the humanity of all human beings is equally recognised. For this to happen there is a need to have a plan of action in which Third World states, intellectuals and civil society organisations play important roles.

The Role of Third World States

Representatives of Third World states should stay united and keep pushing for the reform of the Security Council. This reform agenda shall relentlessly claim a permanent seat for a developing country at the Security Council. The agenda should also push for the strengthening of the UN General Assembly, which should be given more prominence in term of decision and law-making power. Third World states must stand by each other in fora such as the Non-Aligned Movement (NAM) and forget self-interest in world affairs. This approach yielded positive results in 1986 when developing nations united as NAM to push for the adoption of the UN Declaration on the Right to Development.[62]

The Role of Intellectuals

Intellectuals should declare the injustice of the current world system and encourage critical thinking by using the TWAIL and other approaches that highlight the methods of the coloniality of power. In this perspective, it is vital to ensure that the narrative of resistance becomes part and parcel of the international law discourse, characterised by suggestions for tangible changes in current international law regimes.[63] Moreover, African scholars and others proponents of global justice from various fields shall critically examine their disciplines from an Afrocentric perspective and craft their work in Africology. This will enable the world at large to understand how Africa has contributed to the development of civilisation and thus should be treated at the same level as other parts of the world.

In addition, proponents of TWAIL and decoloniality should reach out to and unite with all those groups that are disenfranchised by the current world system. In this perspective, Afro-centrist, Asio-centrist and Latin American advocates should collaborate with feminists and other subdued groups to develop a harmonious and viable alternative to the Northern academic discourse[64] which promotes the hegemony of the Global North.

The Role of Civil Society

Embarking on scholarship for justice or scholarship activism in the Global South is vital as it will educate the masses on the violation of the principle of equality by the Global North for hegemony purposes. Such education would lead to the creation of social movements in the Global South and prepare civil society to mobilise everywhere to stand for the weak and dominated nations.

The role of civil society is clearly recognised by Article 71 of the UN Charter, which compels the Economic and Social Council to make arrangements to ensure that civil society organisations including Africans are consulted on global policy at the UN. Therefore, given the power of the UN Security Council, African organisations seek significant access to the policy arena and decision making ultimately belonging to states.[65] African organisations attempt to fight for Africa's interests in their push for global justice. They play a significant role in raising awareness and capturing the public conscience on matters of importance to Africa and the Global South. African organisations especially have often gathered around the Pan-Africanist ideology to ensure that their issues are given special attention.[66]

Nonetheless, African organisations cannot succeed alone, hence the need to strike alliance with all the disempowered, to work with and become part global civil society while advocating for Africa's interests. This global civil society united by the objective to ensure a better life for all and not the domination of a few shall be given a meaningful right to participation in law-making in international organisations. Chmini correctly notes that "global populations adversely affected by international laws and policies must have a say in the institutions that prescribe and enforce them."[67] As these social movements grow they are likely to filter significantly into the UN system and other international organisations. In this perspective, besides giving equal representation and equal votes to states, the UN should follow Sir Lauterpacht, who back in 1925 called upon the international community to give a significant role to non-state actors in the law-making process in these words:[68]

> The definition of the rule of international law as historical events to which their establishment can be traced, is, I think, correct; but there is no reason to restrict these historical events to those only which are evidenced by acts of statements or written documents; the legal conviction and the sense of rights of masses of men [sic] is a historical fact of not less force.

This implies the involvement of non-state actors such as NGOs (for example) in law-making. I recognise that NGOs' participation is faced with difficult questions related to logistics on which ones should be chosen and why, questions on their legitimacy and legal personality. Nevertheless, NGOs' participation would represent a counter power to "superpower" in law-making in international organisations. Furthermore, the involvement of civil society would enhance the legitimacy of international law-making. Anderson and Rieff said:

> International NGOs have gradually taken a leading role in providing what is declared to be legitimate, and politically legitimizing, input of the world people across a myriad of issues and causes […]. International NGOs come together to advocate for the peoples of the world, those who could otherwise have no voice, given the actors they seek to influence, which include both economic actors and the world's superpower, are globally unregulated.[69]

There is a need to involve independent delegates, those who are free "from parochial nationalist or state interest [and able] to identify common purposes and solutions across other lines".[70] Their involvement should go beyond mere informal round-table meetings and panel discussions at the General Assembly and its Committee, where they make no real impact as it is currently the case. Their involvement must be beyond formal "invitation to the special session and conferences convened under the auspices of the General Assembly, and lately through the biennial high-level dialogue",[71] where they are spectators or can at most lobby for a General Assembly Resolution on a specific subject, because they do not have the right to vote.

Notwithstanding the difficulties linked to efficient NGO involvement in international law-making, it is worth trying because the current exclusionary, or rather hegemonic, approach to international law violates the principle of sovereign equality of states and hinders the realisation of global justice.

Concluding Remarks

The aim of this chapter was to investigate the extent to which the international law concept of sovereign equality is used to ensure the hegemony of the Global North in global institutions. Crafting the analysis in the TWAIL which seeks global justice, the chapter found that indeed sovereign equality is just another tool of coloniality, another instrument for Western hegemony. In reaching this conclusion, the chapter demonstrated that the sovereign equality of states concept, which in principle should have been the backbone of equality and harmony between states, is merely rhetorical. Sovereign equality is not a reality at the UN level, where the Security Council and, more importantly, its permanent members dictate their position informed by their self-interest to developing countries. Similarly, the same body is the law-making body of the world by virtue of the binding character of its decisions. Indeed the Global North is the alpha and omega of the world system in terms of decision- and law-making.

The chapter also demonstrated that even outside the UN Security Council, Northern states will not hesitate to violate a developing country's sovereignty by attempting to arrest their officials without any consideration for international rules. The chapter also showed how platforms such as the World Bank, the IMF and the WTO limit developing countries' right to equal participation in world affairs. In doing so, these institutions make sure that voting rights are proportional to the financial power of member states and put intensive pressure on poor countries, which are consequently unable to take part to the proceedings in world affairs.

Despite this disquieting picture, the chapter suggested that in attempting to establish a world system in which states are equal, it is imperative for the so-called "Third World" states to unite and keep claiming a permanent seat on the UN Security Council and always present a collective position in world affairs. In addition, intellectuals and all proponents of decoloniality, of TWAIL, all disenfranchised or marginalised groups and all advocates of global justice should unite in their declaration and condemnation of world injustices. This concerted action shall inspire civil society to march towards the UN and, more importantly, claim a significant place at this institution and push for a "real" equality of states.

Notes and References

1. Ndlovu-Gatsheni, S. J. (2012). Coloniality of Power in Development Studies and the Impact of Global Imperial Designs on Africa. Inaugural Lecture delivered at the University of South Africa, Senate Hall, 16 October. Retrieved from http://uir.unisa.ac.za/bitstream/handle/10500/8548/Inugural%20lecture-16%20October%202012.pdf.pdf.txt?sequence=4.

2. Ndlovu-Gatsheni, 2012, p. 1.

3. Anghie, A. (2004). *Imperialism, sovereignty and the making of international law.* Cambridge, England: Cambridge University Press.
   Chimni, B. S. (2006). Third World approaches to international law: A manifesto. *International Community Law Review, 8,* 1; Pahuja, S. (2005). The postcoloniality of international law. *Harvard International Law Journal, 46*(2), 459–469.

4. Chimni, B. S. (2011). The world of TWAIL: Introduction to the special issue. *Trade, Law and Development, 3*(1), 18.

5. Anghie, 2004.

6. Kokott, J. States, sovereign equality. Retrieved from http://www.mpepil.com/sample_article?id=/epil/entries/law-9780199231690-e1113&recno=3&.

7. Kokott, J. States, sovereign equality.

8. Treaties of Peace Between Sweden and the Holy Roman Empire and Between France and the Holy Roman Empire, 14 October 1648.

9. Sammons, A. (2003). The "Under-Theorization" of universal jurisdiction: Implications for legitimacy on trials of war criminals by national courts, *Berkeley Journal of International Law, 21*(111), 4.

10. GA Res. 34/103, December 14, 1979. The United States and three other UN member states opposed this.

11. UN General Assembly, 1970. *Declaration of Principles of International Law Concerning Friendly Relations and Co-operation Among States in Accordance with the Charter of the United Nations*, 24 October.

12. See The Friendly Relations Declaration, section 1 allocated to the solemn proclamation of principles; also Kokott, States, sovereign equality.

13. Krisch, N. (2005). International law in times of hegemony: Unequal power and the shaping of the international legal order. *The European Journal of International Law, 16*(3), 377.

14. Westlake, J. (1910). *International Law* (Vol. 1), Cambridge, England: Cambridge University Press, p. 321.

15. Lauterpacht, H. (Ed.). (1955). *Oppenheim's International Law* (Vol. 1), London, England: Longman.

16. Kokott, States, sovereign equality.

17. Kokott, States, sovereign equality.

18. Krisch, N. (2005). International Law in Times of Hegemony: Unequal Power and the Shaping of the International Legal Order, *The European Journal of International Law, 16*(3), 378.

19. Kokott. States, Sovereign Equality.

20. Art 23 of the UN Charter.

21. Arts 55 (a) and (b) and 56 UN Charter; also art 22 of the Universal Declaration of human rights. Though Western countries agreed in Monterry, Mexico, to give 0.7% of their

GDP for development assistance, not only it is not enough, most of them give less than that and it is based on self-interest and not in the spirit of UN Charter informed by international solidarity. For more on this see Shah, A. (2012). Foreign aid for development assistance. *Global Issues,* 8 April. Retrieved from http://www.globalissues.org/article/35/foreign-aid-development-assistance.

22. Kokott. States, Sovereign Equality.

23. UN, 1974. Resolution adopted by the General Assembly 3281 (XXIX), A/RES/29/3281.

24. Gorelick, M. 2006. 'The sixty–first General Assembly: Transcending rifts on development and beyond'. *UN Chronicle*, 43 (4), p. 3.

25. Kokott. 'States, Sovereign Equality'.

26. Pahuja, S. (2005). The postcoloniality of international law. *Harvard International Law Journal, 46*(2), 462, 459–469.

27. Kokott. 'States, Sovereign Equality'.

28. Pagden, A. (2006). The empire's new clothes: From empire to federation, yesterday and today. *Common Knowledge, 12*(1), 36 & 41.

29. Anghie, 2004.

30. Anghie, 2004.

31. Sreenivasan, T. P. (2011). UNSC: Resistance to Revolutionary Change. *Indian Foreign Affairs Journal*, 6(3), 281–292.

32. Mieville, C. (2005). *Between equal rights: A Marxist theory of international law*: Leiden, Netherlands: Martinus Nijhoff, p. 267.

33. Mieville. 2005, p. 270.

34. According to Article 38 of the International Court of Justice (ICJ) statues the sources of international law[?] are: international conventions, whether general or particular, establishing rules expressly recognized by the contesting states; international custom, as evidence of a general practice accepted as law; the general principles of law recognized by civilized nations; and subject to the provisions of Article 59, judicial decisions and the teachings of the most highly qualified publicists of the various nations, as subsidiary means for the determination of rules of law.

35. UN. 1969. The Vienna Convention on the Law of Treaties signed at Vienna 23 May 1969, entry into force: 27 January 1980.

36. The Vienna Convention, Art 2 (1) (a).

37. Olivier, M. 1997. 'Informal International Agreements under the 1996 Constitution'. *South African Year Book of International law*, 22, 66.

38. UN Charter, art 102 (1), which provides for both forms of instruments to be registered and made public in these terms: "Every treaty and every international agreement entered into by any Member of the United Nations after the present Charter comes into force shall as soon as possible be registered with the Secretariat and published by it".

39. Boyle, A. (2007). Soft law in international law making. In M. D. Evans (Ed.), *The making of international law* (p. 142). Oxford, England: Oxford University Press. For more on 'soft law', see Baxter, R. (1980). International law in her infinite variety. *International Comparative Law Quarterly* 29, 549–566; Chinkin, C. M. (1989). The challenge of soft law: Development and change in international law. *International Comparative Law Quarterly* 38, 850–866; Dupuy, P. M. (1991). Soft law and the international law of environment. *Michigan Journal of International Law* 12, 420–435.

40. Olivier, M. (1997). Informal international agreements under the 1996 Constitution. *South African Year Book of International law*, 22, 66.

41. Boyle, A. (2007). Soft law in international law making. In M. D. Evans (Ed.), *The making of international law* (p. 142). Oxford, England: Oxford University Press. For more on 'soft law', see Baxter, R. (1980). International law in her infinite variety. *International Comparative Law Quarterly* 29, 549–566; Chinkin, C. M. (1989). The challenge of soft law: Development and change in international law. *International Comparative Law Quarterly* 38, 850–866; Dupuy, P. M. (1991). Soft law and the international law of environment. *Michigan Journal of International Law* 12, 420–435.

42. For more on the development of customary international law, see D'Amato, A. (1971). The concept of custom in international law. Ithaca, NY[?]: Cornell University Press; Sahl, S. (2007). Researching customary international law, state practice and the pronouncements of states regarding international law. Retrieved from http://www.nyulaw global.org/globalex/Customary_International_Law.htm.

43. Article 25 of the UN Charter.

44. Article 27(3).

45. Dugard, J. (2007). *International law — A South African Perspective*. Cape Town, South Africa: Juta, p. 486.

46. Dugard, J. (2007). *International law — A South African Perspective*. Cape Town, South Africa: Juta, p. 486.

47. Even though soft law has some value, it remains non-binding in principle. On the value of soft law, see Weiss, E. B. (2003). Conclusion: Understanding Compliance with Soft Law. In D. Shelton (Ed.), *Commitment and compliance: The role of non-binding norms in the international legal system*. Oxford, England: Oxford University Press, pp. 535–553.

48. Chimni, B. S. (1999). Marxism and international law: A Contemporary analysis. *Economic and Political Weekly*, *34*(6), 337–349.

49. Krisch, N. (2005). International law in times of hegemony: Unequal power and the shaping of the international legal order. *The European Journal of International Law, 16*(3), 396.

50. Umozorike, U. O . (1979). *International law and colonialism in Africa*. Enugu, Nigeria: Nwamife, p. 138.

51. Dugard, J. (2007). *International Law — A South African Perspective*. Cape Town, South Africa: Juta, 488.

52. The concept of *jus cogens* designates an international law obligation which transcends states' concern; it engages the interest of the world at large.

53. For more on this case, see Bekker, P. (2002). World court orders Belgium to cancel an arrest warrant issued against the Congolese foreign minister. *American Society of International Law Insight*. Retrieved from http://www.asil.org/insigh82.cfm.

54. See the Yerodia case, ICJ decision of February 14, 2002; also Bekker, 2002.

55. See Art. XII Sec. 5 Articles of 1945 Agreement of the International Monetary Fund; Art. V Sec. 3 Articles of the 1945 Agreement of the International Bank for Reconstruction and Development.

56. What is the WTO? Retrieved from http://www.wto.org/english/thewto_e/whatis_ e/whatis_e.htm.

57. Keet, D. (2011). Proposals on the role of trade within the New Partnership for Africa's Development (NEPAD) — challenges and questions. As quoted by S. A. Djoyou Kamga (2011). Human Rights in Africa: Prospects for the Realisation of the Right to Development under NEPAD (Unpublished LLD Thesis, University of Pretoria).

58. Chimni, B. S. (2008). Marxism and international law: A Contemporary analysis. *Economic and Political Weekly, 34*(6), 337.

59. Hardt, M. & Negri, A. (2000). *Empire.* Cambridge, MA: Harvard University Press, p. 133.

60. Mieville, C. (2005). *Between equal rights: A Marxist theory of international law*: Leiden, Netherlands: Martinus Nijhoff, p. 291.

61. Chimni, B. S. (2006). Third world approach to international law: A manifesto. *International Community Law Review 8*, 15.

62. United Nations Declaration on the Right to Development. General Assembly Resolution 41/128 of 4 December 1986.

For more on the process of adoption of this Declaration see Djoyou Kamga, S. A. (2011). Human rights in Africa: Prospects for the realisation of the right to development under NEPAD (unpublished LLD Thesis, University of Pretoria 146–151.

63. Chimni, B. S. (2006). Third world approach to international law: A manifesto. *International Community Law Review 8*, 22.

64. Chimni, B. S. (2006). Third world approach to international law: A manifesto. *International Community Law Review 8*, 22.

65. https://www.globalpolicy.org/component/content/article/177/31816.html.

66. Murithi, T. K. (2011). The United Nations: Between paternalism and partnership. In K. Kondlo and C. Ejiogu (Eds.), *Africa in Focus—Governance in the 21st Century* (p. 249). Pretoria, South Africa: HSRC press.

67. Chimni, B. S. (2007). A just world under law: A view from the south. *American University International Law Review, 22*(2), 218.

68. Lauterpacht, H. (1925). Westlake and Present Day International Law. *Economica, 15*, 307; also Boyle, A., & Chinkin, C. (2007). *The making of international law.* Oxford, England: Oxford University Press, p. 36.

69. Anderson, K., & Rieff, D. (2005). Global civil society: A sceptical view. In H. Anheier, M. Glasius, & M. Kaldo (Eds.), *Global Civil Society* 2004/5 26 & 28; Also Boyle, A., & Chinkin, C. (2007). *The making of international law.* Oxford, England: Oxford University Press, p. 37.

70. Boyle, A., & Chinkin, C. (2007). *The making of international law.* Oxford, England: Oxford University Press, p. 37.

71. Boyle, A., & Chinkin, C. (2007). *The making of international law.* Oxford, England: Oxford University Press, p. 77.

Part II

Decoloniality, Disciplines, and Ideology

Chapter 5

Devil on the Cross: Ngugi wa Thiong'o's Politics of Decolonization

William Mpofu

Here a writer has no choice. Whether or not he is aware of it, his works reflect one or more aspects of the intense economic, political, cultural and ideological struggles in a society. What he can choose is one or the other side in the battlefield: the side of the people, or the side of the social forces and classes that try to keep the people down. What he or she cannot do is to remain neutral. Every writer is a writer in politics. The only question is what and whose politics?[1]

I am insisting that in any society, anywhere, in any age, there are two types of rulers: namely the artist who provides and sustains the fundamental ideas, the foundation of society, and the political chieftain, who comes to power with the aid of his soldier and rich business brethren, who merely puts these ideas into practice in ruling or misruling society.[2]

Introduction

In *Devil on the Cross*,[3] Ngugi wa Thiong'o is at once "the prophet of justice" and a village story-teller, the magisterial "Gicaandi player." He creates an electrifying fictive universe that describes the hellish lives of peasants and workers in a post-independence setting in Africa on the one hand, and the grotesque excesses of the compradorial capitalist ruling class on the other.

Drafted first in the Gikuyu ancestral language, on toilet paper, during Ngugi's detention in Kamiti Maximum Prison, the novel is a narrative of refusal and rebellion by the peasantry and the workers. The peasants and the workers in their "tattered clothes" crucify the "Devil" of colonialism and imperialism by day. By night, the rich people in "dark suits and ties" bring the "Devil" down from the "cross" and they worship him. It is because of this resurrected "Devil" of coloniality that the dream of an independent and prosperous Africa has turned into a nightmare. Incomplete decolonisation and the hellish climate of poverty and deprivation that are visited on the peasants and the workers are the handiwork of the "Devil" of coloniality and its puppets, the post-independence black elite. However, in Ngugi's captivating folkloric universe, the "voice of the people is the voice of God," and a judgement will be levied on the rich and the powerful that have invited colonialism back into the land that the peasants and the workers had liberated.

Most readings of *Devil on the Cross*, as this chapter will demonstrate, have limited themselves to the obviously Marxist posture of the novel, where workers and the peasants seek to dethrone the exploitative ruling class to establish utopian communism. Other critics might be sold to an appreciation of Ngugi as a lonely communalist whose sympathy with peasant and worker politics is a yearning for the idyllic pre-colonial era, where even "if a bean fell from the sky" the people would "split it" among themselves and "share" it in the true spirit of African village democracy. Away from these at once compelling and even convincing readings of *Devil on the Cross*, and appreciations of Ngugi's fiction, this chapter privileges a decolonial reading of the novel as a work of epistemic disobedience, couched from the locus of enunciation of "colonial difference" by a writer whose work is enmeshed in the political struggles of the peasants and the workers in the "zone of non-being," represented in a post-independence African location.

Yet other readings of *Devil on the Cross* and critiques of Ngugi have placed his fictive visions and imaginative creatures in the realm of postcolonial literature and thought. Demonstrably, while Ngugi does describe the sexual exploitation of women and the abuse of the poor by the rich "robbers and thieves" in imagery and grammar that compares to that of postcolonial theorists such as Achille Mbembe, the gist of *Devil on the Cross* refuses the confines of postcolonial thinking in that it insists on the presence of the "Devil" of coloniality in post-independence African contexts. The emphatic presence of the resurrected "Devil" and his works forbids imagination of the "post-" that postcolonial theory envisages. Long after juridical colonialism has been de-stooled, political and social conditions of coloniality continue in Ngugi's fictive universe as they do in the lived experiences of Africa to squeeze life out of the poor and to squeeze the poor out of life.

In *Weep Not Child*,[4] Ngugi uses the novel to decry how Africans who were forced to fight in World War One became tools of Western superpowers; those who did not die in the war came back home to poverty as they found their ancestral lands taken by the colonists. In desperation the black African World War returnees were forced to be squatters who lived in compounds working for the white settlers. In *The River Between*,[5] Ngugi shows how the Christian religion of the white man was used to uproot Africans from their history and divide them into feuding believers and non-believers. In all these mentioned works, Ngugi's diagnosis of the causalities of poverty and alienation of Africans during and after colonialism places blame on an unequal global system that has peripherised peasants and workers in the Global South to non-beings and pawns on the chessboard of the vampiric capitalist world system.

As an artist, Ngugi sees his role as that of a "prophet of justice," revolutionary thinker and teacher whose side of politics is with the people and not against them. In true Fanonian fashion, Ngugi believes in the redemptive nature of liberating violence. The novel ends with Wariinga, the tortured peasant and worker heroine of the novel, shooting to death, among others and first, the rich old man who impregnated and dumped her to poverty and ignorance as she dropped out of school. This chapter will from here flesh out some observations on Eurocentric cultural fundamentalism and imperialism in protest to which Ngugi and many other decolonial writers in the Global South write. From there, the potency of decolonial thought as a lens of 'knowing the world' and appreciating Ngugi's fictive imagination will be enunciated. Relying on the words and practices of his characters in *Devil on the Cross,* this chapter will seek to demonstrate Ngugi's decolonial politics and epistemic disobedience, which has seen him producing his literature first in his native Gikuyu language before translations to the English language.

Eurocentric Fundamentalism

In what he calls the "ego politics of" Eurocentric "knowledge," Ramon Grosfoguel describes how in saying "I think, therefore I am" Rene Descartes inaugurated Eurocentric fundamentalism of knowledge. There developed a current in the West that it possessed wisdom of what was true and good for the whole universe regardless of space and time. The view of the West about the world became a "God's eye view" whose sight cannot be challenged or vision disputed:

> The latter is a point of view that hides itself as a point of view, or, put differently, the point of view that assumes having no point of view.

We are dealing, then, with a philosophy in which the epistemic subject has no sexuality, gender, ethnicity, race, class, spirituality, language, or epistemic location within power relations, and a subject that produces truth from an interior monologue with himself without relation to anyone outside him. That is to say, we are dealing with a deaf philosophy, a philosophy without a face, which feels no gravity. This faceless subject floats through the sky without being determined by anything or anyone.[6]

Armed with this at once arrogant and tyrannical ego-politics of knowledge and understanding, the West could then impose its religion, philosophy and interests on the Global South without a crisis of conscience or an iota of guilt. It is this fundamentalism of Eurocentric knowledge that produced the "civilizing" missions of slavery and colonialism, where the Euro-American empire arrogated to itself the right to recover the Other from the bestial and restore it to humanity by whatever means and violence necessary. Anibal Quijano notes that this toxic imperial Eurocentric mode of knowledge seeks to distort what Africans and other subjects in the Global South know about themselves:

The Eurocentric perspective of knowledge operates as a mirror that distorts what it reflects, as we can see in the Latin American historical experience. […] Consequently, when we look in our Eurocentric mirror, the image that we see is not just composite, but also necessarily partial and distorted. Here the tragedy is that we have all been led, knowingly or not, wanting it or not, to see and accept that image as our own and as belonging to us alone. In this way, we continue being what we are not. And as a result we can never identify our true problems, much less resolve them, except in a partial and distorted way.[7]

The image of African subjects and others in the Global South as reflected and distorted in the Eurocentric mirror of knowing is an image of inferiority and inadequacy. What is European and white, together with all aspects of life associated with it, becomes the standard of all measurements. For that unfortunate reason, Wariinga, the heroine in *Devil on the Cross* (p. 11), after being exploited by men who think 'women are flowers to decorate their beds' and after attempting suicide in a bid to escape a hellish life of abuse, poverty and unemployment, began to convince herself that:

Her appearance was the root cause of all her problems. Whenever she looked at herself in the mirror she thought herself very ugly. What she hated most was her blackness, so she would disfigure her body with skin lightening creams like *ambi* and *snowfire*, forgetting the saying: that which is born black will never be white. Now her body was covered in dark and white spots like the guineafowl. Her hair was splitting, and it had browned to the colour of moleskin because it had been straightened with red iron combs.[8]

Firmly planted in Wariinga's mind was the falsehood that being black is ugly and it is the source of all misfortunes, including poverty and unemployment. She began to yearn to be white, and desperately wish that she could escape her blackness by use of chemicals and ointments. This self-hatred accompanied by self-mutilations does not end with the burning of the skin and the hair, but it extends to the psyche and chains the mind to a status of self-doubt and inferiority.

Not only does Eurocentric epistemic fundamentalism cast into doubt the sense and sensibility of beauty of the African subject, it goes on to re-invent the creator being or God after its own image and agendas. It is no longer the God of humanity but the God of the white man, a God that he gives as a civilising gift to those that he conquers and seeks to dominate and control. The monopolisation of the God figure and his use as a scare instrument to frighten Africans and others in the Global South into fear of damnation and burning in hell are effective technologies of colonialism and coloniality. Minister Josiah Strong, a 19th century American evangelist, preached that:

> It seems to me God, with infinite wisdom and skill, is training the Anglo-Saxon race for an hour sure to come in the world's future. The lands of the earth are limited, and soon will be taken. Then will the world enter upon a new stage in its history—the final competition of the races. Then this race of unequaled energy, with the majesty of numbers and the might of wealth behind it, the representative of the largest liberty, the purest Christianity, the highest civilsation, will spread itself over the earth.[9]

Disguised as the will of God, Eurocentric fundamentalism marches across the globe dressed in the innocence of the gospel and the virtue of salvation for all. Behind the veil of godliness, the crimes of slavery, colonialism and imperialism have been committed by the Euro-American empire with impunity and a titanic ego. Whether disguised as civilisation of the natives, development of the Third World or its democratisation, Euro-American expansionism carries always the darker side of violence and large-scale destruction. From the journeys and "discoveries" of Christopher Columbus and the intrusions and interventions of Cecil John Rhodes up to the North Atlantic Treaty Organisation (NATO) intervention in Libya in 2011, Western expansionism dresses itself with some good news for the native while its true purposes and ends remain to be the vampiric siphoning of resources and labour. The above words of Minister Strong are emphatically symptomatic of the Eurocentric fundamentalism that equips the mentality of the archetypal imperialist.

As the African proverb goes that "before the leopard eats another, it first accuses it of smelling like a goat," the Euro-American empire has done nothing in Africa before diagnosing a certain lack, deficit or a certain excess of some unwanted attribute that only the West are equipped to remedy, if not by 'humanitarian intervention' then by military force of arms. In an artisanal observation and description of this "Greeks that carry gifts" attitude of the West to the Global South, Ramon Grosfoguel (2012:97) notes that:

> During the last 520 years of European/Euro-North-American capitalist/patriarchal modern/colonial world system, went from "convert to Christianity or I kill you" in the 16th century to, "civilise or I will kill you" in the 18th and 19th centuries, to "develop or I will kill you" in the 20th century, and more recently, the "democratise or I will kill you" at the beginning of the 21st century. We have never seen respect or recognition of indigenous, Islamic, or African forms of democracy as a systematic and consistent Western policy. Forms of democratic alterity are rejected *a priori*.[10]

Thus, the Western way of life and politics will, by carrot or by stick, be imposed on the Global South. It is the West that hold monopoly of the truth and of what is good for all humanity. Even Western violence is for reasons of kindness wherever it is visited upon those that are named enemies in particular times. Grosfoguel recalls how Enrique Dussel observed that the European ego-politics of "I think, therefore I am" was preceded by 150 years of "I conquer therefore I am," which is a fitting arrogant slogan of imperialists who see their eyes as the eyes of God and their knowledge of the world as God's wisdom. It is this colossal Eurocentric ego of knowledge and power that Wariinga and other peasants and workers in Ngugi's *Devil on the Cross* are challenging when they sing: "Kenya does not belong to you imperialists, pack up your bags and go, the owner of the homestead is on his way."[11] It is a gigantic power structure of imperialism and coloniality that through his pugilistic fiction, Ngugi seeks to conscientise the masses of poor workers and peasants into challenging and dethroning. Eurocentricism is at once fundamentalist and tyrannical, it is domineering and violent against all that opposes it.

Beyond Marxism: a Decolonial Theoretical Reading of *Devil on the Cross*

Karl Marx was right that "the philosophers have only interpreted the world, in various ways; the point, however, is to change it."[12] Theory and philosophy may describe and name the world in a multiplicity of compelling ways, but what the human condition requires is change for the better, and advancement from conditions of deprivation to those of satisfaction and adequacy. M. S. C. Okolo, whose important book has popularized the reading of "African Literature" not just as entertainment but as serious "philosophy," has largely read and written of Ngugi as a writer in "Marxist aesthetics" of literature. Okolo, while observing that "Marx has no defined theory on literature," opines that according to the Marxist literature of Ngugi:

> Literature then should function as a reflection of the economic arrangements in society and the nature of relationships they foster. Its purpose is to analyse society in its own terms, to present a fictional world that is a lifelike representation of the real world. Writers should approach their task as a social act that entails evaluating the mode of production in society, the nature of the relationship between the various classes, and how to bring about a revolutionary end to the oppression of one class by another.[13]

From what Okolo says and what Marx and Engels (1968:51) say (that "the ruling ideas of each age have ever been the ideas of the ruling class"), the Marxist way of reading literature sees the trouble in the world as the trouble of one class of rich capitalists exploiting poor workers (and peasants). There is no doubting throughout *Devil on the Cross* that Ngugi himself espouses Marxism and envisions a form of communist future for his struggling workers and peasants, whose catechism of struggle (p. 210) says:

I believe that we workers are one clan
I believe that in the organisation of workers
Lies our strength
I believe that Imperialism and its local representatives are the
Enemies of the progress of the workers and the peasants
And of the whole nation …

This 'workers anthem' rhymes in sound and in meaning with the international Marxist slogan of "workers of the world unite." It is the argument of this chapter that there is more to Ngugi's revolutionary fiction than there is to Marxism and its limits, which this chapter seeks to briefly explain. From a decolonial perspective, a perspective this chapter elects to use in reading Ngugi's fiction, there is doubt that the worker that Karl Marx talks of is the same worker that Ngugi writes about, let alone the peasant. In short, a European worker and peasant and an African colonial and post-independence peasant and worker might share the same name but are not the same subjects to the same power that allegedly oppresses them. The Orwellian aphorism of "some workers" being "more equal than others" might be applicable here.

Ramon Grosfoguel debunks Marxism as located inside empire and as not fundamentally antagonistic to imperialism and coloniality. Although Marxism sings the anthem of the proletariat that must dethrone the oppressive class of capitalists, it is not removed or insulated from the pulls and pushes of epistemic racism and the ego-politics of conquest:

> Marx situates his geopolitics of knowledge in relation to social classes. Marx thinks from the historic-social situation of the European prole-tariat, and it is on the basis of this perspective that he proposes a global/universal design as the solution to the problems of all humanity: communism. What Marx maintains in common with the Western Bourgeois philosophical tradition is that his universalism, despite hav-ing emerged from a particular location — in this case the proletariat — does not problematise the fact that his subject is European, masculine, heterosexual, white, Judeo-Christian, etc. Marx's proletariat is a con-flictive subject internal to Europe, which does not allow him to think outside the Eurocentric limits of Western thought.[14]

The limits of Marxism, therefore, and its handicaps in effectively reading the combative literature and Afrocentric fiction of Ngugi, is not only its locus of enunciation in the North, but also its failure to read what Walter Mignolo calls "colonial difference," which locates the African subject in the periphery, and "imperial difference,"[15] which positions the Western subject at the centre. The experience of colonialism, coloniality and racism that Ngugi's workers and peasants are confronting is not exactly uniform with that of Marx's work-ers, who were not exactly at the receiving end of the stick of empire in the context of coloniality and its racist expression. By this failure to read and be alive to the "colonial difference" of African workers and peasants, in this blind-ness which emanates from its "imperial difference," Marxism, from a decolo-nial vantage point, collapses to another imperial technology of dominating the Global South and enveloping it as an appendage of the titanic ego-politics of empire.

Just like Western modernity itself—which covers itself in tantalizing illu-sions of civilisation, human rights, development and such other human goods like democracy and peace, while its real logic is the pursuit of resources that lie under the feet of the natives in the Global South—Marxism appears to deploy the grammar of unity and struggle for all workers, while behind this guise, it conceals the same vampiric universalism that see in the native a thing rather than a citizen. A labourer rather than an empowered human being. Grosfoguel insists that:

> The 20th century communist project was, albeit from the left, yet another Western global imperial/colonial design which under the Soviet empire attempted to export to the rest of the world its universal abstract of communism as the solution to global problems. Marx reproduces an epistemic racism much like that of Hegel, which does not allow him to grant non-European peoples and societies either temporal coevalness or the capacity to produce thought worthy of being considered part of the legacy of humanity or world history.[16]

In the true fashion of Western democracy, developmentalism and human rights, communism was supposed to be received in Africa and the Global South at large as a good benevolently developed above and ready to be consumed by the recipients, who are expected to be eternally grateful for the generosity of the master. The recipients were to suspend their own beliefs, if necessary forget their own history, and adapt this new social and political technology, tried and tested in the West, which was to be the panacea to all their problems. In the eyes of Marx, says Grosfoguel, "non-European peoples and societies were primitive, backwards, that is Europe's past."[17] He saw them as infantile peoples who had not developed enough to enjoy equality and respect. For that reason "in the name of civilizing them and pulling them out of the ahistoric stagnation of pre-capitalist modes of production, Marx would support the British invasion of India in the 18th century and the United States invasion of Mexico in the 19th century." Fundamentally, Marxist communism was not opposed to imperialism and the thingification of the natives in the Global South. Clearly, this darker side of Marxism does not sit well with Ngugi's peasants and workers, who valorize Mau Mau guerillas who bravely confronted British colonialism and quote Gikuyu, the wise ancestor and founder of their nation.

While Marxism with its limitations described above sees the problem with the condition of the world as the capitalist class that exploits and oppresses the proletariat, decolonial thought as a critical theory sees coloniality as "the darker side" of "Western modernity" as the global power structure which reproduces the imperial ego-politics of marginality and thingification of those constituents of humanity that populate the Global South. It is important at this juncture to seek a clear definition of coloniality as a power structure and flesh out its difference from colonialism. Defining coloniality, Nelson Maldonado-Torres said:

> Coloniality is different from colonialism. Colonialism denotes a po-
> litical and economic relation in which the sovereignty of a nation or
> a people rests on the power of another nation, which makes such a
> nation an empire. Coloniality, instead, refers to long standing patterns
> of power that emerged as a result of colonialism, but that define cul-
> ture, labour, intersubjective relations, and knowledge production well
> beyond the strict limits of colonial administrations. Thus coloniality
> survives colonialism. It is maintained alive in books, in the criteria
> for academic performance, in cultural patterns, in common sense, in
> the self-image of people and so many other aspects of our modern
> experience. In a way, as modern subjects we breathe coloniality all
> the time and every day.[18]

Torres's definition of coloniality fits the political and social conditions of a post-independence country like the one that is fictionalised in *Devil on the Cross*. In the fictive universe of the novel, juridical colonialism had been dethroned by the workers in "tattered clothes," but the black business and ruling political elite in "dark suits and ties" resurrected it for their own interests and the interest of global capitalism. This social and political condition of Africa, where the post-independence era turned into another epoch of poverty, political repression and disillusionment for the African masses, has occupied historians and other social scientists in Africa for a long time now.

With remarkable erudition, Paul Tiyambe Zeleza, himself an artisanal historian and story teller, observed that Africa's fictive imaginists, the novelists and poets, were ahead of other academics and social scientists in observing that the dream of independence in Africa was becoming not only elusive but was turning into a haunting nightmare. Zeleza notes that in the proverbial earliness of baboons that see the new moon before the villagers do:

> Long before these African social scientists had discovered the social
> movements in the 1980's, African (creative) writers, almost all from
> the dawn of independence, knew that the masses were dissatisfied and
> hungry for meaningful change. The rhetoric of nation building and
> development could not fool Ousumane Sembene's restive workers,
> Ngugi wa Thiong'o's militant peasants, Bessie Head's exploited rural
> women, and Buchi Emecheta's urban working class women. Achebe
> and Ayi Kwei Armah showed the economic and cultural hollowness
> of modernization, before African and Africanist scholars from the

1970s, through the lenses of dependency theory imported from Latin America, saw that the venerated god had no clothes.[19]

Zeleza writes to the observatory alertness and courageous intellectual and fictive energy of Africa's storytellers, such as Ngugi and many others, who were the first among Africa's thinkers to point out that it was not yet uhuru, and that the promised goods of independence that the masses with their sweat and blood ordered had not been delivered, or that the delivered goods were damaged and spoilt well beyond use. In *Devil on the Cross*, Ngugi effectively describes, in emphatic images, what happens to ordinary people when the ordered social and economic merchandise of independence are delivered in a corrupted and poisonous state. Seeing what has happened to the dream of independence, one of Ngugi's characters, Wangari (p. 40), bemoans the treachery and painful paradox of what has become of the post-independence country:

> You say that if a bean falls to the ground we split it among ourselves? That we shed blood because of the great movement that belonged to us, the people of Kenya, Mau Mau, the people's movement, so that our children might eat until they were full, might wear clothes that kept out the cold, might sleep in beds free from bedbugs? That our children should learn the art of producing wealth for our people? Tell me this: who but a fool or a traitor would not have sacrificed his own blood for those glorious aims? I, Wangari you see before you, was a small girl then. But these legs have carried many bullets and many guns to our fighters in the forest ... and I was never afraid ... Our people, when I recall these things, my heart weakens and I want to cry.... [T]he modern Harambee is for the rich and their friends.[20]

Wangari's bitterness and anger is shared among many peasants, workers and students in post-independence African countries. "The rich and their friends," who have taken up the reins of power and control of the African state, are not delivering the fruits of independence, in spite of the fact that juridical colonialism has been dethroned, and that black sons and daughter of the soil are now in power. In a much more pulsating and spectacular manner, in *Matigari*,[21] Ngugi resurrects a Mau Mau fighter named Matigari, who comes to haunt the country, asking stubborn questions about what happened to independence and the sacrifices of the brave fighters and the masses. The theme of betrayal of independence occupies Ngugi's fiction in elaborate detail and account.

In the true fashion of coloniality, the survivor and successor power of colonialism that remains to dominate not only the economies and polities, but the

lives and the cultures of post-independence subjects in the Global South, in
Devil on the Cross, Gatuiria (p. 58), an educated young man who is concerned
about the ravages of "English cultural imperialism" on the culture of his people,
complains bitterly of the corruption and tragic loss that have befallen his people. Imperialists have not only stolen the people's lands, exploited their labour
and recruited the new black political elite into being intermediaries of global
capitalism who oppress their people just as the white settlers did, but they have
also vandalized the cultures, traditions and religions of the people, leaving
them as rootless and nameless beings with no history or identity to lean on.
Gatuiria asks:

> Let us look about us. Where are our national languages? Where are
> the books written in the alphabets of our national languages? Where
> is our own literature now? Where is the wisdom and knowledge of
> our fathers now? Where is the philosophy of our fathers now? The
> centres of wisdom that used to guard the entrance to our homestead
> have been demolished, the fire of wisdom has been allowed to die,
> the seats around the fireside have been thrown on to a rubbish heap,
> the guard posts have been destroyed, and the youth of the nation has
> hung up its shields and spears. It is a tragedy that there is nowhere
> we can go to learn the history of our country. A child without parents
> to counsel him—what is to prevent him from mistaking foreign shit
> for a delicious national dish?[22]

The bitterness of Gatuiria does not only remain in Ngugi's fiction. In fact,
it can be said that Gatuiria is only Ngugi's mouth piece. An entire book, *Decolonising the Mind*,[23] was dedicated by Ngugi to the struggle for liberation
of African minds, languages and cultures from cultural imperialism. Ngugi's
activism for revived African languages and cultures has marked him out as
not just an occasional Marxist novelist, as most readings of his work have mis-
taken him to be. The proletariat versus the ruling capitalist class struggle which
dominates the Marxist definition of struggle is just but a small province of
Ngugi's literary vocation. He goes beyond, not only to unmask coloniality in
post-independence African contexts, but also to unleash decolonial insights
that have seen his characters such as Gatuiria pleading for an African Renaissance of languages and cultures.

The spectacle of coloniality as represented in *Devil on the Cross* (p. 76) is
dramatised in the cave, where the ruling business and political elite have organised "a competition to select seven experts in Modern Theft and Robbery."[24]
This scene of the novel presents a melodramatic event where leading tycoons
and moguls testify how they have robbed the poor and how they have paid

homage and served international capitalism at the expense of local peasants and workers. Gitutu wa Gataanguru, a local tycoon whose self-given name that bespeaks coloniality of taste and sensibility is "Rottenborough Groundflesh Shitland Narrow Isthmus Joint Stock Brown," tells the gathering how using "cunning" as his "guide" he has made himself obscenely rich in the land of the poor by hoarding land to create famine, and how he has sold the scarce land to land-hungry peasants for obscenely high prices. Kihaau wa Gatheeca, another business mogul, boasts of how he has used his illicit wealth to enjoy "other people's wives," who give him such "a glorious feeling of victory." Gatheeca makes his riches from his "Modern Day Nursery School," which is headed by a "white woman" whose whiteness fools people into thinking that the nursery school dispenses superior education for their children, who get a chance to play with white dolls and toys. To outdo other thieves, Nditika wa Nguunji (p. 176) suggests the capitalists should invent technology to manufacture body parts so that the rich can have spare body parts, including spare sexual organs to have a double take at life. He concludes by saying "a rich man never dies; we could purchase immortality with our money and leave death as the prerogative of the poor." Only when his wife entertains the idea of also having "two things" does Nguunji see the tragedy of his ideas (p. 180).[25]

Of all the grotesque ways of punishing the poor, Gitutu's (p. 107) contributions dramatise the satanic nature of coloniality and its designs. While most of the ideas are meant to entertain the reader and create the comedy that goes with fiction, below the humour lies serious commentary on how capitalism and coloniality, as the darker side of modernity, in effect squeeze the poor out of life and squeeze life out of the poor, leaving them as shells in the service of empire:

> There are two ideas that I would like to develop now. The first concerns ways and means of increasing hunger and thirst for land in the whole country, this will create famine, and the people will then raise top grade tycoons ... as soon as hunger and thirst have increased beyond their present level, we who have the land will be selling soil in small pots and tins so that a man will at least be able to plant a seed in them and hang them from the roof of his shelter..The other idea I would like to follow up is how we top grade tycoons, can trap the air in the sky, put it in tins and sell it to peasants and workers, just as water and charcoal are now sold to them, imagine the profit we would reap if we were to sell the masses air to breathe in tins, or better if we could meter it! We could even import air from abroad, imported air, which we could then sell to people at special prices! Or we could send our own air abroad to be packaged in tins and bottles — yes be-

cause the technology of foreigners is advanced! And then it will be sent back to us here labeled Made in USA, Made in Western Europe, Made in Japan, This Air is Made Abroad; and other similar ads.[26]

As light humoured as they seem, Gitutu's ideas are reflective of the designs of coloniality whose effects have occupied the interest of scholars and social scientists in the African academy for a long time to date. The scarcity of land, environmental pollution that has occasioned the dearth of pure oxygen to breathe, is no laughing matter in Africa. The use of Africa as a source of raw materials that are siphoned and processed in the West to be exported back as finished products in fancy labels and sold for impossible prices is also a worrying concern of students of development, history and economics in Africa. The at once comic and at the same time tragic hallucinatory dreams of Ngugi's fictive thieves and robbers in the cave are a scathing indictment of the treacherous post-independence political and social conditions in the African setting.

With noticeable ability, which is unfortunately limited by his theoretical grounding and project, postcolonial theorist Achille Mbembe describes the actions, forces and excesses of personas and communities in post-independence locations such as those fictionalised by Ngugi in *Devil on the Cross*. Mbembe says what he describes as the "post-colony" is punctuated with "elements of the obscene and the grotesque." In Mbembe's 'post-colony' the setting is "characterised by a distinctive style of political improvisations, by a tendency to excess and lack of proportion." It is such a punitive world, in whose unfriendliness to the poor "the champions of State power invent entire constellations of ideas; they adopt a distinct set of cultural repertoires and powerfully evocative concepts. But they also have to resort, if necessary, to systematic application of pain" in the case of the post-independence locality of *Devil on the Cross*, even the calculated administration of death through hired assassins against activists and opponents. The dehumanization of the oppressed and of the oppressor, who are both enveloped in de-humanity because of their joint imbrications in giving and receiving humiliation, results in "the mutual zombification of both the dominant and those whom they apparently dominate." In the "post-colony" Mbembe says:

> Beyond this concern specifically with the mouth, belly and phallus, the body itself is the principal locale of the idioms and fantasies used in depicting power. But if, as we have suggested, it is the festivities and celebrations that are the vehicles, par-excellence, for giving expression to the commandment and for staging its displays of magnificence and prodigality then the body in question is firstly a body that eats and drinks, and secondly a body that is open — in both ways.[27]

In his own fictional description Mbembe achieves describing the obscenities of excess consumption, debauchery and licentiousness that are peopled by characters such as Gitutu and Nguunji, whose bodies are described in caricature and excess. The dreams of selling soil in tins and manufacturing extra and spare organs, including reserve sexual organs, and the yearning for artificial immortality fit squarely in the bizarre and bestial world pictured by Mbembe. Decay and decadence describe the gluttonous wants for more and more riches, the celebration of crime and illicit gains bespeak a devilish corruption that flowers in gratuitous consumption and even adulterous copulation. An emphatic economy of pornography of life and politics ensures. The misfortune of Mbembe's excellence of observation, however, is that it collapses and ends there, in the description. It is condemned to collapse by its beginning, in the faulty belief that there is a postcolonial reality. Mbembe's truth about the conduct and excesses of his characters in the "post-colony" is immediately suffocated, and smothered to falsehood by the narrow confines of postcolonial theory and thinking.

In its denial of the existence of a "post-colony" and the belief that post-coloniality is an invented mythology that tends to conceal rather than reveal the enduring reality of coloniality, decolonial thought insists that while juridical colonisation was dethroned, new black faces installed in government, and colourful flags flown to melodious national anthems and party slogans, the hangover of imperialism and colonialism remains, reproducing itself in the new structures and personalities in government and in business. The obituary of Mbembe's idea of a "post-colony" is probably signed by Ramon Grosfoguel, who offers that:

> One of the most powerful myths of the twentieth century was the notion that the elimination of colonial administrations amounted to decolonisation of the world. This led to the myth of a "postcolonial" world. The heterogeneous and multiple global structures put in place over 450 years did not evaporate with the juridical political decolonisation of the periphery over the past 50 years. We continue to live under the same colonial power matrix. With juridical political decolonisation we moved from a period of global colonialism to the current period of global coloniality.[28]

In accord with Grosfoguel, this chapter reads the grotesque and bizarre celebrations of theft and exploitation of the peasants and workers in the den of thieves and robbers in *Devil on the Cross* as symptomatic of coloniality and testimony to the presence (and not the "post-") of the "Devil" of coloniality, who in alliance with the ruling political and business class continues where

administrative colonialism left. In *Devil on the Cross* (p. 82) the departing settler, who foresaw the impending defeat of colonialism:

> Called his loyalist slaves and servants to him. He taught them all the
> earthly wiles he knew, and especially the trick of sprinkling theft and
> robbery with the sweetest-smelling perfumes, and the trick of wrap-
> ping poison in sugar-coated leaves, and many tricks for dividing the
> country's workers and peasants through bribery and appeals to tribe
> and religion. When he had finished, he informed them that he was
> about to leave for his home overseas.[29]

Facing defeat, colonialism planted the seeds of coloniality to perpetuate itself and
its ends beyond its lifespan in the colony. It left behind chains in the minds of
the colonised, tricks and greed in the new black rulers, cunning and appetite in
the business class and long umbilical cords that tied them to the empire, represented by "foreign thieves and robbers" who were in attendance at the cave. Jean-
Paul Sartre graphically describes how, well in advance, colonial captains worked
over time to groom the black political and economic elite that was to do their
bidding after they had left the colonies, under the mythical project of decolonisation which marked the erection of coloniality as the new game in global power
relations between North and South. It happened, says Sartre, that the settlers:

> Possessed the Word and the rest borrowed it. Between the former and
> the latter, corrupt kinglets, feudal landowners, and an artificially cre-
> ated false bourgeoisie served as intermediaries. In the colonies, the
> naked truth revealed itself, the mother countries preferred it dressed;
> they needed the natives to love them, like mothers in a way. The Eu-
> ropean elite set about fabricating a native elite, selected adolescents,
> marked on their foreheads with iron, the principles of Western culture,
> stuffed into their mouths words which stuck to their teeth, after a brief
> stay in the mother country, they were sent back, interfered with, these
> living lies no longer had anything to say to their brothers, they echoed
> from Paris, from London, from Amsterdam […].[30]

The individuals who took over the reins of polities and those of economies
at the departure of juridical colonialism were creatures of colonialism, systemic
products with a predetermined agenda that had interests of the mother country
safe in their stewardship. These "walking lies" were mythical heroes and lib-
erators who became the proverbial wooden handle of the iron axe that cut the
trees in the forest and when the trees saw it they said, "But the handle is one
of us." In the hands of these "walking lies" global coloniality does not need
white representatives and overtly racial settlers, the programmed blacks can

do it even better. In its blindness to such dynamics as these, postcolonial theory becomes a little too narrow to effectively comprehend the workings of the world where colonialism has effectively installed in its former place the "Devil" of coloniality. From here, this chapter graduates its attention to an examination of Ngugi's epistemic disobedience, which represents a fruition of his work in decolonial thoughts and practices that fly well above the suffocating limits of Marxism and postcolonial theory.

Ngugi's Decolonial Epistemic Disobedience

In his work, upon which the large body of literary criticism in the West still relies for insights as to what constitutes good literature, Aristotle in *Poetics* mapped out five qualities of what he termed the sublime in works of imitative fiction and representational poetry. The exalted literary attributes are "grandeur of thought, vehemence of position, style, nobility of diction and phrase and elevated composition."[31] The individual artist was expected to exhibit competence in the Western conventions of composition and rendition of artistic communication. To date most Western and non-Western literature still sticks to the founding pronunciations of authorities like Aristotle, Longinus, Horace and other critics. The interest of this chapter is in how Ngugi wa Thiong'o and other combative decolonial African writers have disobeyed these Western conventions to generate modes of African expression and rendition that rhyme with the cultural pulse of African history and culture. To start with, Gatuiria, Ngugi's young artist in *Devil on the Cross* (p. 227)[32] composes a song—not from his closet as an individual artist, for the display of his sublime abilities, as the Aristotelian conventions demand, but a song for "many voices" and the "nation," in accordance with communal African traditions where the artist as the "Gicaandi player" is one with the community, the "mouth" of the nation, its eyes and ears.

In the important book *Towards the Decolonisation of African Literature*, Chinweizu et al. deliver an elaborate vision of how Afrocentric writers should, in relevance to African sensibility, mine inspiration and artistic influence from the rich cultural landscapes of African oral traditions. To Chinweizu and others, African writers and their critics should abandon the colonial habit of viewing African literature as an overseas province of Western literature, but as one literary tradition with its own heritages and histories in the orature of Africans. It is a misfortune that the conventional critics should view:

> African Literature through European eyes. If at all they know that
> African culture is under domination, they seem to think that it must

remain so. Most of them would be ashamed to admit it, but the fact of the matter is that these African critics view African literature as overseas department of European literatures, as a literature with no traditions of its own to build upon, no models of its own to imitate, no audience or constituency separate and apart from the European, and above all, no norms of its own.[33]

Not so with Ngugi. Much in defiance of the rather simplistic readings of his work as a mere Marxist literary megaphone or postcolonial protest artist who draws influence from his early readings of Western literary classics in the colonial school, he comes up with a rebellious mixture of an appropriation of English prose mixed with African story-telling and song narratives. The very title *Devil on the Cross,* as David Cook and Michael Okenimkpe argue, "refers to the ironic inversion of the story of the crucifixion, it is now the Devil, ruthless genius of the cash nexus, who in a vision is crucified by workers and peasants."[34] Ngugi subsumes the biblical story, twists it and turns it to make it obey the message and tone of his own story.

Much debated of Ngugi's ideas on African literature has been his proposal, and one which he is religiously practicing, of writing in his mother tongue first, and then for the benefit of other audiences translating his works to Swahili and then English. In aversion to cultural imperialism and sensitive to alienation, Ngugi has over time marked himself out as a militant opponent of the wholesale consumption of Western imperial cultural products. It is Ngugi's strong view that European languages are imprisoning and inimical to the true expression of the African experience. He asks the question:

> Is an African Renaissance possible when we the keepers of memory have to work outside our own linguistic memory? And within the prison house of European linguistic memory? Often drawing from our own experiences and history to enrich the already rich European Memory? If we think of the intelligentsia as generals in the intellectual army of Africa including foot soldiers, can we expect this army to conquer when its generals are held prisoner? And it's worse when they revel in their fate as captives.[35]

The writing of African literature in English or any other imperial language is for Ngugi a limiting colonial misfortune that needs to be challenged. The profits of this idea and practice to African literature can be debated, but what this chapter draws from it is Ngugi's determination to stay true to Afrocentric and endogenous modes of literary expression that rhyme with his people and culture. Language borrowed from the colonial master cannot be relied upon as a tool to dethrone him and the infrastructure of oppression and cultural imperialism. Well beyond the "epistemic racism" of Marxism and the suffocating limits of postcolonial theory, Ngugi remains rooted in the firm landscapes of the orature and culture of his people. In defiance of the consuming Western "ego-politics" of knowledge informed by the "I think, therefore I am" tyranny of thought and meaning that believes European thought to be an undebatable universal good, Ngugi "shifts the geography" of reason to speak from the locus of enunciation of the Global South in what Walter Mignolo calls "epistemic disobedience."[36]

At the end of the novel Wariinga is not the pathetic suicidal soul that she was at the beginning. She is a successful mechanical engineer who throws karate kicks in self-defence. The workers, peasants and students, in defiance of the consequences of imprisonment and death, chase the thieves and the robbers out of the cave, and Wariinga shoots dead the rich old man who stole her youth, impregnated her and refused responsibility. The total message of the novel is that of struggle, resistance, and rebellion against given meanings and impositions. Ngugi is at once "the prophet of justice" and the "Gicaandi player" who cannot refuse the cries of the community and the nation to tell their story in their language and cultural sensibility. He is the ruler artist defined by Okot P'Bitek,[37] who produces the ideas by which society must be ruled, and he produces them not as their Marxist intellectual "vanguard" but a decolonial "rearguard" that works, walks and talks together with the people.

Conclusion

The project of this chapter has been to understand the decoloniality of Ngugi wa Thiong'o's political fiction as represented in his classic, *Devil on the Cross*. Seeing himself as a "prophet of justice" the narrator of the story, who is Ngugi's mouth piece, is presented to the readers as a communal artist, the "Gicaandi player" who receives pleas from the community to tell their story, and he does so in the language and cultural sensibility of the people. In its Afrocentric and decolonial posture, Ngugi's work as witnessed in *Devil on the Cross* confronts Eurocentric fundamentalism of knowledge and culture head on. Well beyond the "epistemic racism" that limits the Marxist understanding of the African experience of coloniality that the workers and the peasants endure, and the suffocating inadequacies of postcolonial theory, which purveys the myth of a "post-" colonial experience, Ngugi discharges a militant decoloniality of thought and practice that amounts to "epistemic disobedience" that is practiced and couched in the locus of enunciation of the Global South, and of "colonial difference." In its combative unmasking of coloniality and radical pursuit of a "decolonial turn" in rejecting imperial languages and subsuming imperial Aristotelian conventions of expression by twisting and domesticating them to the African experience, Ngugi's fiction effectively shakes off the label of simplistic Marxist and postcolonial literature.

Notes and References

1. Wa Thiong'o, N. (1997). *Writers in politics*. Portsmouth, England: Heinemann.
2. P'Bitek, O. (1986). *Artist the ruler: Essays on art, culture and values*. Nairobi, Kenya: Heinemann.
3. Wa Thiong'o, N. (1982). *Devil on the cross*. Essex, England: Heinemann.
4. Wa Thiong'o, N. (1988). *Weep not child*. London, England: Penguin Books.
5. Wa Thiong'o, N. (2008). *The river between*. London, England: Heinemann.
6. Grosfoguel, R. (2012). Decolonising Western universalism: Decolonial pluriversalism from Aime Cesaire to the Zapatistas. *Transmodernity: Journal of Peripheral Cultural Production of the Luso-Hispanic World, 1*(3), 87–103.
7. Quijano, A. (2007, March/May). Coloniality and Modernity/Rationality. *Cultural Studies, 21*(2/3), 168–178.
8. Wa Thiong'o, N. (1982). *Devil on the cross*. Essex, England: Heinemann.
9. Strong, J. (2010). Gale Encyclopedia of Biographies, Answer.com. http://www.answer.com/topic/josiah-strong.
10. Grosfoguel, R. (2012). Decolonising Western universalism: Decolonial pluriversalism from Aime Cesaire to the Zapatistas. *Transmodernity: Journal of Peripheral Cultural Production of the Luso-Hispanic World, 1*(3), 87–103.
11. Wa Thiong'o, N. (1982). *Devil on the cross*. Essex, England: Heinemann.
12. Marx, K., & Engels, F. (1968). *Selected writings in sociology and social philosophy*. Harmondsworth, England: Penguin Books.
13. Okolo, M. S. C. (2013). *African literature as political philosophy*. London, England: Zed Books.
14. Grosfoguel, R. (2012). Decolonising Western universalism: Decolonial pluriversalism from Aime Cesaire to the Zapatistas. *Transmodernity: Journal of Peripheral Cultural Production of the Luso-Hispanic World, 1*(3), 87–103.
15. Mignolo, W. D. (1999). *Coloniality at large: The Western hemisphere in the colonial horizon of modernity*. New York, NY: Duke University.
16. Grosfoguel, R. (2012). Decolonising Western universalism: Decolonial pluriversalism from Aime Cesaire to the Zapatistas. *Transmodernity: Journal of Peripheral Cultural Production of the Luso-Hispanic World, 1*(3), 87–103.
17. Grosfoguel, R. (2012). Decolonising Western universalism: Decolonial pluriversalism from Aime Cesaire to the Zapatistas. *Transmodernity: Journal of Peripheral Cultural Production of the Luso-Hispanic World, 1*(3), 87–103.
18. Maldonado-Torres, N. (2007, March/May). On the coloniality of being: Contributions to the development of a concept. *Cultural Studies, 21*(2/3): 240–270.
19. Zeleza, P. (2003). *Manufacturing African Studies and crises*. Dakar, Senegal: CODESRIA.
20. Wa Thiong'o, N. (1982). *Devil on the cross*. Essex, England: Heinemann.
21. Wa Thiong'o, N. (1993). *Matigari*. London, England: Africa World Press.

22. Wa Thiong'o, N. (1982). *Devil on the cross*. Essex, England: Heinemann.

23. Wa Thiong'o, N. (1994). *Decolonising the mind: The politics of language in African Literature*. Harare, Zimbabwe: Zimbabwe Publishing House.

24. Wa Thiong'o, N. (1982). *Devil on the cross*. Essex, England: Heinemann.

25. Wa Thiong'o, N. (1982). *Devil on the cross*. Essex, England: Heinemann.

26. Wa Thiong'o, N. (1982). *Devil on the cross*. Essex, England: Heinemann.

27. Mbembe, A. (1992). Provisional notes on the post-colony. *Africa Journal of the International African Institute, 62*(1), 343–510.

28. Grosfoguel, R. (2007, March/May). The epistemic decolonial turn: Beyond political economy paradigms. *Cultural Studies, 21*(2–3), 211–223.

29. Wa Thiong'o, N. (1982). *Devil on the cross*. Essex, England: Heinemann.

30. Sartre, J. P. (2001). *Colonialism and neo-colonialism*. London, England: Routledge.

31. Aristotle. (1965). *Classical literary criticism*. Middlesex, England: Penguin.

32. Wa Thiong'o, N. (1982). *Devil on the cross*. Essex, England: Heinemann.

33. Chinweizu, et al. (1985). *Towards the decolonisation of African literature*. London, England: Routledge.

34. Cook, D., & Okenimkpe, M. (1997). Ngugi wa Thiong'o: An exploration of his writings. Oxford, England: Heinemann.

35. Wa Thiong'o, N. (2009). *Remembering Africa*. Nairobi, Kenya: East African Educational Publishers.

36. Mignolo, W. (2011). Epistemic Disobedience and the Decolonial Option: A manifesto. *Transmodernity: Journal of Peripheral Cultural Production of the Luso-Hispanic World, 1*(2), 41–66.

37. P'Bitek, O. (1986). *Artist the ruler: Essays on art, culture and values*. Nairobi, Kenya: Heinemann.

Chapter 6

A Decolonial Critique of Multi-Inter-Transdisciplinary (MIT) Methodology

Tendayi Sithole

Introduction

The debate about the discipline is as old as the discipline itself. This also includes decoloniality as the rallying point of criticism against the discipline. The discipline is the regulation of meaning, something which is contextual, but this regulation was and is still made in the ways that create absolutism, in the sense that the idea of the universal rests with the Euro-American empire. The discipline, hailing from this geographic and epistemic locus, is seen as knowledge and knowledge is seen as the discipline. What does not emerge, however, is subjectivity in its entirety—that is, the subjectivity of those who are at the margins of the Euro-American empire, an empire that assumes the positionality of the centre for the purpose of universalism.

The entry point here is to try to excavate some essential aspects of decoloniality engaging disciplinarity to reveal its forces of coloniality. The forces of coloniality, of course, hide the darker side of disciplinarity. What disciplinarity does not offer, and what multi-, inter-, and transdisciplinarity (MIT) to some extent does, is the epistemologies from below, particularly as these pertain to the African subject. These epistemologies are informed by cognitive justice and, nevertheless, they continue to wage struggle within the belly of disciplinarity. This chapter argues that disciplinarity is foundational and constitutive to coloniality. And, to some extent, this is still the case with MIT. In doing so, the chapter deploys decoloniality as a rallying point and proposes a few thoughts on disciplinary decadence, shifting the geography of reason and the ecologies of knowledge.

The Case for Decoloniality

Decoloniality is mobilised to revisit the silences and epistemological vio-lence, an epistemicide that resulted in the globalisation of Euro-American knowledge and the displacement of other knowledges. This is necessary in that the positionality of the African subject is that which informs knowledge claims. These knowledge claims are a constitutive part of the existence of that which is denied existence, and therefore they are claims informed by existential questions. It is necessary to state that decoloniality enables the foundation to understand, interrogate and challenge the decolonisation of the African subject. The rearticulation of African subjectivity is the formation of the African subject as the subject in the full sense of the word. In other words, the subject that has the capacity to think for itself and which possesses knowledge. It is through decoloniality that the African subject can free itself from the subjection that stems from disciplinarity. Decoloniality is necessary in that the discipline con-strains rather than enables.

According to Mignolo, decoloniality originates in the Third World. Decolo-niality diagnoses and searches for a project of political imagination to give new forms of life, forms of life that were denied to the African subjection which is in the belly of oppression.[1] Decoloniality constitutes a different agenda which places itself in the darker side of modernity and which exposes what modernity hides.[2] If modernity is salvation why is it that it creates inequality, injustice, and exploitation—the very basis of the ex-colonised's death? It is the task of decoloniality to reveal the lie embedded in the project of modernity. Modernity creates evils that shackle the African subject, and there is a problem in such a world with its postcolonial condition to reappropriate and reproduce the colonial structural tendencies which are embedded in modernity. For Walsh, there is a need for new communities of thought that are embedded in the struc-tural positionality of the African subject—that is, the subject which should be understood in terms of its structural positionality that is oppressed, mar-ginalised and subjugated on the periphery of the Euro-American empire.[3] In other words, decolonial epistemic perspective informs the continuous struggles which claim and practise their affinity with the African subject, with its exis-tential conditions as a lens. It is a form of political project which aims to raise the possibility of new and other worlds. What is emphasised here is a form of thought and existence which is decolonial in orientation.[4]

Decoloniality is deeply rooted in genealogies of understanding which examine coloniality as long-standing patterns of power that emerged as a result of colonialism and which define social, economic and cultural conditions in absence of the colonial administration.[5] This means coloniality is the result, survival, metamorphosis, continuity and maintenance of subjection. So, this makes it necessary for decoloniality to be grounded in histories and lived experiences created by colonialism and sustained by coloniality and, as such, it aims at breaking away from coloniality, which ratifies subjection. For this to be possible, decolonial epistemic perspective in its totality is informed by and entails praxis of a different kind, a praxis that confronts the hidden and cobwebbed deceptions of coloniality found in power, knowledge and being.

The Haunting Presence of Disciplinarity

Disciplinarity assumes its ever-presence, that it is something that will never wane, never to be transcended as far as the articulation of the discipline is concerned. It means, then, the discipline is still with us and it will not go away. The presence of the discipline is claimed to be the configuration of knowledge and, according to this view, there cannot be knowledge in its scientific and sophisticated view in the absence of the discipline. So, the conventional common view is that the presence of the discipline has to remain intact for the construction and articulation of knowledge. As Savransky argues, disciplinarity constitutes epistemological rigidity and certainty which is fundamental to the foundational canon(s) and constitutive to the discipline.[6] It is in the annals of the discipline that those which fall outside the representational scope of the Euro-American episteme should be relegated to the margins of barbarity or if not, at worse, face epistemicide. Smith argues that the discipline can be redeemed when the strategy concerning knowledge construction is the object of analysis, which is the foregrounding of reinvention of the discipline.[7] The discipline is knowledge and there cannot be knowledge proper outside the presence of the discipline and to some extent, there cannot be knowledge in its valid form without creating specialised knowledge. The purpose being solely that such specialisation is tantamount as the ammunition to make the discipline to be something that is able to solve the problems that come with modernity.

It is essential to confine the discipline qua knowledge within the content of modernity since both are said to be key in the shaping of modernity and also providing solutions to problems within modernity. As such, it is clear that the discipline is the important centre in the construction of specialised knowledge, which is key to solving problems brought about by modernity, or which modernity seeks to challenge, and is indeed the making of the world in its political, social, cultural and economic sense. Such construction of the world is one that is aimed at creating particular kind of subjectivities which deepen the understanding of the nuances of the complexities around which the discipline functions. According to Farred, the discipline stands on the act of erasure: by being expansive, it actually leaves many things unsaid.[8]

The very fact of its certainty, purity, difference, universalism (to name just a few) are the pointers which, on the other hand, reveal the very weakness of the discipline. The discipline is, therefore, through its frames, methods and modes of inquiry, 'the surest mark of "erased" knowledge'.[9] The construction of the world on the basis of knowledge is the collapse and erasure of other *knowledges*. These kinds of knowledge, which are produced through the confines of the discipline, both normalise and pathologise different kinds of behaviour and identities.[10] The organisation of *knowledges* has been that of knowledge, where the Euro-American empire coalesces everything and brings everything into its centre to form knowledge. As Gordon notes, 'notions of knowledge were so many that *knowledges* would be a more appropriate designation'.[11]

The haunting presence of disciplinarity is testimony to the fact that the configuration of knowledge has been that of its singular nature, where *knowledges* do not exist. According to Gordon, the modes of producing language are evidently enlisted as things in the service of colonisation, thus leading to epistemic colonisation. As Ndlovu-Gatsheni diagnoses, epistemological colonisation is the invasion and destruction of African imaginaries that contribute to the decapitation of African subjectivities, making it impossible to engage in any form of political imagination, shaping genealogies, missions, horizons and futures of African subjectivities.[12] Epistemic colonisation occurred and is sustained by means of epistemic violence which wore the mask of Euro-American epistemology. This is the deliberate non-existence of singularity in order to make way for modernity uninterrupted, and the discipline has been the master in making the solitude of knowledge and not allowing *knowledges*. This is the banality of Euro-American cul-de-sac as the way to legitimise itself.

Though the discipline is seen in that light in modernity—that is, that of solving problems to understand the complexities of modernity—what is not brought to light is what purpose this serves in terms of the discipline being the auxiliary of the colonial project, and today in the era of emancipation, where the Euro-American is still othering the 'Other'. The 'Other' is the subject at the margins of the empire, specifically the African subject. Why is it accepted that the discipline is the embodiment of knowledge? Or put in another way, why is knowledge thought of within the confines of the discipline? These questions highlight the linkages between the discipline and knowledge and they symbolise a unified entity, which is thought of as inseparable and which reifies the presence of knowledge instead of knowledges. This assumed inseparability between discipline and knowledge means that knowledge cannot emerge, for the discipline should be thought of as knowledge and knowledge as discipline. However, it needs to be pointed out that knowledge is not prison to the discipline, even within the context of the university and its pedagogic practices, but then, it is projected as such and this is affirmed by its positionality as something of solitude within the confines of modernity.

At another level, the university which houses the discipline in the form of departments, the latter discharging the knowledge through construction, reflection, validity and critique with the aim of graduateness, this is the knowledge in the specialised form. As Smith notes, one discipline cannot answer a complex variety of questions pertinent to the existential conditions of the African subject.[13] What makes the discipline exist and persist in its tradition even in this time of its crisis is the demand for consistency, which collapses into maximum consistency in order to be consistent.[14] This consistency is the one in which the haunting presence of the discipline is locked into, because as a defensive position it is able to produce its own regime of truth and yet parade it in the form of absolutism. This absolutism indeed produces the epistemic order of worldly things in that the acts and practices of self-hood within the confines of knowledge and disciplinarity as the mode of articulation is indeed that which is convenient to make the Euro-American empire the centre.

The Epistemic Order of Worldly Things

The discipline cannot be divorced from the order of worldly things—that is, the hierarchy of knowledge in relation to the configuration of the world. The world as it is represents hierarchies of asymmetrical power and relations which are rooted in subjection and also the othering of those who are at the margins of the Euro-American empire. Subjection affirms the positionality of the Euro-American empire as the centre of knowledge which must be spread even outside the margins of the empire. Ndlovu-Gatsheni is concerned with 'how colonial modernity pushed African forms of knowledge into barbarian margins of society and out of the academy'.[15] The order of the world is the order of epistemology and to some extent, this assumes the false identitarian project that epistemology is the world in its monolithic sense. It is in the arrangement of the Euro-American empire that knowledge is seen, and this alludes to the importance of the discipline. Gordon evokes the dimension of epistemological colonisation which is pervasive and which is claimed not to exist.[16] This is seen and justified as necessary for modernity. What does not exist are the forms of lives which exist under this colonisation since epistemology is seen at the abstract level, separated from being a political project having a great bearing on the existential conditions at the receiving end of subjection.

If modernity is to be the order of worldly things, then epistemology in the sense of the discipline is in the service of modernity, and it will be argued here that this is the modernity which guises itself as redemptive, whereas it is the opposite. In other words, modernity assumes the naturalism of the order of worldly things and as such, creates a condition where epistemology is seen as the basis underlying the justification of that order, which is asymmetrical and fueled by subjection of epistemic interventions from the margins. The epistemic nature of the discipline has been that of purporting the project of modernity, and in no way there has been a critique of modernity as coloniality. This means that modernity has not been exposed in its scandalous form as something that is inherent in the discipline and which by all accounts gives the redemptive picture of the Euro-American empire, parading it as a model. It is in this arrangement that the epistemic order of worldly things means that other parts of the world should imbibe modernity and mimic it in order to rise in the ranks of epistemic purity. Though the latter is something which is a mirage for those who are in the margins of the empire; they are not seen as equals, even if they can project themselves as that, it means that they are not in the worldliness.

The exclusive nature of worldliness assumes that epistemology in the state of the discipline is something that has modernity, which is civilisation, redemption, enlightenment, progress, public good. The intervention here is to engage modernity in what Mignolo refers to as its darker side, where the appearance of modernity is not its positive nature, something which is suspended at the margins of the Euro-American empire.[17] The darker side of modernity constitutes racism, violence, and destruction, all of which can be understood as subjection. Modernity is the site of castration of subjectivities and even not allowing the formation of political imaginations. The order of worldly things here appears in the ways in which modernity is elevated in the guise of prudence, and this is something that shows the deception that is part of it.

To move further, it is important to point out that the order of worldly things can be looked at in the ontological sense, wherein the cartography of the world constitutes a line which is both metaphoric and real. Santos argues that the cartography of modernity with its abyssal line of thinking should not be messy, since it may lead to messy practices.[18] The practices are, however, messy, in that ethics are abandoned in the other line of the abyssal thinking. So this is the cartography of modernity, which does not show its darker side. In Santos's understanding, the existence and the drawing of the abyssal lines are both literal and figurative. Also, for Santos, the co-presence of these two abyssal lines of thinking suggests the deep impossibility of co-presence. This lays testimony to the fact that differences are running deeper and deeper, and these differences represent the form and content of power relations. It is clear that in this state of affairs, power relations are asymmetrical. This is the cartography which is the constitutive part of subjection.

The abyssal line to which Santos alluded is one that divides the world in the Manichean sense of prudence/evil axis. As Santos states, modernity spreads globally, violating all forms of life on the other side of the abyssal line in order to redeem them from their barbarity to civility, while on the contrary, modernity is the axis of evil itself, as it does not create civility but barbarity par excellence. The asymmetry of power is also visible in the level of conversation. According to Walsh, the asymmetric process of interaction is visible between the relationality of the local level and the global level.[19] The abyssal lines demonstrate clearly how those who are in the empire are at the receiving end of civility and enjoy the benefits that come with modernity and as such are those who are the centre of the construction of the world and controllers of subjectivities. The subjects who are in the colony are said not to be fit to possess epistemic power; they can represent themselves as agents of history, but only as objects to be represented. The epistemic order of worldly things concerns those who are humans (those at the centre of the Euro-American empire) and non-humans (those at the margins of the empire). To be worldly and in its orderly favour is to be at the centre of the empire, and to be at the margins means not being worldly. As such, non-humans cannot be worldly. If this is the logic of the order of worldly things, it means then that epistemology is not universal since there are those who are excluded and denied of it. Those who are at the margins are seen as objects and epistemological reservoirs to be processed. In other words, they are epistemological raw material and cannot have the state of priority as they are waiting to be processed as finished products.

Multi-Inter-Transdisciplinary Decadence

What does the coming of Multi-Inter-Transdisciplinarity have to do with the state of the discipline? Does this mean that the discipline is in crisis, or does it imply a panacea to something that is problematic in the discipline? What is at stake with the discipline if there is something at stake with these three forms of disciplinarity? Though MIT takes rigour, openness and tolerance as fundamental principles, what is at stake and for whose benefit is the need for MIT? As Basarab notes, MIT is not about substituting but enriching each discipline.[20] This then means MIT is a mode of fertilisation where there is a constant search for new lived experiences and this is good for the rigour necessary for knowledge. Basarab argues that MIT allows tolerance of different disciplines and creates harmony. MIT is said to move away from a supposedly indisputable canonical knowledge system.

It is important to provide a brief distinction for MIT, which is rooted in the aim of bridging the gap between disciplines. Basarab provides the following distinction. Multi-disciplinarity is studying the research topic in several disciplines at the same time, inter-disciplinarity is the transfer of methods from one discipline to another and trans-disciplinarity is the study between disciplines, across different disciplines and beyond all disciplines. As Farred argues, MIT is 'founded on the notion of the discipline — or, aspects or tendencies within a single discipline — working with, intersecting, or overlapping with another'.[21] For the purpose of this chapter, the three are lumped together solely for the reason that they are moving beyond the discipline in its traditional sense. Also part of it is the fact that they are offering some sort of a remedy to the discipline. So the three therefore, despite their differences, are referred to as MIT from here on. As Basarab notes, MIT is the demand for transference, dialogue and reconciliation. On this basis, MIT is seen as the epistemic break from the discipline in the singular and plural sense, but that actually does not mean that the discipline is brought to an end. For the mere fact that the world "disciplinary" features in MIT means that the condition set is to enhance, complicate, sophisticate and hybridise the discipline. Whether it is in its state of ailment and decadence is something which is contested in MIT, but suffice it to say here as the point of argument that modernity is in crisis, hence MIT as well. What MIT calls for is the shaking of the rigidity of the discipline and of course at different degrees. The justification being that what is brought into being is the deeper understanding of epistemological and ontological phenomena.

The fundamental question to be asked is the presence of the canon within the discipline itself and under which knowledge it is constructed, which knowledge is foundational to its modes of articulation and subjectivity. In what ways is MIT dealing with the problem of Euro-American purview of knowledges as disciplinary knowledge? It is not clear to what extent MIT is addressing the question of epistemic violence which exists by means of closure, censorship and other modes of disciplinary power structures. In relation to the question of power, it is not clear in what ways MIT aims to make the epistemic break from the power structures that enhance and strengthen disciplinarity. It will be argued that MIT is still within the confines of the discipline, and like the discipline before it, it is still entangled by disciplinary decadence. Disciplinary decadence as Gordon defines it is that which sees itself in the sense of the world and which is deontologised and absolute by turning away from living thought.[22] Disciplinary decadence, as Gordon states, is having the mind-set of the empire that it must outlive all and beyond its purpose. Like the empire itself, the discipline is in a state of decay, hence it cannot solve the crises brought about modernity.

Disciplinary decadence constitutes disciplinary affliction, which exposes the isolation of the discipline and it being stuck in the cul-de-sac of the phenomena in which it is engaged. It is isolated from fundamental questions and offers a limited point of view. As Gordon notes, disciplinary decadence is caught in disciplinary envy in that it sees all disciplines from its standpoint. Though MIT undermines this monolithic view, what MIT is still trapped in is disciplinarity itself rather than engaging in something beyond the discipline. Emphasis on strict disciplinary domains is restricted in that the sole purpose is to discipline radical thought, something which is not the leitmotif of MIT. Disciplinary decadence is the process of critical decay within disciplinarity. This means that whatever has to do with the discipline, and specifically in this case, MIT, where the discipline is seen to be rescued by means of appraisal, critique and modification in order to solve complex problems of modernity, both epistemologically and ontologically, it means that there is a need for a bit of reflection. This reflection is necessary, and more so if it stems from decoloniality, to diagnose the decadence of the discipline, examining where the wrath of common sense (within the guise of objective and scientific knowledge) has taken its toll by means of disciplinary dogma, which is affirmed by the foundational thought and practices of the canon.

Does it mean now that in this era where the authority of the canon is being challenged, there should be the insistence that there is no disciplinary knowledge? It is in this era where the canon used to assume a towering status and monolithicism, with some mild criticism of course, but the problem is the limit of the horizon since they have been locked within disciplinarity. The unthinking of the canon within the canon of the discipline is seen as something accepted, but that cannot be done in most cases with the canon coming from the margins of the empire. So, thinkers who are canons are not those who are at the margins of the empire, but only those who are at its centre. The discipline, even in this era of decadence, is still holding onto its locus as being that of the empire, where conceptual, theoretical and methodological tools should emerge from the confines of the empire. To be confined in the annals of the empire is to assume the state of disciplinary purity, and this is seen as the epicentre of reason and critique. To be still confined, even in this era of disciplinary decadence, means that the ontological perceptions of those who are outside the empire are denied and the imposition of sterile epistemological interventions still insist to be relevant in this era of disciplinary decadence.

The discipline is still the modes of epistemological classification, which is seen as essential for the purpose of knowledge specialisation. MIT is intervening as something that aims to complicate this classification, and this is done in order to allow the expansion of the horizon of knowledge and also its breadth and reach. But then, the Euro-American canon still exists whether it is relevant as something that is not reflected openly. As such, the Euro-American canon as something problematic is glossed over, and the critique of this state of affairs is seen as a defensive mode of victimology. The canon in its classical sense is the one in which there is no world outside the configuration of the Euro-American empire.

Disciplinary decadence has not been a point of reflection with regards to MIT. The reason for the very act of decay within the discipline has been the pathologising and dehumanizing attitude towards the African subject. If, then, this has not been a serious point of reflection in MIT, it does not, however, harbour that subjection tendency; the mere act of being silent on epistemic violence means that it is still in disciplinary decadence. Overcoming disciplinary decadence, as Gordon notes, is overcoming epistemic colonisation.

Multi-Inter-Transdisciplinarity and the Reinforcement of Coloniality

Coloniality should not be seen as colonialism, but rather as the epoch that survives colonialism. Coloniality emerged from the contact points of the colonial encounter, articulating the modes of operation and appropriation of restructuring the world to give the same effect as colonialism did, and made way for subjection to be strengthened. Walsh amplifies this thus, 'While colonialism ended with independence, coloniality is a model of power that continues'.[23] This means it is the encounter, and this is seen through its indefinite continuity and metamorphosis. For Walsh coloniality is both a concept and a lived reality. Similar to Walsh, Maldonado-Torres has it that coloniality should be understood within the realm of war, conquest, and violence—the conditions of misery which always see the ex-colonised at the receiving end.[24] It means that coloniality still carries with it the baggage of colonialism, but it seeks to modify itself by hiding what it is. This is done by means of naturalising, normalising and institutionalising injustices to the subaltern. In other words, it hides its true essence, leaving the status quo intact. According to Maldonado-Torres, coloniality, just like colonialism, through the pretension of modernity radicalises and naturalises the ethics of war.[25]

Coloniality produced the very antithesis of life with regards to the African subject. The form of life lived by the African subject is that which is inherited from the industrial complex of subjection, which maintains the structures that reproduce it. This industrial complex of subjection can be the forces that do shape the psyche—that is, the subjectivity of the African subject, a particular kind which perpetuates subjection. The African subject cannot shape the structures which it did not create. In most cases, the African subject emerges from the existential structure of being marginalised and excluded. The purpose of this is to make the African subject incomplete and to gravitate towards adaptive existence to the structures keeping the status quo of subjection intact. In relation to these structures, there are two options, the first being to destroy or create new ones, while the other one, which is pervasive, is to adapt and transform these structures. With regards to the second option, it clearly indicates that the African subject cannot imagine the remaking of the world outside the structures of subjection.

There is a need to rethink and even to go beyond thinking, not to repeat, even in the point of exhaustion. There is a need to deploy other ways of seeing. MIT is trapped within coloniality in the sense that where knowledge lies is where coloniality lies. The reinforcement of coloniality in MIT is the proliferation of coloniality. Therefore, MIT does not solve the problem of coloniality. It is in the trappings of coloniality that MIT is not able to produce subjectivities infused by liberation, but only those informed and structured around emancipation. As such, coloniality gains permanence and sophistication in that it hides and proliferates within the decentralisation of the discipline which is still informed by the Euro-American canons and methodologies. It is important to highlight still that the locus of enunciation of MIT is still Euro-American, where the discipline originates and is still articulated from. Therefore, it follows that there is no possibility of MIT losing all that which is plagued by the discipline itself.

Coloniality makes it possible not to reveal the epistemological and ontological scandal that is hidden in the discipline, and which still remains a blind spot in MIT. The epistemological and ontological scandal is the exclusion of African subjects, where African subjects do not exist in the metaphoric and the real sense. The issue of non-existence is brought about by the absence of fundamental questions which have to do with the formation of African subjectivities and which of course call the discipline to come to an end rather than to reform itself. MIT and coloniality resonate with a 'world still dominated by Western particularistic worldviews that have been universalised and globalised'.[26] Then, MIT enforces coloniality in that it aims to proliferate and pluriversalise Euro-American knowledge systems and still transplant them to the margins of the empire. This is the same as the practice of carrying over to the colony questions which were the critique of modernity to as if their purpose were to end coloniality itself, whereas the opposite is indeed the case.

What decoloniality seeks to reveal is that this is the era of disciplinary decadence. The scandal of disciplinary decadence is the inability of the discipline to account for the problems brought about by modernity, the one supported by the discipline and the ones which the disciplines sees as impossible to resolve. This means that in being in a state of decadence, the discipline fails to live up to what is central to it, and that is being of relevance. The failure to be relevant means that the discipline and the canon it stands on are outside the form of lives which are fueled by the power of imagination. It is important to imagine ways in which the construction of the canon cannot liberate itself at this moment. This is particularly acute at the margins of empire where disciplinarity and the canon were just imposed, with a little bit of critical adaption here and there, but the full form being that which works in the favour of the Euro-American empire. The disciplines as they are through the canon, methodology, critique, conceptualisation and theory are allowed to be critical, but not decolonial. Decoloniality is necessary to expose the disciplinary decadence which hides behind reason, scientific merit, factuality, accuracy and objectivity, to name but a few, and also the tendency of epistemological absolutism.

Teleological Suspension: Toward Epistemic Disobedience

What is needed is to take the epistemological struggle of the African subject as that which is a constitutive part of political and ontological questions. This will mean that the epistemological struggle will be a decoloniality, with its varied traditions, a desire to establish a plural canon of thought transcending the monolithic pretentious of the Euro-American epistemologies which assume totality.[27] It is important here to draw from Gordon's notion of teleological suspension, where questions are raised as things pertinent to think at the margins of the discipline.[28] In other words, these are the questions that question what is inherent in the discipline, or the ones which the discipline poses whether they are of importance or not. Teleological suspension, as Gordon states, requires the shifting of the geography of reason. This means the questions should be posed from the sites which have been deemed bereft of thought, ontology and epistemology—hence the justifications that they must be represented and acted upon. The capacity of those in the clutches of subjection to ask must be rediscovered. In short, it is the capacity of the racialised, colonialised and excluded to have the capacity to ask questions.

The epistemic decolonial shift, which is the movement of the geography of reason, clearly indicates that knowledge about Africa should be looked at through the locus of enunciation of Africa and not that of the empire—that is, Euro-American imperial global designs which are the constitutive parts of modernity, modernity which is also the constitutive part of coloniality, since both cannot survive without the other. Modernity is informed by the expansionism of Western civilisation, which is seen as the absolute civilisation over other forms of civilisations. This goes hand in hand with hegemonic narratives projected as absolute to mask the injustices that come with subjection.

The shifting of the geography of reason is necessary to that which aims to disentangle itself from the tentacle of coloniality, which is embedded in the discipline. For there to be the geography of reason there should be a teleological suspension, in which the conventions of disciplinarity and the source through which the thought emerges, its telos, are suspended. Teleological suspension is necessary to even imagine ways of thinking and unthinking that are also outside the disciplinarity of MIT. Since MIT is entangled in the discipline, teleological suspension is that which faces up to disciplinary decadence, and it ferments new forms of thought from the margins of the empire in order to provide the new grammar of being and new forms of articulations. For this to come into existence, teleological suspension does not assume that which replaces the discipline or aiming to take it out of the abyss of modernity, but rather, it is a new way of making that which has never been the loci of thought to be the loci of thought. It is about bringing new subjectivities to the fore and imagining ways in which other knowledges, outside the discipline and the Euro-American canon, become the new tools of knowledge constructions.

Teleological suspension is in direct opposition to epistemic dependency and dependency colonisation. The two are rooted in the form of thought patterns which aim to keep the Euro-American episteme intact. Behind this pattern is the forceful, even violent act of inclusion and seclusion. The two operate in tandem within the operation of modernity by including only knowledge of the Euro-American empire in the discipline, while excluding those from the colonies. This creates a condition where those who are in the colonies should depend on those who are in the empire for knowledge, and by no means are they allowed to construct knowledges themselves, but they must imbibe the Euro-American knowledge. Teleological suspension sees knowledge as something that is detached from the subjects. But knowledge is in fact the constitutive part of the subject where in the lived experience of the subject demanding liberation emerges. It is through teleological suspension that the subject becomes synonymous with the construction and articulation of knowledge as an important part of subjectivity. The existential conditions of the subject do come at the centre, and the lived experience becomes an object of study by the subject, drawing from resources of knowledge that are not seen as having epistemological status and had been excluded from the canon.

Within the context of MIT, it is important to probe whether MIT will still face up to the crisis of disciplinary decadence. MIT is not teleological suspension as it is within the confines of the discipline. Since the discipline is caught in the myopia of absolutism, linearity and rigidity, MIT comes as the antidote to that. But then, what teleological suspension calls for is going further by suspending the conventions of the discipline to allow space for knowledges excluded and marginalised due to not having fit the template of disciplinarity. So, teleological suspension is the emergence of undisciplinarity, where the political ontological project of colonised subjects is liberation. MIT is blind to disciplinary mechanisms such as subjection, for it sees the integration, collaboration and transcending of the discipline as something that is the antidote to the discipline, whereas it is not.

MIT and its oppositional postmodernist posture critique universalism, master narrative, linearity of history, hierarchy of totalisation and puts emphasis on plurality, heterogeneity, margins or peripheries.[29] Though this will be laudable and seen to have been sharing sentiments with decoloniality, what does not emerge is the locus of enunciation and the critique of epistemology itself. It is clear that MIT does not critique the very essential concerns implied in questions that decoloniality asks, such as: which knowledge is at stake and whose purpose does it serve? Thus the very act of singularity of knowledge instead of knowledges is problematic. The problem is that MIT has been acting like the agent of change for the discipline, which needs of course to be exorcised of its colonial virus, maybe, the very act of becoming that which needs to be dismantled. MIT with its postmodernism and postcolonial dose is actually the very meta-narrative it seeks to critique; it is to some extent the exclusivity of Euro-American self-presentation. It is the critique of the meta-narrative by the very nature of its fragments, which is the crisis. MIT has created the loosening of disciplinarity and is creating what Castro-Gomez calls 'epistemological fiefdoms'; MIT is complicit in guarding and administering the canon of each discipline.[30] The dominant narrative is rooted in Euro-American modernity as its starting point and it fails to express ethical and political aspirations needed decolonial knowledge.[31]

Santos submits that knowledge is not conceived in abstractions but in practices and interventions—that is, knowledge is a political project.[32] Knowledge is not created, produced and socialised for the sake of its own interests, but to reach particular ends, and with the political project of modernity—to organise the world and to ratify subjection of the African subject. As Santos posits, knowledge is '[e]mbedded in different Western and non-Western cultures,' and that such experiences are used as 'different categories, symbolic universes, and aspirations of a better life'.[33] The understanding of the coloniality of knowledge should be through the lens of understanding the world system, which has been constructed by the hegemonic Eurocentric paradigm for the past 500 years for the purpose of domination, exploitation and oppression.[34]

According to Santos, modernity is the epistemic empire with the mutual interdependence exhibiting the accomplished manifestation of abyssal thinking.[35] This means modernity promotes a monopoly of universal abstraction which is embedded in the dichotomy of true and false.[36] In the darker side of modernity lie other forms of truths, that is, in the other line of abyssal thinking. The colonised zone of existence is said to constitute beliefs and practices which are exotic, marginal and idolatrous in practice—which cannot be considered forms of knowledge. So the relegation of other knowledges on the other line of abyssal thinking suggests that they are barbarian, since they are said to be devoid of Western civilisation. As Lander points out, such relegation amounts to knowledges of abyssal epistemology being reduced to myths and superstition.[37] Abyssal epistemology discredits other forms of knowledge and in this sense it is a form of fundamentalism. This is hidden behind the codes of objectivity, universality, and scientific truth with the notions of verifiability, reliability and validity. Lander amplifies this perspective to point out that Western knowledge is known as scientific knowledge, which is embedded in truthfulness, universality and objectivity, while it relegates other forms of knowledge outside the concept of knowledge itself.

Coloniality of knowledge is a form of world and knowledge, and on the opposite side of it, there are other forms of worlds and knowledges, the very antithesis of coloniality of knowledge.[38] Knowledge creation and transformation is a hegemonic project which always responds to actors' desires and needs as well as institutional demands, the very basis that informs and strengthens modernity.[39] It is clear that theorising the African subject in spaces within modernity negates the radical content of the critical theory which is essential for the subjectivity of the African subject. The likes of Antonio Gramsci, Jacques Lacan, and Michel Foucault, to name but a few, acquire the canonical status to the extent that they are used as theoretical tools to study Africa. This form of canon loses sight of the languages and narratives that are located in the subaltern locations of the world, because they are a form of critical thinking located within modernity. This really implies that it is a form of thinking that is alien to the lived experience of the African subject, and its knowledge bears not much relevance even if the application or duplication is made to fit into the subaltern.

Also, the African subject runs the risk of reproducing modernity in the subaltern by asking similar questions to those of modernity. This really implies that the project itself is limiting and self-defeating as far as Africa as a geography of reason is concerned. Africa as the ex-colonised zone, the zone of that inhibited by the African subject, should not be understood as a mere object of study but as a geo-political location that has its own forms of knowledge and regimes of truth which claims no universality—a view of the world which should co-exist with others. Such co-existence does not imply being integrated in the global design systems, the very sites of epistemic violence and racism, but one that (co-)exists in its own right. In other words, Africa should not be understood as a region, but an epistemic space. It is in these epistemic spaces where counter-hegemonic discourses exist which question the very basis of modernity and its concealment of its darker side. As Escobar states, epistemology and philosophy include the need to understand subject position to assert the construction of meaning to reflect and understand the darker side of modernity.[40] This is what Maldonado-Torres calls radical diversality, which refers to 'a critique of roots that bring into light both coloniality and the epistemic potential of non-European epistemes'.[41]

What is called for in fact is epistemic disobedience as the way to exorcise the toxic knowledge and to bring to birth the ecologies of *knowledges* informed by African subjectivities. That is, the insurrection of the kind of *knowledges* which stand on what Ndlovu-Gatsheni calls the six core concerns of African subjectivity, namely: African self-rule, self-regeneration, self-definition, self-understanding, self-knowing and self-articulation. For this to come into being, epistemic disobedience should assume the form of politics of necessity.

On Theodicy and the African Subject as a Judge

For the African subject to assume the role of a judge, it must have the capacity to judge, and this rests both on epistemology and ontology. The African subject has been judged, and as such, been outlawed. For Maldonado-Torres, the capacity to judge is the ethico-political act of the decolonial gift which affirms the very existence of the African subject.[42] The political gift in the context of decoloniality does not take place in the continual sense of being offered; it is, in paradox, taken before they are offered. As Maldonado-Torres notes, the subjects who are dispossessed cannot give, and subjects who do not regard other subjects as not being subjects cannot give anything to those subjects. This paradox is at the heart of epistemology and ontology, which, as they stand, are informed by the colonial logic of gift and dispossession as means of subjectivity. So, what does it mean for those who are dispossessed to assume the capacity of a judge? This will then mean, as the partial answer that those who are banned from being judges as those who actively engage in affirming their existence in their own terms. In doing this, they will engage in teleological suspension.

Teleological suspension is about the law of the damned (African subjects at the margins of the empire who are squeezed out of the ontological content by means of subjection), the law of will to live in liberation and, at the epistemic level, to fight for liberation from epistemic violence. The law of the African subjects as judges is the continued resistance, the insurrection of thought criminalised in most of the discipline in that it gives power to those whom the discipline was supposed to discipline. The law of the damned is the law of demands, and these demands are not only socio-political but largely ontological demands, which are insatiable as they assume the character which cannot be satisfied. Satisfaction will only happen if everything is started again — that is, the end of the Euro-American discipline and knowledge as the only thought, to become that which co-exists with others.

What teleological suspension calls for is an awareness that there is theodicy. There is a crisis of theory and method. Epistemic liberation is a condition that is necessary to pursue. The politics of possibility come into being through the search for liberation and the exorcism of the colonial virus. The ethics of liberation are at the centre of epistemology and ontology, and these are the things that MIT does not dwell on. And to suggest that MIT is liberation is a mistake; it is better to confine MIT as the act and the project of emancipation. Mignolo states that the African subject as a judge is where 'critical thoughts [are] emerging in the colonies and ex-colonies'.[43] Decoloniality makes visible the underside of modernity — it is the critique of criticism. Meaning it criticises the theories which are also critical of modernity, but which are within the bounds of modernity, like post-structuralism, postmodernism and post-colonialism. This is the thought that responds to and critiques modernity in its mutating form — that is, coloniality as it hides its locus of enunciation by claiming to be objective, totalising and universal. As a particular kind of critical thought, it unpacks critical theory and its genealogy of thought and opposes the fundamentalist position of comparing, measuring, evaluating and judging human experiences.[44]

Decoloniality is not a theoretical dead-end but the 'search for other possible knowledges and worlds'.[45] Therefore, there needs to be fundamental questioning — that is, the capacity of those who are said to be outside the realm of knowledge to be the judges about their own existential conditions and their lived experiences. The capacity to ask questions is the route which allows African subjects to assume the position of judges. This is the form of subjectivity which has been largely prohibited, and this is also something with which MIT does not engage. African subjectivity at the site of knowledge has to form the centrepiece in which MIT cannot feel comfortable to see the end of the discipline, and this might have to do with MIT's silence, not questioning coloniality, which is rife in the discipline. What is called for is the creation not of the known subject, but the knowing subject. Through epistemic disobedience this will create new ways of knowing and *knowledges* created in the new light.

Why are the poststructuralist and postmodernist, and even the postcolonialist to some extent, so hell-bent in attacking liberatory ontological and epistemic projects like decoloniality? It will be submitted here that in these 'posts', the African has never assumed the capacity as a judge. This is because the manner of affirmation and self-presentation is within the Euro-American discipline, as the tools to judge and the criteria to judge do not rest with African subjects themselves. To assume the capacity as a judge means that the African subject becomes the agent of history; they present their forms of subjectivity and are therefore no longer acted upon by others. The problem which MIT has also not looked into is that subjects living in the colonised theoretical framework or epistemic sites cannot liberate themselves since what comes from these is coloniality itself. That is why disciplinarity is about the erasure of contradiction and not allowing the emergence of other canons or even a challenge from *knowledges (*as opposed to knowledge). The canon is situated in and relevant to the Euro-American empire and it is exported and reinforced by means of the discipline and it is packaged as knowledge to the margins of the empire.

As Gordon notes, the African subject should engage in the radical anti-colonial critique by means of teleological suspension.[46] For this suspension to occur, Gordon demands that there must be differentiality between reason and rationality, to really account for the epistemic conditions of social life. The discipline is more in line and embedded in rationality than reason because it is rationality which resists teleological suspension. Such resistance is to be expected since teleological suspension means the end of rationality. However, as Gordon notes, there is a need to be suspicious of reason as well, since its articulation and justifications amount to rationality and even common sense. It is in common sense that the rigidity of the discipline is reified and whatever challenges it (for example, a radical anti-colonial critique) is easily dismissed.

What helps this theodicy survive even in its mode of crisis is what Smith refers to as 'authoritative judgement'.[47] This has been the task within the epistemic circles confined to the Euro-American centre since it is said to be the custodian of knowledge. Therefore, judgment is said to rest with those who have the capacity to judge, and as such, not those who are judged. The subject position of being a judge means the judge acts in the form of rewards and punishment, and from the standpoint of knowledge as opposed to *knowledges*. Those who are judged have no say; what is external to them is that which has the capacity to judge. The problem here is that *knowledges* do not have any merit and the judgment against them will be made from the standpoint of knowledge. The lived experience of those who are judged does not matter as a reference point of judgment.[48] Then it means that judgment itself is theodicy.

Therefore, teleological suspension even points out the decadence at the level of the Euro-American theory and method, and calls for the suspension of both method and theory, and to push for proliferation of other methods and theories outside the centre of the empire—its margins. The opposition to meta-theory and absolutist methodologies is to prevent the reduction of phenomena to universal application. MIT takes localisation, globality and contextuality of knowledge into account, but rarely does it centre the African subject as the subject with the capacity to judge. What is absent in MIT is the question of the Euro-American canon as the judge and reference point through which judgment is made. Canonisation as the process at work comes through construction, validation, and purity as constitutive parts of knowledge and the discipline from which it is foundational and constituted. The canon is the reference point of judgment on methods, theories and other toolkits of knowledge. The canon qua judgment is clouded with the fetish of certainty, detachment, universalism and absolutism for the higher end of pursuing objective knowledge. MIT does not engage fully with the problem of singularity of knowledge, and because it calls for the plurality of the discipline, so it must be for the discipline and the canon it rests on.

When the African subject assumes the position of the judge it means that the geography of reason has reached a fundamental turn, and as such, the horizons of thought and action are indefinite. This means the politics of ontology in the sense of knowledge are informed by the possibility of decolonizing the world and its futures and giving life and subjecthood from where it has been denied. The position of the African subject as a judge is necessary as the existential conditions of subjects are knowledge in themselves and life is that of survival due to the existential conditions of being in death-zones. Such zones are operating through reason and justification of disciplinarity, using epistemic violence as a tool. These death worlds are omnipresent and they constitute horror which is glossed over by the discipline, meaning that the discipline does not have any bearing on the ontology of subjects squeezed by subjection. The position of the African subject as a judge means decoloniality. Decoloniality is resistance, critique and the indefinite search for other worlds, futures and options in the interests of the African subject, and the will to liberation.

Towards Ecologies of Knowledges

Decoloniality argues for all other knowledges to exist. This is the very idea of challenging knowledge in its singularity, with its claim of universal applicability. What is being advocated is ecologies of knowledges leading to a pluriversalised idea of worlds. Savransky coins the term 'onto-epistemological pluralism' to account for knowledges in their role and making being cast in a new light.[49] These new ways of knowing are knowledges created by those who are being excluded in the realm of the singularity of knowledge. As Savransky notes, 'onto-epistemological pluralism' opposes Euro-American epistemological exclusion and epistemicides by pursuing modes of knowing and representation so that the epistemological demands of those who are oppressed come to life. What is brought to the fore is that which has been caught by the tentacles of subjection. It is the emerging opposition forces affirming themselves to create other worlds and ecologies of knowledges rather than seeking to be integrated into the world and its universal knowledge.

The emergence of such knowledges destroys the very structure of subjection and its mode of containment. Ecologies of knowledges rebel against the very idea of knowledge, the very basis of reason it stands on. Ecologies of knowledges seek to firmly attach knowledges to ontological positions.[50] This takes seriously the fact that knowledges emerge from the materiality of ontological conditions and positions. This forms part of the views about and of the world, as opposed to world views, since the latter suggests the singularity of the world, with knowledge as the master signifier, as opposed to knowledges of worlds. They dwell on the shift of geography of reason, which locates the subject away from where the subject thinks. This shift is necessary as thought emerges from where the body *qua* lived experience assumes location. This thus permits the articulation of the shift of geography of reason and grounding it from the theory emerging from lived experience. The geography of reason affirms that 'the location of terrain has shifted, that the most recent systematic mutations might suggest new directions or the situated politics of knowledge making'.[51] Ecologies of knowledges affirm differentiality of knowledges. For the mere fact that they are in their plurality, it therefore means they are different. This opposes the totalising tendency of the Euro-American episteme, which promotes sameness while in its articulation it engages in epistemicides.

The conception of the world of course is where many worlds fit and where the emergence of subjugated histories and knowledges come into being. Ecologies of knowledges wed epistemology and ontology together as the form of standpoint. Ecologies of knowledges suppose the ethico-political act of thinking Africa—its knowledge and live experience from the vantage point of insurrection. Ecologies of knowledges denote situated knowledges. These are knowledges situated in the existential conditions of African subjects. As such, ecologies of knowledges give leeway to forms of lives which have been liquidated by subjection. Their illegitimacy as not being knowledges from the Euro-American episteme's loci of judgment is the master code under rupture.

Ecologies of knowledges are not thought from the zero-point position and linear thinking, but from the very positionality of the subject's location.[52] There exist signs of exhaustion in the crisis-ridden paradigm that is dominant.[53] Euro-American knowledge propagates itself as 'the locus which formulates collective goals valid for everyone'.[54] This is used as a gesture same to that of the state knowing what is best for its citizens and subjects by having the role that confers it having legitimacy over the means of violence. According to Rodriguez, ecologies of knowledges contest the idea that knowledge resides with Euro-American subjects, who are modern and complex as opposed to primitive and inferior other.[55] This perpetuated the idea of hierarchising, racialising and dehumanising those who are said not to be the producers of knowledge. This idea justifies the colonisation of knowledges into knowledge and Euro-American subjects determining what qualifies as knowledge and what does not. It is through these means that knowledge, in which structures and operations of power are hidden, is the construction of the other, the figure alienated by the knowledge itself. So, the purpose of knowledge is to impose disciplining of the mind and body—that is, inventing the other to serve the interests of the Euro-American empire.[56]

Ecologies of knowledges call into question 'the rationality of the cannons of conquerors and the preaching of missionaries'.[57] They object to epistemologies of ignorance which are propagated by the very act of epistemicides. As Santos states, 'Colonialist ignorance consists in refusing to recognize the other as an equal and converting the other into an object'.[58] The process of domination and disfiguring has gone along with epistemic ignorance (which is deliberate ignorance) to eliminate resistant forces against which it imposes itself. Ecologies of knowledges are armed with what Santos calls 'a new critical gaze', which means the new ways of knowing and seeing from the locus of enunciation of those who are at the receiving end of subjection.[59] For Santos, this new critical gaze is giving new tools to an archeological task of excavations and searching for subjugated and marginalised knowledges and constructing new epistemes informed by liberation. Taking this form, Connery argues that 'this interrogation requires new foci and new urgency in these times of differential crisis'.[60] Connery suggests that ecologies of knowledges should open up parameters conducive for political and epistemological imagination.

Conclusion

What the discipline does not offer and MIT to some extent does is a breaking away from coloniality of knowledge epitomosed by disciplinary decadance in Euro-American traditions of knowledge. Epistemologies from African subjects who are at the receiving end of subjection facilitated by discipline create a state of colonising minds. It is only through their own self-presentation and canonisation that African subjects will be subjects in the full sense — not having claim to epistemological privileges, but being foundational and constitutive to their own ecologies of knowledges. What infects both the discipline and MIT is coloniality, which is foundational and constitutive to them, with their nuclei of the Euro-American empire, to be spread and transplanted to the other. However, it needs to be pointed out that in this era of disciplinary decadence, the discipline is still in crisis. To avert itself from this crisis, it clings to coloniality as a lease on life.

At the heart of coloniality is the problem of epistemicides, denials, and displacements inherent in Euro-American epistemic practices and the projection of its epistemic power. Ecologies of knowledges go beyond what MIT and the discipline aim to rescue, aiming not to add to the problems that Euro-American epistemology brought unto itself. MIT and the discipline do not take coloniality into account, hence they are trapped within coloniality, which they seek to reproduce. So, they are in the problem of disciplinary decadence, which is the crisis of modernity itself. Decoloniality, which is embedded in ecologies of knowledges, with a strong dose of epistemic disobedience and the necessary shift of the geography of reason, still stand as formidable forces for creating a world where many worlds fit. It is through decoloniality that another ethico-political world is possible.

Notes and References

1. Mignolo, W. D. (2011). Geopolitics of sensing and knowing: On (de)coloniality, border thinking and epistemic disobedience. *Postcolonial Studies, 14*(3), 273–283.

2. Mignolo, W. D. (2007). Introduction: Coloniality of power and de-colonial thinking. *Cultural Studies, 21*(2–3), 155–167.

3. Walsh, C. (2007). Shifting the geopolitics of critical knowledges: Decolonial thought and cultural studies 'others' in the Andes. *Cultural Studies, 21* (2–3), 224–239.

4. Ibid.

5. Maldonado-Torres, N. (2008). *Against war: Views from the underside of modernity.* Durham, NC: Duke University Press.

6. Savransky, M. (2012). Worlds in the making: Social sciences and the ontopolitics of knowledge. *Postcolonial Studies, 15*(3), 351–368.

7. Smith, M. J. (2000). *Culture: Reinventing the social sciences*. Buckingham, England: Open University Press.

8. Farred, G. (2011). "Science does not think": The no-thought of the discipline. *The South Atlantic Quarterly, 110*(1), 57–74.

9. Ibid., p. 60.

10. Smith, *Culture*.

11. Gordon, L. R. (2011). Shifting the geography of reason in an age of disciplinary decadence. *Transmodernity, 1*(2), 95–103, p. 95.

12. Ndlovu-Gatsheni, S. J. (2011). Colonial matrix of power and the African intellectual/epistemological crisis. Unpublished Paper.

13. Smith, *Culture*.

14. Gordon, Shifting the geography of reason.

15. Ndlovu-Gatsheni, Colonial matrix of power and the African intellectual/epistemological crisis, p. 1.

16. Gordon, Shifting the geography of reason.

17. Mignolo, Introduction: Coloniality of power and de-colonial thinking.

18. Santos, B. S. (2007). Beyond abyssal thinking: From global lines to ecology of knowledges. *Review, 30*(1), 1–33.

19. Walsh, Shifting the geopolitics of critical knowledges.

20. Basarab, N. (2002). *Manifesto of transdiciplinarity* (Trans. Karen-Clau Vos). New York, NY: State University of New York.

21. Farred, "Science does not think", p. 58.

22. Gordon, Shifting the geography of reason, p. 98.

23. Walsh, Shifting the geopolitics of critical knowledges, p. 229.

24. Maldonado-Torres, N. (2007). On the coloniality of being: Contributions to the development of a concept. *Cultural Studies, 21*(2–3), 240–270.

25. Maldonado-Torres, *Against war*.

26. Ndlovu-Gatsheni, Colonial matrix of power and the African intellectual/epistemological crisis, p. 61.

27. Ibid.

28. Gordon, Shifting the geography of reason.

29. Santos, B. S. (2010). From the postmodern to the postcolonial — and beyond both. In E. G. Rodríguez, M. Boatcâ & S. Costa (Eds.), *Decolonizing European sociology: Transdisciplinary approaches* (pp. 225–242). Surrey, England: Ashgate.

30. Castro-Gomez, S. (2002). The social sciences, epistemic violence, and the problem of the "invention of the other". *Nepantla, 3*(2), 269–285.

31. Santos, From the postmodern to the postcolonial.

32. Santos, Beyond abyssal thinking.

33. Ibid., p. 37.

34. Grosfoguel, R. (2007). The epistemic decolonial turn: Beyond political-economy paradigms. *Cultural Studies, 21*(2–3), 211–223.

35. Santos, Beyond abyssal thinking.

36. Ibid.

37. Lander, E. (2002). Eurocentrism, modern knowledges, and the "natural" order of global capital. *Nepantla, 3*(2), 245–268.

38. Escobar, A. (2007). Worlds and knowledges otherwise: The Latin American modernity/coloniality research program. *Cultural Studies, 21*(2–3), 179–210.

39. Mignolo, W. D. (2007). Introduction: Coloniality of power and de-colonial thinking. *Cultural Studies, 21*(2–3), 155–167.

40. Escobar, Worlds and knowledges otherwise.

41. Maldonado-Torres, N. (2004). The topology of being and the geopolitics of knowledge: modernity, empire and coloniality. *City, 8*(1), 29–56.

42. Maldonado-Torres, N. (2006). Cesaire's gift and the decolonial turn. *Radical Philosophy Review, 9*(2), 11–138.

43. Mignolo, Introduction: coloniality of power and de-colonial thinking, p. 155.

44. Ibid.

45. Walsh, Shifting the geopolitics of critical knowledges, p. 234.

46. Gordon, Shifting the geography of reason.

47. Smith, *Culture*.

48. Ibid.

49. Savransky, Worlds in the making.

50. Rodriguez, E.G. (2010). Decolonizing postcolonial rhetoric. In E. G. Rodríguez, M. Boatcâ & S. Costa (Eds.), *Decolonizing European sociology: Transdisciplinary approaches* (pp. 49–67). Surrey, England: Ashgate.

51. Connery, C. L. (2012). Reflections on the politics and locations of knowledge making in a time of crisis. *Concentric, 38*(2), 45–63.

52. Mignolo, Geopolitics of sensing and knowing.

53. Santos, From the postmodern to the postcolonial.

54. Castro-Gomez, The social sciences, epistemic violence, and the problem of the "invention of the other", p. 271.

55. Rodriguez, Decolonizing postcolonial rhetoric.

56. Castro-Gomez, The social sciences, epistemic violence, and the problem of the "invention of the other".

57. Rodriguez, Decolonizing postcolonial rhetoric, p. 230.

58. Santos, From the postmodern to the postcolonial, p. 230.

59. Ibid.

60. Connery, Reflections on the politics and locations of knowledge making in a time of crisis, p. 47.

Chapter 7

A Decolonial Analysis of the Coloniality of the Discipline of Anthropology

Nokuthula Hlabangane and Zodwa Radebe

Introduction

The discipline of anthropology has throughout its history been beset by a myriad of challenges, chief among which is to do with its epistemic underpinnings and epistemological locatedness. Although we may assume that all social sciences are imperial, anthropology undoubtedly acquired a special role and status in this constellation.[1] Fundamentally, the challenges of anthropology centre around the fact that historically and theoretically, its subject matter (an object made at least as much as found) has been people it represents as the Other. Anthropology is predicated on the colonial impulse of understanding and conquering peoples in far-away lands.[2] The curiosity about people thought of as different from the researcher, who in many instances is located in the Western metropole, has led to the exoticisation of these people. The difference is not just difference for its own sake but is presented as cultural inferiority, occupying a position lower down in the purported evolutionary scale. Anthropology is influenced by two different traditions: British anthropology, which draws from ethnology, and American anthropology, known as cultural anthropology, which is influenced by Franz Boas.[3] What binds these different traditions is their primary object of study; as Levi-Strauss defines it, "Anthropology is the science that makes humanity the primary object of investigation".[4] It is this objectification of other races that connects anthropology with the world

131

order which excludes the natives. From this point of view, anthropology becomes a critical component in sustaining this world order.

The rise of modernity gave birth to many philosophical and existential questions. Different disciplines came into being in an attempt to address these questions. Anthropology was one of them. According to Wolff and Cipolloni,[5] anthropology emerged from the eighteenth century intellectual context of the Enlightenment. They argued that the Enlightenment was fundamentally anthropological as it was acknowledging global diversity, interpreting human societies, and bridging cultural differences. Essentially anthropology was born out of a need to understand an Other who was to be conquered and submerged. While the Enlightenment was advocating for liberty and equality, the rise of modernity brought about exploitation through capitalism, which led to slavery and colonialism. The argument that anthropology was an invention of the Enlightenment and as such is associated with the values of liberty and equality gives anthropology a noble background. While it is true that the Enlightenment did influence the thinking in anthropology with theorists such as Boas,[6] the so-called father of modern anthropology, advocating for the acknowledgement of difference, and arguing that each society has its own way of organising life which is not better or worse than other ways of life, this was in stark contrast to modernity, which purported a unilineal evolutionary scale. This dilemma was to stay with the discipline in implicit and explicit ways throughout its history. On one hand, cultural relativism, while acknowledging and accepting of difference, informs the very impulse to "discover" and comment on (cultural) difference in a world in which there is consensus that pristine cultures no longer exist. But because anthropology is primarily concerned about an Other, that difference has to be fabricated at worst to justify uniquely "anthropological" knowledge. Commenting on this quandary, Stillwaggon[7] remarks that "the writing of ethnographies often has the unfortunate result of inventing differences between people around the world. Although the works can be merely descriptive snapshots of a people, by implication they are comparative in nature because what they describe is noteworthy."

This chapter speaks to the colonial foundations of anthropology and how these continue to bedevil the discipline. In particular, the chapter speaks beyond rethinking anthropology, as is the subject of many manuscripts, to unthinking the discipline, which is a far more radical approach as it goes to the core of the discipline and what it has espoused all this time. Ribeiro and Escobar[8] argue that while all anthropologies have had dissenting figures, alternative knowledges, failed experiments and occasional epochs of creativity and revolt, these have largely functioned within established boundaries and have not changed the discipline fundamentally. Ultimately, the chapter proposes a de-

colonial deconstruction of anthropology that questions not only the basic concepts of the discipline but also its overall relevance in the contemporary world.

Anthropology and Domination

To understand the many challenges which arise from its own self-question-
ing as well as the critique from those at its margins, one will need to go back
to anthropology's historical foundations. Much is said about the different anthropological approaches and theories emanating from Britain and the US, for
instance, but its colonial foundations tend to be glossed over, ignoring the institutional and political contexts in which ideas unfold and blossom. The same
can be said of South African anthropology, which tends to focus on the schism
between Afrikaans and English anthropology. According to Nyamnjoh,[9] debates over the epistemological and racial politics inherent in the Western academic study of natives still rages in universities to this day. These relate to
gatekeeping practices that are legendary in South Africa, for instance. These
"gatekeeping" practices are wide-ranging and ubiquitous, as are their effects.
They will be understood from a decolonial standpoint that asserts a "coloniality
of being", a "coloniality of knowledge" and a "coloniality of power". That is
to say that anthropology is implicated in the colonialization of people, in that
the division of labour is always such that "the West" in its various manifestations always studies "the rest" in ways that are colonial in nature as well. Anthropological knowledge is also problematic in that it tends to freeze the Other
in a perpetual state of "culture" as opposed to "reason" and "development".
From this point of view, cultural difference is assumed rather than proven, re-
sulting in "cultural relativism" becoming "cultural absolutism". In this sense
then, anthropological knowledge has tended to unwittingly justify an unjust
world order. Herein is found the nexus of knowledge and power.

Anthropology was born out of the European expansion and colonial project.
While theorists such as Karl Max[10] were challenging the ills born of modernity,
such as capitalism, and predicting their fall as they were not sustainable, the
beneficiaries of modernism were defending their benefits. Ethnology, a study
that tried to reconstruct the past of primitive societies,[11] was key in defending
the benefits of modernity. Scientists such as Johann Blumenbach studied the
human race using ethnological methods and from these studies claimed that
Europeans were the only advanced race.[12] Blumenbach was not the only one
making this argument; Thomas Jefferson, who had argued that "all men are
created equal" in the *Declaration of Independence*, later argued that there was
a rank of races which was natural.[13] And these were supported by Samuel G.
Morton,[14] who also proved that Negros were inferior and therefore justified

slavery. The claims made by these scientists shaped the racial constructs that we see even today. Worldviews emanating from Europe and America that excluded other races from citizenry rights were qualified by these scientists and are the foundation of the contemporary world order.

However, these ethnological scientists did not make these claims unchallenged. Scientists such as Frederick Douglass, an African American scholar, responded in an essay entitled "The Claims of the Negro, Ethnologically considered" by challenging the idea that "the human race are of multitudinous origin, naturally different in their moral, physical, and intellectual capacities". He argued that the claims of natural difference between human beings perpetuate and justify slavery. He was supported by Joseph-Antenor Firmin,[15] a Haitian anthropologist who in 1885 published *De l'egalite des races humaines* (On the Equality of Human Races), where he argued that all races were equal. These counter arguments paralysed ethnology, reducing its role to the anthropology of museums, and its focus to 'disappearing societies'.[16] It was Franz Boas who resuscitated anthropology with his main argument that culture was relative.

Despite claims of cultural relativism, anthropology has been found to be complicit in, if not actively involved in, the politics of domination. Its concepts tend to freeze the native and thus deny him history.[17] In this representation, the native is found to be devoid of history, knowledge, humanity and reason, and is yet to evolve to full humanity. Anthropology as a discipline that speaks on behalf of a mute other has been rendered null and void, as the "native" has not only disappeared but he has also not found his voice. Anthropology thus faces a crisis of representation. The politics of representation and the politics of difference have proven to be the undoing of the discipline in its recent history. In particular, theories about how the nexus between knowledge and power works to maintain and reproduce domination within modern social science have undermined the legitimacy of the discipline to those on whose behalf it purports to speak. African(ist) anthropologists face a particular crisis that arises from this nexus of knowledge and power, which maintains not only Western power but also who can legitimately have the authority of being a distinguished anthropologist.[18] Native anthropologists are systematically excluded from legitimacy, as their theories are thought of as not scientific because they do not have the necessary distance to achieve objectivity. There is a price of the admission for African anthropologists wishing to join this clan: assimilation. The existence of anthropologies totally isolated or opposed to Western anthropologies is impossible as even nativist perspectives have had to go through processes of validation that are largely Western-mediated. On the other hand, anthropology is conceivably influenced by developments in places it travels to; as Ribeiro and Escobar[19] put it, "If cultures travel, anthropology travels the world and can be enriched and transformed by its encounters with different local situations". However, it is also true that there are different travellers and ways of travelling that place us immediately within fields of global power which are characterised by unequal exchanges. So while anthropology is theoretically open to other worldviews, there are real forces that thwart this. Its colonial and anti-African roots remain intact to a large extent. Contestation tends to revolve around re-thinking the discipline, with the result of tweaking concepts here and there. Unthinking the discipline becomes unthinkable in this scheme of things.

There is an incessant hair-splitting about the exact complicity of anthropology in the colonial project. This is a bid to redeem the discipline somewhat from its colonial foundations. Was it the hand-maiden of colonialism or is its role more nuanced and thus more complicated than that? This particular argument is advanced by so-called native anthropologists, amongst others, who are looking for ways to redeem the discipline and create a possibility for new anthropologies which are not hostile to Africa and its people.[20] This possibility is thwarted by the fact that there is no escaping the roots and influences of the discipline. However, there is credence in the assertion that if culture travels, so does anthropology, and for this reason it is amenable to outside influences. This may very well be the case if anthropology still wore and maintained its innocence. Anthropological knowledge has been accused of constructing and reinforcing inequality. African anthropology thus bears the burden of defending the dignity of Africa and its people from Western-derived concepts and worldviews that confirm notions of a dark Africa. From this point of view then, African-based anthropologists usually hold an oppositional view to Western-based anthropologists, with the former seeking to defend and uphold the dignity of Africa and its peoples and the latter seeing Africa from the vantage point of Western modernity frameworks.[21] To this end, some argue that those who have been Othered by the categories of anthropology have been placed in a peculiar relationship to the institutions of modernity, including the academy. Existing power dynamics are such that researchers of African descent are unable to "study up" and are thus forced to study "themselves". While this has potential to bring forth new conversations that are framed in new terms, arguments advanced from auto-ethnography are usually viewed with suspicion. The inability of the discipline's epistemological and methodological tools to offer understandings of Africa and its complexities is thus a continuing critique against the discipline. Fundamentally, the methodologies of the discipline are confounded by the social identities and institutional locations of academics, which shape the questions they ask and the conclusions they reach. Reiterating this point, Sichone[22] argues that anthropologists from the West lack the necessary grounding in the local cultural practices and yet write about African cultures with authority even after a brief encounter with an arbitrary array of informants. This somewhat pedantic observation actually raises the important point that anthropological knowledge's dependence on the anthropologist as the primary research and interpretive tool is its greatest weakness and one that needs deconstructing — who is always the researcher and who are mostly likely the researched? Further, how are the two imagined?

Critique of Anthropological Knowledge

The following sections will, piece by piece, look at anthropological concepts *extraordinaire*, from which anthropology's crisis of legitimacy flows. Central to anthropology is the "culture concept". The culture concept supposedly reflects a people's total way of life, including their values, symbols, customs, traditions, etc. Areas as diverse as the economy, religion and social organisation have attracted the anthropological gaze. From this can be read their development status with the West as a point of reference, with African economies, for instance, regarded as simple, religions as superstitious and social organization as undifferentiated. The culture concept has come under siege with the advent of globalization, which, in many respects, cancels out the difference upon which anthropology is predicated. Paradoxically, sameness is said to manifest itself on the very cultural diversity that the discipline is concerned with, applauds and celebrates. This refers to the ultimately unworkable idea that despite or perhaps because of their differences, all societies embody the same cultural value and worth.[23] Difference is the very essence of what ethnographers seek to unearth. "If the history of the discipline is anything to go by, there is not a single ethnological paradigm — whether evolutionism, functionalism, structuralism or culturalism — to name only the major ones — that has not been criticised for dividing the world between we and other, superior or inferior. There is not even one that has not been found guilty of the ultimate ethnological transgression — ethnocentrism".[24] The leap from ethnocentrism and racism is not too wide.

Having pointed to the infirmities of the culture concept, Geertz[25] went on to proclaim its indispensability not only to anthropology as a discipline but to understandings of human kind in general as he points out that everyone, everywhere and at all times seems to live in a sense-suffused world and is a product of a history of notion-formation. While there is merit in the sentiment that "each man calls barbarism whatever is not his own practice — for we have no other criterion of reason than the example and idea of the opinions and customs of the country we live in", not all notions and knowledges are evaluated on the same hierarchical plane. Hierarchies of knowledge are predicated upon hierarchies of social and political power. The claim that anthropology, in its many guises, is a universal discipline in spite of its Western foundations is not without contradiction. The newly-advanced idea of "world anthropologies" seeks to advance the assertion that anthropology is indeed a universal discipline, reflecting universal philosophies and concerns in ways that are not prejudicial to any society. While elements of and for world anthropologies are better conceived of in moments of marginality and dissent,[26] the foundational principles of the discipline, including its Eurocentric gaze and associated prejudices and limitations, confound this and have proven detrimental to the wellbeing of the discipline. As such, anthropology has faced the question of its demise on more occasions than is the case for other disciplines. While its many points of resurrection are a sign of resilience and ability to adapt to some, others point to its continued irrelevance in whatever guise. Note is here made that anthropology does not have one definitive theory that is shared by what are now known as "anthropologies". For instance, Ribeiro and Escobar[27] distinguish between empire building and nation building anthropologies. They position their practitioners differently in knowledge and political fields — the former tends to study distant others while the latter studies its own internal others. The implications of this difference go beyond political locatedness and commitments; it affects theory production because those working within their own societies have to adapt or transform established concepts from the centre or create new ones within a much more politicised world. They follow received scripts in the name of a universal science with little room to unthink these concepts. In this vein, Mafeje argues that African anthropologists can only mimic or import from the centre and use the local experience to validate concepts and assumptions conceived elsewhere.

Anthropology's initial guise was that of "butterfly counting"[28] in response to the purported demise of original cultures. These perceptions were influenced by evolutionary modernist thoughts and the concomitant civilising mission. In this way, the Othering tendencies of anthropology served to perpetuate and consolidate the us vs them, centre vs periphery and modern vs barbaric dichotomies, with the West as a reference point. In turn, such conceptions served to justify colonial violence — what has been called "modernity's hidden face". Anthropology firmly belongs within the structures of modernity. Anthropology, it has been said, is an integral part of the intellectual division of labour among academic disciplines, which accorded it the "savage slot", that is, the role of studying the "primitive" or what is not "the West".[29] "Modern knowledge is also Eurocentric in that it suppresses and subalternises the knowledge of those see as lying outside the European locality".[30] Critiques of anthropology have argued for the provinciality of anthropology despite its claims as a universal science. Anthropology arose under specific circumstances and is rooted in a particular way of conceiving the world that is not necessarily shared by all. It has Eurocentric roots and purports Eurocentric values. This is important because it at once undermines and highlights the context-situatedness and particularity of anthropological concepts, values and worldviews. This is even more imperative if we are to consider the violence that has been wrought by the discipline on those studied. Anthropological concepts and philosophies also place us immediately within fields of global power, that is, in spaces shaped by unequal exchanges between hegemonic and non-hegemonic centres.[31] Anthropology reflects regional, national and international "structures of alterity", asserting that the connection between anthropology and world politics applies to all anthropologies, but with particular poignancy to hegemonic anthropologies. By hegemonic anthropologies is meant the set of discursive formations and institutional practices associated with the normalization of academic anthropology chiefly in the US, UK and France.[32]

Despite this subalternisation of knowledge of those lying outside the European locality or because of it, Africa has continued as a research laboratory for the metropolitan academy. While the us vs them categorisation and the attendant civilising impulse of the discipline have been somewhat toned down in response to criticism, it can be argued that it is quite impossible for the discipline to shed these tendencies altogether without redefining its essence as an academic discipline within Western modernity. For one, it is difficult to justify the discipline beyond its "butterfly-collecting" tendencies. Anthropology, unlike other social science or humanities disciplines, has no intrinsic value other than to make commentary on "culture", however that is conceived. The final analysis is that the culture concept and thus anthropology cannot help but be caught in difference making.

Ribeiro and Escobar[33] assert that "questions about knowledge are questions about modernity". From this point of view, modernity is seen as an inescapable universal. "Modern knowledge is based on logocentrism—the belief in the logical truth as the only valid foundation for a rational knowledge of the world—a world made up of knowable and orderable things".[34] It has been the preoccupation of the discipline to be concerned about how much difference is difference. The question to ask then is to what end is this difference highlighted? Moreover, while African anthropology promises to question and thus undermine the basic tenets and conceptual frameworks of anthropology proper,[35] this can only be a cosmetic rearrangement that will not change anthropology and its premises fundamentally. So, while African anthropology promises to decentre Western epistemological traditions by unpacking African ways of knowing, creating its own traditions, this is undermined by, amongst other things, the over-reliance on native interpretations that often tend to re-produce colonial discourse about the native culture, amidst the continuing and influential legacy of colonial discourses.[36] Questioning and responding to the assertion that anthropology can reconfigure itself, Mafeje[37] argued that the dis-cipline cannot be redeemed, citing primarily the fact that the demise of its Other has rendered it null. From this point of view then, anthropology belongs to the past rather than the future. It can be argued that the violence wrought by the discipline cannot equal its benefits, which are negligible if we are to look beyond the advancement of individual careers. In this vein, Wolcott ar-gues, "The stark reality is that we are pretty much for it ourselves […] al-though we do desperately wait to tell it like it is and help others tell their stories through us, we remain in control of, and always have something to gain, by telling".[38] That is why even today anthropology largely still studies the Other, as the Other is its core business. The discipline is unable to extricate itself from its modernist foundations.

The final product, we argue, is nothing more than adding to the record of what man has said throughout history.[39] We do not think that anthropology does fulfil the promise that groups of people will be better understood, as even its methodologies are fraught with limitations. In the final analysis then, an-thropology is akin to running around in circles with no definite end-point, as we can no longer cite anthropological knowledge with any authority, especially in light of the resistance of anthropologists in the periphery who have found a voice with which to speak back and contest dominant anthropological par-adigms. Moreover, if we accept that all knowledge is about modernity, then anthropological knowledge is particularly entangled in this way. Anthropology does not seem to have much to offer in dealing with the challenges of the 21st century except to highlight cultural pluralism, which is in itself not found but made. This preoccupation of the discipline highlights its voyeuristic impulses. The question of objectivity is central to contemporary debates in anthropology. Notwithstanding the postmodern critique of anthropology, the discipline con-tinues to claim to be scientific in its approach, implying the soberness of the anthropologist and thus down-playing his situatedness and political entangle-ment. Taking issue with this stance, Said points out, "No one has ever devised a method for detaching the scholar from the circumstances of life, from the fact of his involvement (conscious or unconscious) with class, a set of beliefs, a social position or the mere activity of being a member of a society".[40] How do we then trust that "findings" are independent of the situated ethnographer? It is sheer arrogance for anthropology to argue for objectivity, to "posit truth as something independent of the thinking subject and make the thinking subject the condition of possibility all truth".[41] The truth is "everything depends on the point of view, the angle, the perspective, and whosoever determines the point of view and succeeds in getting others to follow will establish the system of analysis".[42] From the above arguments it is fair to deduce that what anthropology thrives for is essentially the point of view of the anthropologist, not objectivity. As such, power differentials are always implicated in any anthropological enterprise. Responding to these limitations, detractors of the discipline have advocated that the anthropologist and the discipline itself be anthropologised, i.e. be put on the same analytical plane as those researched. This chapter is such an attempt.

Postmodernism has not only brought into question the authority of Western knowledge in general, it has further highlighted the weaknesses of anthropological knowledge in particular. For anthropology to achieve its primary objective, which is to understand the 'other' societies or communities, it needs a tool that can be viewed as scientific. Radcliffe-Brown argues that "Social Anthropology should be based on systematic field studies carried out by trained anthropologists using scientific methods of observation".[43] Ethnography therefore must be seen as scientific so as to produce acceptable results. On the other hand, communities, as objects of study, need to fit in the criteria that is set up or the hypothesis put forward. For communities to fit in, we argue, they must therefore be created or invented.[44] These communities must be simple, they must be primitive, and they must also be small. Levi-Strauss supports the claims we are making when he says, "One of the peculiarities of the small societies which we study is that each constitute as it were, a ready-made experiment, because of its relative simplicity and the limited number of variables required to explain its functioning".[45] While the discipline has sought to respond to these earlier limitations by, for instance, conceding that societies are seldom small, discrete entities that are amenable to anthropological experiments, so to speak, this general thinking still exists. For instance, anthropological knowledge is notorious for its focus on the mundane, the everyday made exotic. This focus on local knowledge and experience is, in fact, a great disservice to people, who while for all intents and purposes function at a "local" level, are not shut off from broader socio-political systems. To continue to insist on the salience of the "local", and in many instances, to the exclusion of a broader analysis that maps out the connection between the local and the global, is to fabricate an exotic people who fit in the anthropological stereotype. This poses a challenge to the basic anthropological concepts such as "culture". In response, Mafeje asks, "[T]o what extent is their[46] [anthropologists'] universalistic jargon reflective of the local 'situations' or translatable into vernacular languages?"[47] This question is often left un-answered. Therefore, as Clifford argues, "Ethnographic accounts of other societies and cultures are manmade constructs, the invention of rather precocious ethnological imagination, in short, fictions".[48] It becomes important to ask why and to what end are these "fictions" insisted upon. We argue that beyond offering career prospects to its practitioners, the discipline has largely stayed faithful to its modernist impulses.

It is in this context that we begin to understand the frustrations expressed by Kenyatta, amongst others, who argued that anthropology is "the duplicity of western pretender to philanthropy who claimed to monopolise the office of interpreting the African's mind and speaking for humans".[49] Having trained as an anthropologist himself, Kenyatta could not see how he could use anthropology to respond to the challenges of Kenyans at the time; hence he abandoned it. Kenyatta is not the only African(ist) anthropologist who was frustrated by anthropology. Mafeje,[50] himself a professor in anthropology, argued that anthropology was a child of imperialism and therefore needed to die, as he could not see how it could be redeemed. Mafeje is supported by Argyrou[51] in his call for the demise of anthropology. For Argyrou, anthropology's objective is impossible "because ethnographers are caught in the ontological double-bind of trying to be both subjects and objects, both the creators of the world of sameness and the creatures in the world they have created".[52] As natives, it has been easy to study anthropology but very difficult to become anthropologists precisely because of this above-mentioned conundrum, where the anthropologist is both player and referee at the same time.

In practical terms then, knowledge about the Other was used by colonial administrators to control the native, the idea of the Occident and the Orient.[53] While obsessed about the local, anthropology was not shy to advance meta-narratives that transcend the local. The culture concept remains a defining one for the discipline of anthropology and as such is its meta-narrative. This to the extent that Geertz remarks, "Whatever its problems and however dialectically expressed it is not likely to go entirely away unless anthropology does".[54] Geertz's major contribution to anthropology was centered on his re-theorization of the concept of "culture". This re-theorization had two very closely interlocked dimensions—an ontological one (what culture is) and an epistemological one (how we can know it).[55] The problem with this idea is that it is almost impossible for one, insider or outsider, to grasp so vast a thing as an entire way of life and finding ways to describe it.[56] Questions about continuity and change, objectivity and proof, determinism and relativism, otherness and commensurability confound this ambition.[57] Is it even possible to pin-point where one culture ends and another begins? From this point of view, then, she argues that anthropology proceeds amid charges of irrelevance, bias, illusion and impracticability. It is from this point of view that the "culture" concept, while the mainstay of the discipline, is also one of its greatest liabilities.

Another criticism of culture is the idea of culture as a deeply sedimented essence attaching to or inhering in particular groups of people.[58] This is a symptom and remnant of colonial thinking. In this scheme of things, the West is accorded rationality and its citizens individuality and complexity. The rest are thought of as cultural, its citizens undifferentiated as they are bound by cultural thinking. For instance, Fried[59] argues that one of the anthropological notions *par excellence,* the tribe, has no empirical basis, that it is a figment of anthropologists' imagination that confirms anthropology and the West's image of a Dark continent, inhabited by savages. In this conception, tribes were seen as breeding populations with unbridled sexual mores. Fried[60] asserts that while not readily spoken, such thoughts about Africa remain. This as evidenced by anthropological notions of HIV/AIDS vulnerability in Africa, which Farmer,[61] amongst others, asserts are in the vein of Africa as Other. Rather than being a construct of Africa, tribes are a result of Western invasion and the concomitant formation of the state. He writes, "The invention of the state, a tight, class-structured political and economic system, began a process whereby vaguely-defined and grossly overlapping populations were provided with the minimal organization required for their manipulation, even though they had little or no internal organisation of their own other than that based on conceptions of kinship, the resultant form was that of the tribe". From this point of view, tribes are neither economic, cultural, political nor ideological groups. Fried[62] goes on to note that in many instances, tribes became known by names other than those they called themselves. "Names easily become part of the political means of divide and conquer, after which, by providing markers and reminders of social distance, they may function to maintain a system of exploitation. Like genealogies and religions, like myths, prayers and legends, names play a shifting but constantly active role in the chartering ideology of every human society".[63] This lends credence to the assertion that all history is constituted by discourse formations. To this end, he asserts that "in some of the most far-sighted critiques one finds a questioning of the epistemological, institutional and political foundations of Anglo-American anthropology". This "postmodern" moment influenced essentialist conceptions of "culture", emphasising conversely the historical, polyphonic, political and discursive character of any "cultural fact". Ortner[64] asserts that the ontological and epistemological dimensions of culture are coming apart. For instance, questions about what culture is — its ontology — are confounded by questions about the coherence of life ways, the degree to which they form connected wholes, are homogenous, shared, discrete, and the possibility of specifying where one culture leaves off and the next begins.

Geertz, in particular, took issue with typologies, grand theories and universal generalisations and rejected abstractionism and reductionism as methods for the social sciences.[65] In this vein, Geertz suggests that relativism "disables judgement", while absolutism "removes it from history".[66] He advocated a middle path between relativism and absolutism as a basis for culture theory. A related dilemma that faces anthropology is "what kinds of relationships can/may/should obtain between the resolute localness and face-to-faceness of ethnographic work and the vastness, complexity and especially non- or a- localness of such formations".[67] This raised the question of whether anthropology's identity is defined by its commitment to the production of ethnographic texts, with their emphasis on the local context and the concomitant "seeing is believing" mantra that places the ethnographer as a witness to culture rather than as cultured himself. The suggestion here is that "culture" in the traditional anthropological and upgraded Geertzerian sense is simply less and less relevant to the contemporary world.[68] The above limitations taken together with the contradictions posed by the confluence of cultural relativism and difference, both cornerstone paradigms in anthropology, leaves the discipline bereft of any enduring and matter-of-fact epistemological grounds. The issue of meaning-making as against the notion of "cultural systems" was in some measure a response to these dilemmas. However, another caveat arises from the recognition that meaning-making is central to questions of power in that symbolic constructions of meaning are actively made by real historical actors and can therefore not be devoid of political ideology. Ironically, the notion of "having a culture" or "being a culture" has become politically crucial to many communities previously labelled as "cultures" by anthropologists. This tactic is being adopted as a political tool in competition for scarce resources. At the same time many ethnic groups and many contemporary postcolonial intellectuals take exception to being studied as specimens of cultural difference and otherness.[69]

As a general rule, in anthropology cultural analysis was placed above analyses of social and political events and processes. Cultural analysis was seen as an end in itself. The importance placed on cultural analysis vis-à-vis social, political and economic considerations perpetuates the exoticisation of those studied by anthropologists. Their silence on the inequitable distribution of goods and power justifies these inequalities. Further, the question of agency in anthropology needs deconstruction. To this end, conceptions of agency as dialectical are proposed. "Anthropology may be what anthropologists do, but anthropologists do what they do by doing it with and perhaps sometimes to others." Fabian,[70] in particular, has raised this point, sharply criticising anthropology's tendency to affirm difference as distance in its construction of its Other. In response, Fabian advocates for coevalness; that is, for anthropological fieldwork to be possible, the ethnographer and the interlocutor must exist in the same time plane. From this point of view, difference and distance between those with whom and to whom anthropologists do anthropology is constructed to justify anthropological notions of an Other. In this way, the anthropological Other is made, and therefore, not real.

Beyond Postmodernism: Towards the Decoloniality of Anthropology

Postmodern emancipatory politics have exposed the politics of representation, insisting that all knowledge is embodied and particularised. Contestation is, as a result, the order of the day. Yeatman[71] argues that postmodern emancipatory politics do not abandon the values of modern universalism and rationalism as they depend on the very premises of modernism that they seeks to dismantle. While postmodernism paves the way for other knowledges and imagining other worlds, its starting point is always modernity.

> From the standpoint of those who are contesting their status as Other, postmodernism appears as the efforts of the modern imperial, patriarchal master subject to manage the extent and direction of the crisis for his authority. Postmodernism has no emancipatory power, it is reaction of a kind that seeks to pre-empt and co-opt. It is a reaction which accommodates by depoliticising the challenges meted against the modern master subject.[72]

Using the imagination of the power structure, anthropology creates the natives, and the natives become exotic and peculiar. Communities are studied outside their broad context and can thus be said to, in fact, be imagined and created. Once the communities are created, they lose their sense of existence, their sense of being. Looking at the history of anthropology in the South African context, Harris asserts that Wilson, one of South Africa's pre-eminent anthropologists, "never attempted to describe the social whole but illustrated how aspects of it were interconnected".[73] This goes against the dictum that there is no text without historical context.[74] Against such wisdom, anthropology negates this understanding in its pursuit to understand the Other. This omission of the native's past by anthropologists such as Wilson is not a coincidence. This could be read as a strategic move to focus on broader contextual issues that affect local communities and expose the impact of colonialism and the role played by anthropology in their domination. Therefore, "this ignoring the institutional and political context in which ideas unfold and blossom" is the deliberate act to overlook even their past that links anthropology with slavery, colonialism, and imperialism.[75] This partly explains why while "they [anthropologists] as South Africans worked very comfortably within [the] confines of the South African political system[,] their work had certain policy implications for the apartheid regime".[76] The omission of context, while anthropology claims to be contextual, helps in re-imagining the natives who are perceived as primitive and therefore in need of civilising interventions from the West.

Perez[77] argues that it is in the interstitial gaps, the unheard of, the unthought, the unspoken, that open up negotiation spaces for the decolonising subject who is in a quest to unmask the prevailing world order and thus imagine a new world. Decolonial readings of anthropology speak to the geopolitics of knowledge and the provincial nature of Eurocentric knowledge, thus opening up spaces for other knowledges that go beyond disciplines that are geographically marked in their essence. Anthropology is due for a fundamental and thoroughgoing decolonialisation that exposes its spatial and theoretical colonialisation of the world. Anthropology has been sustained by a cabal of scholars whose views are cemented by the insistence that theirs is *the* view that captures and describes the proverbial elephant and deal decisively with dissenting voices by distributing privilege in ways that punish such voices.[78] From this point of view, the bureaucratic structures of the university are complicit in muting alternative viewpoints and ways of knowing. African students of anthropology who choose vilified ancestors, such as Mafeje, amongst others, have little hope of advancing in the academy that largely still looks to the West for direction and influence. The politics of publishing are no different either.

Conclusion

Can we imagine a world without anthropological knowledge? This question speaks directly to whether anthropological knowledge offers anything special to humanity at large. We contend in this chapter that in fact, anthropological knowledge has wrought a lot of pain that it has yet to account for. Its concepts, worldview and its foundations have always pitted Western ideals against the rest. Anthropological concepts have tended to mute and distort other knowledges and worldviews. We argue that even the most harsh criticism of the discipline cannot displace or dislocate its fundamental principles. The result has always been re-thinking as opposed to unthinking the discipline. What possibilities does unthinking anthropology hold? For one, this gives an opportunity to understand that difference, while at first a deliberate project, has largely been eroded by the very processes that sought to entrench it. Further, commenting on the local, as anthropology tends to do, can only serve to make, rather than discover, difference. Anthropology's pretence to being a science that offers objective views of the world has been revealed. Beyond this, what can anthropology base its knowledge systems on? It is, therefore, easy to argue for a case of a world without anthropological knowledge. It does not even require that we imagine the unthought and the unspoken to undermine the basic tenets of the discipline. Anthropology stands on shaky ground. The ontological and epistemological dimensions of culture, the very founding concept of the discipline, are coming apart. The rest can only take its cue from this.

Notes and References

1. Ribeiro, G. L., & Escobar, A. (2006). World anthropologies: Disciplinary transformations within systems of power. In G. L. Ribeiro & A. Escobar (Eds.), *World anthropologies: Disciplinary transformations within systems of power* (pp. 1–28). New York, NY: Berg Publishers.

2. Said, E. (1978). *Orientalism*. New York, NY: Vintage.

3. Boas, F. (1897). The social organization and the secret societies of the Kwakiutl Indians. In *Report of the U.S. National Museum for 1895* (pp. 311–738). Washington, DC: U.S. Government Printing Office.

4. Levi-Strauss, C. (1963). *Structural anthropology*. Suffolk: Richard Clay (The Chaucer Press).

5. Wolff, L., & Cipolloni, M. (2007). *The anthropology of the Enlightenment*. Stanford, CA: Stanford University Press.

6. Boas, The social organization, pp. 311–738.

7. Stillwaggon, E. (2006). *AIDS and the ecology of poverty*. Oxford, England: Oxford University Press.

8. Ribeiro and Escobar, World anthropologies, pp. 1–28.

9. Nyamnjoh, F. (2012). Blinded by sight: Divining the future of anthropology in Africa. In *Africa Spectrum, 48*(1), pp. 107–112.

10. Marx, K. (1974). *The German ideology*. New York, NY: International Publishers. (Original work published in 1846).

11. Levi-Strauss, *Structural anthropology*.

12. Blumenbach, J. (1997). The degeneration of races. In E. Eze (Ed.), *Race and the Enlightenment: A reader* (79–91). Oxford, England: Blackwell. (Original work published in 1776).

13. Jefferson, T. (1944). Notes on the State of Virginia. In A. Koch & W. Peden (Eds.), *Life and Selected Writings of Thomas Jefferson*. New York, NY: Modern American Library (Original work published 1787).

14. Morton, S. (1844). *Crania Aegytica: Or, observations on Egyptian ethnography derived from anatomy, history, and the monuments*. Philadelphia, PA: J. Pennington.

15. Firmin, J.-A. (2000). *The equality of the human races.* (C. Asselin, Trans.). New York, NY: Garland. (Original work published in 1854)

16. Moore, J. H. (2008). *Encyclopedia of race and racism A–F.* MacMillan Social Science Library. Volume 1 of Encyclopedia of Race and Racism. Thomson Gale.

17. Comaroff, J., & Comaroff, J. (1991). *Of revelation and revolution: Christianity, colonialism and consciousness in South Africa.* Chicago, IL: University of Chicago Press.

18. Nyamnjoh, F. (2012). Blinded by sight: Divining the future of anthropology in Africa. In *Africa Spectrum, 48*(1), 107–112.

19. Ribeiro and Escobar, World anthropologies, pp. 1–28.

20. Mafeje, A. (2001). *Anthropology in post-independent Africa: End of an era and the problem of self-redefinition: African social scientists reflections* (Part 1). Nairobi, Kenya: Heinrich Boll Foundation.

21. Yeatman, A. (1994). *Postmodern revisionings of the political.* London, England: Routledge.

22. Sichone, O. (2001). The making of makwerekwere: East Africans in Cape Town — A paper for a workshop interrogating the new political culture in Southern Africa: *Ideas and institutions'.* Harare, Zimbabwe 13–15 June.

23. Argyrou, V. (2002). *Anthropology and the will to meaning: A postcolonial critique.* London, England: Pluto Press.

24. Ibid.

25. Geertz, *Culture, custom and ethics,* p. 3.

26. Ribeiro and Escobar, World anthropologies, pp. 1–28.

27. Ibid.

28. Leach, E. (1961). *Rethinking anthropology.* London, England: The Athlone Press.

29. Troillot, M.-R. (1995). *Silencing the past: Power and the production of history.* Boston, MA: Beacon Press.

30. Ribeiro and Escobar, World anthropologies, pp. 1–28.

31. Ibid.

32. Ibid.

33. Ibid.

34. Ibid.

35. Ntarangwe, M., Mills, D., & Babiker, M. (2006). *African anthropologies: History, critique and practice.* New York, NY: Zed Books.

36. Magubane, B. (1971). A critical look of indices used in the study of social change in colonial Africa. *Current Anthropology, 12*(4–5), 419–445.

37. Mafeje, *Anthropology.*

38. Wolcott, F. H. (1999). *Ethnography: A way of seeing.* London, England: Walnut Creek.

39. Geertz, C. (2000). *Culture, custom and ethics (key contemporary thinkers).* Cambridge, England: Cambridge Polity Press.

40. Said, E. (1978). *Orientalism.* New York, NY: Vintage.

41. Argyrou, Anthropology, p. 13.

42. Asante, Molefi. K. (1993). African Environment and Society: Afrocentric Renewal. Presented at the thirty-Sixth Annual Meeting of the African Studies Association, Boston, Massachusetts, December 4–7. No. 1993: 4.

43. Radcliffe-Brown, A. R. (1951). The comparative methods in social anthropology: Historical note on British social anthropology. *American Anthropologist, 54*(2, 1), 275–277.

44. Mudimbe, V. Y. (1988). In *The invention of Africa: Gnosis, philosophy, and the order of knowledge*, advances an even bigger critique of the discipline when he argues that anthropology is complicit in the invention of a particular Africa.

45. Levi-Strauss. 1963. *The effectiveness of symbols*.

46. Note is here taken that while Mafeje was a professor of anthropology, he is actively distancing himself from the discipline by his choice of words. This underscores the point made below that, while the authors are scholars of anthropology, the transition to thinking of themselves as anthropologists is fraught with a lot of contradictions.

47. Mafeje, A. (1991). *The theory and ethnography of African social foundation: The case of the interlacustrine kingdoms*. London, England: CODESRIA.

48. Clifford, J. (1986a). Introduction: Partial truths. In J. Clifford & G. Marcus (Eds.), *Writing culture: The poetic and politics of ethnography* (pages). Berkeley, CA: University of California Press.

49. Kenyatta, J. (1938). *Facing Mount Kenya*. London, England: Martin Secker and Warburg.

50. Mafeje, *Anthropology*.

51. Argyrou, *Anthropology*, p. 118.

52. Ibid.

53. Said, *Orientalism*.

54. Geertz, *Culture, custom and ethics*, p. 45.

55. Schweder, R. A. (2005). Cliff notes: The pluralism of Clifford Geetz. In Geertz, *Culture, custom and ethics* (pp. 1–9).

56. Ortner, S. B. (1999). *The fate of culture: Geertz and beyond*. California: University of California Press.

57. Ibid.

58. Ibid.

59. Fried, M. H. (1975). *The notion of tribes*. New York, NY: Octogon Books.

60. Ibid.

61. Farmer, P. (2001). *Infections and inequalities: The modern plaques*. Berkeley, CA: University of California Press.

62. Fried, *The notion of tribes*, p. 36.

63. Ibid.

64. Ibid.

65. Schweder, Cliff notes, pp. 1–9.

66. Geertz, *Culture, custom and ethics*, p. 3.

67. Ortner, *The fate of culture*, p. 67.

68. Ibid.

69. Ibid.

70. Fabian, J. (1983). *Time and the other: How anthropology makes its objects*. New York, NY: Colombia University Press.

71. Yeatman, *Postmodern revisionings*, p. ix.

72. Said, Orientalism.

73. Harris, B. J. (1984). 'The History of Anthropology Within the Context of the South African Political Economy'. Presented at the Twenty-Seventh Annual Meeting of the African Studies Association, Los Angeles, CA, October 25–28.

74. Mafeje, *The theory and ethnography*, p. 9.

75. Ntarangwe, M., Mills, D., & Babiker, M. (2006). *African anthropologies: History, critique and practice*. New York, NY: Zed Books.

76. Harris, The history of anthropology, p. 18.

77. Perez, E. (1991). *The decolonial imaginary: Writing chicanas into history (theories of representation and difference)*. Bloomington, IN: Indiana University Press.

78. Nyamnjoh, F. (2012). Blinded by sight: Divining the future of anthropology in Africa. In *Africa Spectrum, 48*(1), 107–112.

Chapter 8

Post-Disciplinarity and Forgetfulness of Coloniality in Tourism Studies

Morgan Ndlovu

Introduction

That tourism is one of the popular subjects in the discourses of development concerning the countries of the Third World is no longer disputable. However, the subject of tourism in the Third World has since been clouded by accusations that the operation of the industry is generally underpinned by colonial-type relations and tendencies. Thus, in spite of the positive analyses that tourism in the developing world has contributed to economic growth, reduction of poverty and consolidation of vanishing identities, among other aspects, a number of scholars have remained adamant that the colonial-type relations and tendencies that underpin the operation of the industry in general, such as the negative representations of identities and exploitative political-economic relations, tend to overshadow its positive contributions. While a number of scholars in the field of tourism studies have tended to focus on the practical and explicit impacts of tourism on various aspects of life among the peoples of the Third World, other scholars have questioned whether the manner in which knowledge production in the field of tourism studies takes place reinforces or challenges the status quo of colonial-type relations and tendencies, both in the practice and epistemological frame of the subject. Among a number of scholarly endeavours that have sought to question or find solution to colonial-type relations and tendencies in the study and practice of tourism is that which calls for a post-disciplinary approach to the subject. This chapter examines whether the discourse of post-disciplinarity challenges or reinforces the status quo of colonial-type relations and tendencies in the study and practice of tourism among the countries of the Third World. The chapter's central argument is that in order to effectively cleanse the study and practice of tourism in countries of the Third World of colonial-type relations and tendencies, it is imperative that a discourse such as that of post-disciplinarity takes a 'de-colonial turn' in its approach to the subject of tourism. The chapter is predicated on the notion that there is an indisputable symbiotic interrelationship between the manner in which knowledge production is conducted in the field of tourism studies and the manner in which tourism practices take place among the countries of the Third World.

Why Tourism Studies?

Tourism is one of the most interesting subjects when it comes to the idea of post-disciplinarity. This is not only because the practice of tourism is a business of 'difference' but also because the study of tourism is one of the most debated when it comes to imaginations of a post-disciplinary era in the study of social phenomena in general. Thus, it needs to be mentioned from the onset that one of the most contentious issues about the study of tourism since it was introduced as an academic and/or professional subject is the question of whether the subject can be classified as a discipline. This is mainly because the study of tourism has always been conducted using theoretical tools borrowed from other disciplines such as anthropology, business studies, sociology and geography, among others, leading to questions of whether it is a single, multi- or inter-disciplinary subject.

While scholars such as Tribe,[1] among others, have concentrated on debating whether the study of tourism can be classified as a discipline, the debate on the subject of tourism has also seen a contestation between scholars such as Leiper who argue that tourism studies is more organised and scholastic as a discipline[2] and those such as Jafari who have argued that the study of tourism is 'more expedient, productive and meaningful'[3] when it is undisciplined or interdisciplinary. These academic contestations over the question of whether tourism studies is a discipline, on one hand, and those who argue on whether it must be disciplined or de-disciplined, on the other hand, have seen the discourses on the study of tourism oscillating between those advocating for disciplinarity at one particular moment and those advocating for post-disciplinarity at another particular time-frame.

The question that emerges from the contestations on whether tourism must be a discipline or not is that of who benefits from the discourses that oppose and support disciplinarity and/or post-disciplinarity in the study of tourism at a particular time and location. This question is quite important to examine because the study of tourism, like that of any other field, has some direct or indirect bearing on the lived experience of individuals and communities, hence the need to examine the impact of its discursive articulations on the subalternized peoples of the Third World. This chapter argues that the manner in which the pro- and the anti-disciplinarity discourses are currently being articulated pertaining the study of tourism does not factor into account the plight of the people of Third World with specific reference to the manner in which their voices and ways of knowing are subjugated. Thus, for instance, the debates about the need for post-disciplinarity in the study of tourism do not have in mind the desire to address the problem of 'epistemicides' that continue to be committed by a universalist Western-centric knowledge production system on the ways of knowing of non-Western peoples. This behaviour and attitude in both the discourses that advocate and oppose disciplinarity in tourism studies can be viewed as constituting what the decolonial scholar Maldonado-Torres referred to as the *forgetfulness of coloniality*.[4]

Through his idea of the *forgetfulness of coloniality*, Maldonado-Torres argues that 'the forgetfulness of the damned is part of the veritable sickness of the West, a sickness that could be likened to a state of amnesia that leads to murder, destruction and epistemic will to power—with good conscience'.[5] Thus, the forgetfulness of Western thinkers when it comes to the plight of non-Western people in countries of the Third World generally is a self-centred *will-to-ignorance* and a *forgetfulness of damnation*[6] that not only leads to ontological oppression of the non-Western subject but also to coloniality of knowledge and power.

In the case of the debate on whether tourism studies can be productive as a cohesive discipline or a post-discipline, it can be argued that both the discourses that advocate for disciplinarity and post-disciplinarity in tourism studies tend to *forget* or dismiss the relevance of the colonial experience of the non-Western subject. This makes both the discourse of disciplinarity and post-disciplinarity complicit in disciplining the non-Western subject into a docile and complying subject of Western knowledge because they are both predicated on the false notion that the very canon on which disciplines are rooted is universally justified. This chapter argues that the question of disciplinarity vis-à-vis post-disciplinarity must be attended to at an epistemological level, and as such, what must be questioned in the discourses of post-disciplinarity/disciplinarity is not only the problem of arranging the discipline in terms of academic tribes, but also the very epistemic virtue on which academic disciplines are generally predicated. In this way, the challenges of coloniality and colonial experience in the field of knowledge production can be addressed within the discourse of post-disciplinarity.

In general, that the power of disciplinarity in the field of tourism studies is something that needs to be negated or de-disciplined cannot be disputed, but the question that needs urgent attention in the quest for a tourism studies curriculum or research approach beyond a disciplining scholarship is that of whether the challenge of domination and inequalities in the whole enterprise of knowledge production is also part of the agenda. This question is quite important with specific reference to the peoples of the Third World because their locations on the dominated side of colonial difference, which Gordon described in Fanonian terms as the hellish 'zone of non-being',[7] can mean that they view the world from a different 'locus of enunciation'[8] from those located in the 'zone of being' in the West. Thus, among the majority of subalternized indigenous peoples of the Third World, the fundamental problem with both the practice and epistemic framing of tourism studies within the sphere of knowledge production is that of 'coloniality' — a power structure that survives the end of direct colonialism and continues to sustain asymmetrical power relations and dichotomous conceptions of humanity through racial hierarchization.

This chapter's point of departure is that tourism studies cannot be treated as different from other academic disciplines in the sense that it is, like all other disciplines, permeated by the general behavior of Western logo-centrism when it comes to knowledge production. What this means is that the major problem with tourism studies is, in general, the fundamentalism of Euro-American modernity's sole claim to universality and truth in the field of knowledge production — a development that denies the peoples of the colonized a voice in the field of tourism knowledge production. This, therefore, means that the process of de-disciplining tourism studies cannot be successfully undertaken without understanding how the nature of the practice and epistemological frame of tourism itself constitute the manner in which the world system is organized and hierarchized.

The Idea of Discipline and Its Genealogies

This part of the chapter traces the genealogy of the idea of a 'discipline' and it argues that the idea of an academic discipline serves different purposes at different times, contexts and geo-specific locations. Thus, through the decolonial epistemic lens one of the fundamental questions that this chapter seeks to answer is that of whether the idea of academic disciplines serves a similar disciplinary purpose and/or effect for the Western and non-Western subject. This is quite important because the process of colonial domination of the non-Western world by the Western nations was not only supported by knowledge production, but also by epistemicides on non-Western ways of knowing and seeing the world, especially those that were found to be antagonistic to Western canonical dictum in matters of thought. In other words, the idea of a discipline can serve to achieve domination by bringing about a systematic approach to the colonial project of subjugating the indigenous knowledges of the dominated subject.

In general, the question of academic disciplines and their role in the present cannot be fully understood until we trace the origins of the broader idea of 'discipline' itself. Thus, one of the genealogical backgrounds to the idea of discipline can be traced to the religious idea of 'discipleship'. According to Turner, '*disciplina* were instructions given to disciples' and as such, the idea of disciplines tends to carry some religious connotations.[9] Thus, discipline in the religious context can be seen as having laid the foundation for the modern educational notion of 'body of knowledge'. This background on the religious genesis of the idea of discipline is quite important because it enables us to question whether today the idea of academic disciplines in the field of knowledge production still serves the purpose of producing 'academic disciples', and if so, who stands to benefit and to be punished or chastised out of this quest to cultivate discipleship in the field of knowledge production.

The religious connotations of discipline are even crucial when one considers that the idea of discipleship or discipline links to that of obedience as well as the penal methods of instilling it. Thus, the idea of discipline can also be traced to military training and the church, where penal methods and systems of rule serve as instruments of achieving obedience for the functioning of those institutions. All these genealogical backgrounds clearly indicate that the idea of discipline links to the ideas of obedience, punishment and rules for the achievement of particular purposes. The question that, therefore, emerges out of the genealogical backgrounds to the idea of discipline is, in a world order where epistemicides of some knowledges are committed and one version of what constitute knowledge is imposed on others, what role does discipline play in articulating the relations of power between the dominant and dominated in the field of knowledge production? This question is quite important because clearly the idea of discipline has a social role that it plays in peoples' relations and articulations of power.

Discipline has social importance as a technology of the body, soul and the mind. Thus, according to Weber, discipline can produce personalities and life orders that have an affinity with the discipline of labour force in capitalism.[10] This articulation of the idea of discipline that links it with the Protestant ethic and spirit of capitalism clearly indicates that discipline can be carried out for exploitative relations of power. Thus, Weber's articulation of the origins of discipline together with Foucault's idea of discipline as an instrument of governmentality demonstrate that discipline can serve a positive purpose on the part of the powerful while manifesting itself negatively to the less powerful.[11] In the field of knowledge production, where relations of power are underpinned by colonial forms of domination, this means that discipline can serve to maintain a hierarchal system between those who are at the top and those who remain at the bottom. The question that remains to be answered is that of what role the idea of academic discipline plays in a world system where the Western subject has privileged itself to be the sole producer of knowledge and worldview while committing epistemicides against the non-Western subject. This question is of particular importance to the peoples of the non-Western world because the meaning of discipline in the academic space of knowledge production carries a different connotation to that of the dominant subject in the Westernized environment of knowledge production.

Is Tourism Studies Really a Discipline?

The idea of de-disciplining tourism knowledge and/or practice cannot be a successful exercise unless the question of whether tourism is a discipline is examined. However, in order to establish whether tourism studies is a discipline, it is crucial to determine first what makes a subject a disciple, who is disciplined and for what reasons. This is important because the idea of what constitutes an academic discipline tends to vary across different scholarly positions at different times and geo-specific locations. Thus, for instance, scholars such as Tribe[12] argue that tourism as a subject tends to lack the characteristics of a discipline, while those such as Goeldner,[13] among others, have described it as a discipline. The question that needs to be answered, therefore, is that of what makes an academic subject a discipline.

Different scholars have used different criteria to judge whether the subject of tourism constitutes a discipline. According to Tribe,[14] tourism does not deserve the label of being an academic discipline simply because 'there is not a distinctive logical structure to tourism studies' since its concepts are not a form of a distinctive network but are understood 'generally within the logical structure of their provider discipline'. What this means is that tourism as a subject of study is viewed as un-disciplined mainly because 'it does not provide any truth criteria which are particular to it-self but rather utilizes those criteria which are found in its contributory disciplines'.[15] Thus, tourism's lack of its own internal theoretical or conceptual unity has prompted scholars such as Darbellay and Stock[16] to question whether tourism is a paradigm or episteme.

By a paradigm, Darbellay & Stock meant what Kuhn[17] described as a *disciplinary matrix*, or an *ensemble* of principles and methods shared by a specific scientific community, while by episteme they meant what Foucault described as a field of formation and transformation of knowledge that cannot be reduced to an accumulation or a simple stage of the different bodies of knowledge at any moment of scientific development.[18] Through the notions of paradigm and episteme, Darbellay and Stock[19] argue that while before the 1950s, the attempt to treat tourism as a holistic whole did not succeed in reducing tourism studies to a discipline, the period after 1950s saw a movement that disciplined researchers into a paradigm by a scientific community. Thus, these scholars conclude that the intertwining disciplinary and non-disciplinary developments around the tourism phenomenon mean that tourism can be considered as an episteme. This is mainly because disciplines always take into account other disciplines' frameworks or methodologies, translating them into their own problematization.[20] What can be concluded from this analysis is that the above scholars view tourism as a discipline that consists of both a paradigm and an episteme as constructed from different disciplines, albeit not in identical terms. Tourism studies can, therefore, be viewed as a multidisciplinary field of study rather than an interdisciplinary or a post-disciplinary one, since it is neither underpinned by the organized co-ordination process that mobilizes a dialogue between disciplines to warrant an interdisciplinary status, nor totally lacks a disciplining element to be post-disciplinary.

While the debates about whether tourism is a discipline or not in terms of being a self-contained tribe, having an explicit territorial boundary and specific communal networks in the academy[21] are important, what is often omitted in these debates is the question of the role played by the idea of academic disciplines in the articulation of power relations between Western and non-Western ways of knowing. Thus, for instance, it can be argued that to a non-Western subject all academic disciplines within the Westernized academy are predicated on a fundamentalist Western canon that privileges a Western epistemic perspective as the only perspective capable of knowing, even for the people whose imaginations, knowledges and aspirations are non-Western. In other words, from a decolonial epistemic perspective, in Western-centric academies, there is only one discipline—that which denies the possibility of an 'ecology of knowledges' and the pluriversality of different worldviews in the production of knowledge while privileging a Western worldview over all possible ways of knowing.

In response to the manner in which the voices and perspective of the peoples of the non-Western world are marginalized in the field of knowledge production within the Western academy in general, scholars such as Smith[22] have remarked that 'the term "research" is inextricably linked to European imperialism and colonialism'. Thus, colonizing nations relied on disciplines such as sociology and anthropology to produce knowledge that sustained the colonial project. The disciplines that have always been sustaining the colonial project continue to inform even emerging disciplines such as tourism studies, hence the maintenance of 'coloniality' in the sphere of knowledge production. Thus, at stake is the question of racism and epistemology, where the lighter skinned peoples of the First World have 'knowledge' while the darker skinned of the Third World have 'culture'. What this means is that in order to imagine and build a just and non-imperial or non-colonial understanding of the world, it is not adequate to coordinate and multiply different disciplinary approaches to phenomena, as suggested in discourses on multi- and inter-disciplinary approaches, but it will be necessary to go beyond the idea of discipline in the first place.

Among the peoples of the non-Western world where the whole Euro-centred epistemology that is carefully hidden in academic disciplines has a disciplining effect on their indigenous ways of knowing, it is necessary to adopt Mignolo's idea of 'epistemic disobedience'.[23] Thus, according to Mignolo, the peoples of the non-Western world need to go beyond the assumption that the knowing subject in the disciplines is transparent and disincorporated from the known and untouched by the geo-political configuration of the world, in which people are racially ranked and regions are racially configured.[24] This means that thinking does not come before being, hence we produce knowledge from racially marked bodies within geo-historically marked spaces from which we get the urge to speak.[25] In the context of de-disciplining an academic subject such as tourism studies, this means that we need to be conscious of what Maldonado-Torres referred to as the *forgetfulness of coloniality*,[26] whereby, as in the case of de-disciplining knowledge, we only do it in order to save the West from various global crises that Western 'disciplinary decadence'[27] have failed to solve while forgetting the equally significant task of de-disciplining knowledge in order to allow the peoples of non-Western world freedom to think.

Why a Decolonial Turn in Tourism Knowledge Production?

What has been referred to as 'decolonial turn' by scholars such as Gosfoguel[28] and Maldonado-Torres[29] is quite important for tourism studies because one of the fundamental challenges facing the world today is that of provincializing the West. This is necessary because the constitution of the world system, whose construction was achieved mainly by the conquest and subjugation of one part of the world by the other, has culminated in a situation that is characterized by political, economic, social, cultural and epistemic domination and subordination of non-Western societies by 'Western' European dominators and their

Euro-North American descendants. Thus, the Euro-American sole claim to universality has culminated into a dichotomized world system where Western worldviews and practices take precedent over those of the peoples of the non-Western world. The question, therefore, is how can a world system predicated on relations of subjugation, injustice and inequality in various aspects of life be reconstituted to accommodate the aspirations and worldviews of all the inhabitants who exist within it, without one part of the world privileging itself over others? This question is quite important for a subject such as tourism studies because a number of initiatives, such as post-disciplinarity, have been explored to reverse the injustices and inequalities that were brought about by the advent of the new world system in 1492, when the 'voyages of discovery' began to take place, but up to the present, the peoples of the non-Western world still live under various crude forms of exploitation and oppression. Thus, to the majority of the peoples of the Third World, whose worldviews have since the advent of Euro-American-centered modernity been subalternized by Euro-American modernity, tourism is a modern medium of neo-colonial relations between the First and the Third World. These neo-colonial relations are not only limited to the practice of tourism in the Third World, but also extend to the field of knowledge production through tourism studies since the discipline of tourism, like any other discipline, is a subject that is underpinned by the logo-centric meta-narratives of European culture.

This chapter argues that, in order for the West and the rest to have an equal share in determining the present and the future of a subject such as tourism, it is imperative that the influence of Euro-American-centred modernity with its sole claim to universality is negated. One of the key strategies of negating the totalizing tendency of the Euro-American worldview and its associated practices entails both falsifying its universality and exposing its provinciality — an exercise that can lead to a world characterized by a 'pluri-versality' of worldviews and lived experiences rather than a single universalized one.

Indeed, in its formal and explicit aspect, colonial domination has been defeated throughout the Third World, but this does not mean that the peoples of this part of the world are no longer exploited, dominated and discriminated against as members of 'races', 'ethnicities' or 'nations'. In the same way, the fact that political juridical administrative colonialism has been eliminated in the Third World does not translate to mean that the relationship between the West and the non-Western world is no longer one of colonial domination. In contrast, the cessation of constant and systematic repression over aspects such as modes of knowing, of producing knowledge, of producing perspectives, images and systems of images, symbols, modes of signification, resources, patterns and instruments of formalised and objectivised expression, intellectual or visual,[30] after the demise of juridical administrative colonialism in the Third World meant that social, political, economic and cultural control had to be continued through coloniality—the most general form of domination in the world today. Thus, the process of Euro-centrification of the world has continued unabated even though colonialism as an explicit political order might have been completely destroyed. According to Grosfoguel, '[T]he most powerful myth of the twentieth century was the notion that the elimination of colonial administrations amounted to the decolonization of the world'.[31] This mistake of reducing the problem of colonial domination to an issue of power contestation over juridical-political boundaries of state in national liberation and socialist strategies of anti-colonial struggles have led to the myth of a 'post-colonial' world. Thus, it is within this false premise of a 'post-colonial' world that though 'colonial administrations' have been entirely eradicated in developing states and independent statehood celebrated throughout the Third World, the non-European peoples are still living under what Grosfoguel refers to as 'crude European/Euro-American exploitation and domination'.[32] This means that the concept of colonialism which became the basic template of anti-colonial struggles throughout the Third World was, from the onset, too simplistic to deal with the complexity of colonial domination, whose architecture boast heterogeneous and multiple global structures put in place over a period of 450 years.

Rather than remain trapped within purviews of colonial domination that are espoused in the limiting critique of 'classical colonialism' that tended to underpin the ideology of nationalist and socialist anti-colonial struggles throughout the Third World, progressive scholarship by Latin American scholars such as Quijano, among others, have called for an understanding of colonial domination through the conceptual lenses of 'coloniality'.[33] The concept of coloniality, unlike the critique that underpinned classical colonialism, unveils the mystery of why, after the end of colonial administrations in the juridical-political spheres of state administration, there is still continuity of colonial forms of domination. This is mainly because the concept of coloniality addresses the issue of colonial domination not from an isolated and singular point of departure, such as the juridical-political administrative point of view, but from a vantage point of a variety of 'colonial situations' that include cultural, political, sexual, spiritual, epistemic and economic oppression of subordinate racialized/ethnic groups by dominant racialized/ethnic groups, with or without the existence of colonial administrations.[34] This holistic approach to the problem of colonial domination allows us to visualize other dynamics of the colonial process, which include 'colonization of imagination',[35] 'colonization of the mind'[36] and colonization of knowledge and power. These dynamics of colonial domination enable us to grapple with long-standing patterns of power which Maldonado-Torres argues were and are 'maintained alive in books, in the criteria for academic performance, in cultural patterns, in common sense, in the self-image of people, in aspiration of self, and so many other aspects of our modern experience'.[37] Thus, Maldonado-Torres's position concurs with that of Quijano, who states that 'coloniality operates on every level, in every arena and dimension (both material and subjective) of everyday social existence, and does so on a societal scale'.[38]

The Study and Practice of Tourism in the Third World: The Prospects of a 'Decolonial' Post-Disciplinary Approach

The quest for a decolonial turn in the study of tourism cannot be a compelling endeavour without a clear demonstration of how a decolonial approach can lead to a more de-disciplined practice and epistemological framing of the subject than currently is the case with the discourses of post-disciplinarity. However, before evaluating any prospect of a decolonized post-disciplinary approach in the study of tourism among the countries of the Third World, it is important to explore briefly how the presence of colonial-type relations of power and tendencies in the tourism industry of the non-Western world are currently understood. This is important to understand because the call for a decolonial turn in the study of tourism must lead not only to a better understanding of the industry but also to a possible transformation of power relations in the practice and study of tourism.

By and large, the current articulations of colonial-type relations and tendencies in the tourism industry of the Third World are informed by what can be classified as a cultural studies paradigm and political economy paradigm. The cultural studies paradigm tends to privilege the question of identity when articulating coloniality in the practice of tourism, whereas the latter tends to privilege the economic relations of power. This poses a problem to our understanding of coloniality in the organization of the tourism industry among the states of the Third World because the question of what comes first between identity and economic imperative is a 'chicken-egg' type of dilemma that cannot be resolved. However, the 'chicken-egg' dilemma in the question of what comes first between identity and political economy as we seek to understand colonial-type relations of power in the organization of the tourism industry of the Third World can easily resolved from a de-colonial epistemic perspective, which visualizes coloniality as an entangled package of hierarchically arranged racial, ethnic, gender, sexual, economic, and epistemic relations of power. What this means is that the question of what comes first is irrelevant since these global 'heterarchies of power'[39] came at the same time in the form of an entangled package. Thus, for instance, in the case of the construction of cultural tourism sites such as cultural villages in South Africa, it can be concluded that the skewed political economy that favours the 'white race' and the negative perception of indigenous identities are not only part and parcel of the entangled packaged of coloniality but are also two sides of the same coin.

Despite the fact multi-, inter- and post-disciplinary approaches in the study of tourism can broaden our understanding of the subject, these approaches have a limitation in transforming the manner in which tourism knowledge production is generally conducted. This is important to understand because the manner in which tourism knowledge is currently produced is characterized by the imposition of Western technologies of knowing, seeing and understanding the world upon the people of the Third World. Hence there is a need for a decolonial turn that will enable the non-Western subject to produce knowledge from his/her own perspective of the world.

One of the technologies of knowing and seeing the world in the sphere of tourism knowledge production is the idea of sewn 'research methodologies', which the discipline of tourism has inherited from other disciplines and which serve to re-inscribe those Western ways thinking and reasoning that precede them. In other words, the idea of deploying pre-determined research methods also presupposes findings in research, hence they serve to maintain the dominance of the Western-centric worldview in the process of knowledge production. Thus, the idea of deploying pre-determined research methodologies enables tourism knowledge production among the countries of the Third World to be conducted in such a manner that researchers end up writing *about* and *for* the non-Western subject rather than *with* and *from* the non-Western subject's point of view.[40] This had led decolonial scholars such as Gordon[41] and Mignolo[42] to call for the 'shifting of the geography of reason' and 'epistemic disobedience' in order to allow the dominated subjects of the non-Western world to produce knowledge from where they are located. What this means is that a decolonial turn in the quest for post-disciplinary in the study of tourism can lead to a situation where it is possible for previously denied knowledges such as those of the indigenous peoples of the Third World to co-exist alongside that which is Western, thereby making the 'ecologies of knowledges' in tourism studies a realizable one.

Conclusion

The idea of post-disciplinarity in tourism studies, like that of many other disciplines, is a noble one, but it can only be truly post-disciplinary when it begins to question the very canon on which tourism and other fields that inform the study of tourism are predicated. Thus, it needs to go beyond the question of 'disciplines' as academic tribes and begin to seek ways of taking seriously the knowledges of indigenous peoples, which are generally suppressed by the hegemonic Western worldview in knowledge production. However, in order to take seriously the subalternized knowledges of indigenous peoples of the Third World, the discourses of post-disciplinarity need to make a decolonial turn from privileging the voices, views and ways of seeing of the Western subject and *remember* the wisdoms of the *damned* of the earth within the sphere of knowledge production.

Notes and References

1. Tribe, J. (1997). The indiscipline of tourism. *Annals of Tourism Research, 24*(3), 638–657.

2. Leiper, N. (1981). Towards a cohesive curriculum in tourism: The case for a distinct discipline.
Annals of Tourism Research, 8(1), 69–84.

3. Jafari, J. (1977). Editor's Page. *Annals of Tourism Research, V* [Special edition], 8.

4. Maldonado-Torres, N. (2004). The topology of being and the geopolitics of knowledge. *City: Analysis of urban trends, culture, theory, policy, action, 8*(1), 29–56.

5. Ibid., p. 36.

6. Maldonado-Torres, 2004, p. 40

7. Gordon, L. R. (2007). Through the hellish zone of non-being: Thinking through Fanon, Disaster, and the Damned of the Earth. *Human Architecture: Journal of the Sociology of Self-Knowledge, 5*(3), 5–11.

8. Grosfoguel, R. (2007). The epistemic decolonial turn: Beyond political-economy paradigms. *Cultural Studies, 21*(2–3), 211–223.

9. Turner, B. S. (2006). Discipline. *Theory, Culture & Society, 23*(2–30), 183.

10. Weber, M. (2002). *The Protestant ethic and the spirit of capitalism.* Harmondsworth, England: Penguin.

11. Foucault, M. (1977). *Discipline and punishment: The birth of the prison.* London, England: Tavistock.

12. Op cit., Tribe, 1997.

13. Goeldner, C. R. (1988). The evaluation of tourism as an industry and a discipline. International Conference for Tourism Educators mimeo. Guildford. University of Surrey.

14. Tribe, 1997, p. 643.

15. Ibid, p. 644.

16. Darbellay, F., & Stock, M. (2012). Tourism as complex interdisciplinary research object. *Annals of Tourism Research, 39*(1), 441–458.

17. Kuhn, T. S. (1962). *The structure of scientific revolutions.* Chicago, IL: University of Chicago Press.

18. Foucault, M. (1969). *L'archeologie du savoir.* Paris, France: Belin.

19. Darbellay & Stock, 2012.

20. Ibid.

21. Tribe, J. (2010). Tribes, territories and networks in the tourism academy. *Annals of Tourism Research, 37*(1), 7–33.

22. Smith, L. T. (1999). *Decolonizing methodologies: Research and indigenous peoples.* Dunedin, New Zealand: University of Otago Press.

23. Mignolo, W. D. (2009). Epistemic disobedience, independent thought and de-colonial freedom. *Theory, Culture & Society, 26*(7–8), 1–23.

24. Ibid.

25. Mignolo, 2009, p. 2.

26. Maldonado-Torres, 2004.

27. Gordon, L. R. (2011). Shifting the geography in an age of disciplinary decadence. *Transmodernity, 1*(2), 95–103.

28. Grosfoguel, 2007.

29. Maldonado-Torres, N. (2011). Thinking through the decolonial turn: Post-continental interventions in theory, philosophy, and critique—an introduction. *Transmodernity, 1*(2), 1–15.

30. Mignolo, W. D. (2007). Introduction: Coloniality of power and de-colonial thinking. *Cultural Studies, 21*(2–3), 155–167.

31. Grosfoguel, 2007, p. 219.

32. Ibid.

33. Quijano, A. (2007). Coloniality and modernity/rationality. *Cultural Studies, 21*(2–3), 168–178.

34. Grosfoguel, 2007, p. 220.

35. Quijano, 2007.

36. Dascal, M. (2009). Colonizing and decolonizing minds. In I. Kucurandi (Ed.), *Papers of 2007 World Philosophy Day.* Ankara, Turkey: Philosophical Society of Turkey.

37. Maldonado-Torres, N. (2007). On the coloniality of being: Contributions to the development of a concept. *Cultural Studies, 21*(2–3), 243.

38. Quijano, A. (2000). Coloniality of power, ethnocentrism, and Latin America. *NEPANTLA, 1*, 243.

39. Grosfoguel, 2007.

40. Ibid.

41. Gordon, 2011.

42. Mignolo, 2009.

Chapter 9

Decolonizing Social Psychology in Africa

Puleng Segalo

Introduction

As an undergraduate student of psychology I had to learn numerous personality theories and how these explained and described human behavior. What struck me at first was that all these theories we had to learn were by white males from Europe and the United States, and this left me with the question "How am I supposed to relate to this?" This dilemma stayed with me throughout my undergraduate years until I went on and registered for postgraduate studies in Psychology.

As an honours student we were required to enroll for psychometrics as a requirement towards completion of the qualification. This module required that we learn the various psychological tests/personality measuring instruments. One of these tests was called The Rorschach, which is a projection test consisting of ten inkblots that people have to look at, and describe what they see. Their description assists the assessor to make an assessment of the person's personality/state of mind. One of the assignments we were once given was that we should go administer the test to someone we know, make interpretations/diagnosis/analysis of the results, and present these in class. A fellow student (who was a white girl) presented her results: She reported that she used her gardener (a black man) as a *subject*. She reported that the *subject* appears to be having some unresolved anger issues and shows possible aggressive tendencies. This report was based on the fact that in one of the inkblots, the *subject* reported that he sees a goat skin with drops of blood on the sides, showing that the goat was recently slaughtered. A number of black students in class, including me, challenged her diagnosis and argued that goat skin with blood does not necessarily signify anger, and that it is crucial that the *subject*'s background be taken into consideration before making conclusions. In many African cultures, slaughtering of a goat forms part of many traditional rituals, and upon asking our fellow student, she confirmed that the *subject* was elderly, thereby confirming to us that he might have associated the inkblot with the slaughtering of a goat (in other words, he drew from his lived experience/worldview). This is one of the many examples of how misdiagnosis may happen if we use imported tools uncritically to understand local experiences. Grosfoguel's argument becomes relevant here when he argues that "in western philosophy and sciences the subject that speaks is always hidden, concealed, and erased from the analysis".[1] He further stresses the importance of taking into consideration the geo-political and body-political location of the subject that speaks.

Psychology continues to be guilty of the application of imported knowledge without critically assessing the relevance in other contexts — for example, the South African context. Numerous feminist scholars have argued that as researchers we need to first and foremost acknowledge that as we represent others we do so from a particular location and power structure. With this in mind, it is therefore critical to acknowledge situated knowledges and avoid being quick to pathologize. It is important to ask: what is the position of the subject that speaks? Grosfoguel offers an answer to this when he argues that "by delinking ethnic/racial/sexual epistemic location from the subject that speaks, Western philosophy and sciences are able to produce a myth about a truthful universal knowledge that covers up, that is, conceals who is speaking as well as the geo-political and body-political epistemic location in the structures of colonial power/knowledge from which the subject speaks".[2] This point is further articulated by Pauline Chinn[3] in her work on decolonizing methodologies and indigenous knowledge. Chinn argues that "science as a quest for knowledge developed in the historical context of Europe's search for new lands and economic resources".[4] With a specific focus on the Hawaiian context, Chinn argues that schools were used as vehicles to drive 'monoculturalism' and the idea of a universal truth.

Having had the chance to spend a few years in the Global North, seeing the benefits and having the privilege of observing and experiencing what it is like to study about theories that were developed and spoke to issues that were relevant in the context I found myself in, I was determined and convinced more than ever that psychology and more specifically social psychology in South Africa needs to be decolonized. Continuing to use and apply theories that were developed elsewhere to make sense of people's lived experiences in our writing and teaching in classrooms (social interactions, identity, inter-group relations, gender, and race issues to name but a few) is an example of what Quijano calls "the colonial matrix of power",[5] which assumes one center of producing knowledge and delegitimizing other forms of knowledge production.

With this background in mind, I intend here to discuss how I wrestle with the challenges and dilemmas that I continuously face within my chosen discipline of psychology, and specifically the social psychology sub-discipline. Psychology has been concerned with issues of social justice and the provocation towards action for a more just distribution of resources and strives towards human dignity; however, the lens through which this takes place needs rethinking. There is a need for a critique of the narrow way in which psychology has over the years viewed and theorized social phenomena. For a long time, the discipline of psychology has shied away from alternative ways of exploring people's lived experiences, almost always assuming a universal and singular view of understanding individual and collective experiences.

People's experiences within psychology have for a long time been viewed mostly from a 'pathologizing' standpoint, which, it can been argued, has multiple limitations. Viewed as possible pathology, people's experiences may become universalized, thereby leaving out broader contextual (social, environmental, political, historical, economical, etc.) aspects that have been shown to play a role in the subjective experience of individuals. Psychology has for a long time been quick to diagnose people from an individualistic perspective, almost always positioning the 'problem' within the person. Viewing people's experiences this way occludes how their lived experiences cannot be separated from their histories, cultures, bodies, families, communities; through cognitions, memory, and embodiments; in voice and in silence; and over time.

For over 100 years, so-called depth psychology—Freudian, post-Freudian, Jungian, post-Jungian, Lacanian psychology, phenomenological psychology— has developed practices of recollecting, working-through, symbolizing, and understanding human behavior at an individual level. Unfortunately, many depth psychologists have treated the individual personality as if it were unrelated to a historical and cultural environment. There is a need to step back when we theorize within psychology, and acknowledge the need to critically engage and acknowledge the various contextual aspects that affect people's lives. Questions of power and domination have for a long time been ignored within social psychology theorizing, and as Apfelbaum[6] argues, we cannot claim to represent all if many people remain marginalized, silenced and oppressed by the way we speak and write about them. Martin-Baro,[7] Brinton Lykes,[8] Paulo Freire,[9] Don Foster,[10] and other liberatory psychologists stress the importance of practicing a psychology that is emancipatory and one that acknowledges the psychosocial nature of human experiences. As Liem argues, "offering release to silenced voices might lead to a promotion of "greater self-understanding".[11] Psychological models that attempt to describe human behavior should incorporate the role played by history, politics, class, power and how these interplay for them to be 'relevant' and applicable in various contexts. Failure to do so may lead to universalizing of people's experiences, which tends to be oppressive in nature as it forces people to fit into pre-determined and prescribed labels and categories.

Western Domination of Social Psychology

According to Doxtater, "Euro-scholarship ignores indigenous knowledge for the purpose of promoting its own narrative structures based on Western knowledge that decides what is true".[12] Doxtater further argues that "Western knowledge rests itself on a foundation of *reason* to understand the true nature of the world, yet it also privileges itself as the fiduciary of all knowledge with authority to authenticate or invalidate other knowledge".[13] Drawing from numerous indigenous scholars, Doxtater insists, "Indigenous knowledge is reasonable, deliberate, and useful for making sense of life".[14]

Social psychology as a sub-discipline of psychology, though espousing an expanded purview that considers the social situations in which subjects are found, continues to be populated and dominated by knowledges and theorizing from the West. This is a point also noted by Moscovici in his argument that "US social psychology has been, and still is before us, ahead of us, and around us".[15] It might be helpful at this point to offer some of the ways in which social psychology has been defined and understood. Baron and Byrne—who have written extensively on what social psychology is, whose textbook psychology teachers religiously keep prescribing to students, now in its 13th edition—define social psychology as "a field of study that focuses on the manner in which the behavior, feelings, thoughts of one individual are influenced and determined by the behavior and/or characteristics of others".[16] Later on, in 1997, the authors offered a "reworked" definition where they argued that "social psychology is the scientific field that seeks to understand the nature and causes of individual behavior and thought in social situations".[17] As can be seen from the redefining of what the sub-discipline is about, there seems to be a continuous re-thinking of what social psychology is. Looking at these definitions, there seems to be a shift from a person being influenced specifically/directly by others in his/her environment to a broader focus on social situations. It is also critical to note that feelings (emotions, affect) have lost space in the re-definition. Speaking about the importance of context when theorizing, Moscovici argues that:

The real advance made by American social psychology was not so much in its empirical methods or in its theory construction as in the fact that it took for its theme of research and for the contents of its theories the issues of its own society. Its merit was as much in its techniques as in translating the problems of American society into psychological terms and in making them an object of scientific inquiry.[18]

This argument that Moscovici raises highlights the importance of conducting research on one's own society, making sense of issues that arise within one's context and constructing theories based on research findings. I think it is critical to point to how theories that were constructed in America were based on "translating the problems of American society". Paying attention to this point enables us to see the danger or problematic nature of importing American theories without taking into consideration how they were constructed. For many years, the practice and teaching of social psychology within South Africa relied on these imported texts without critically looking at the challenges of decontextualized application.

One of the prominent South African social psychologists, Kopano Ratele[19] argues that while most of what social psychology in South Africa focuses on emanates from the United States, it should be noted that there are some voices from Europe which also found their way into Psychology lecture halls down here in the South, for example, Henri Tajfel and his theory of social identity, which was later taken further by John Turner, and Serge Moscovici with his theory of social representations. Ratele[20] (speaking about the social psychology textbook that he edited in 2003) informs us that:

Although there has been social psychological research since the beginnings of psychological studies in South Africa in the early twentieth century, and specifically since the 1920s, the present volume is only the second one to be published on social psychology out of South Africa. The first volume, published in 1991, consisted of a collection of 14 chapters by 12 South African psychologists and was edited by Donald Foster and Johan Louw-Potgieter.

The above assertion by Ratele highlights the challenge that continues to face the discipline. It is an illustration of how knowledge continues to be imported. A question that could be asked at this point in furthering Ratele's assertion is: what epistemic lenses do South African psychology scholars write from? As a student and teacher of psychology I continue to be troubled by the fact that very few institutions prescribe South African authored and published texts on social psychology. Even more troubling is how most of these locally authored texts continue to mimic American-produced texts. I need to step back at this point and plead guilty to the offence of continuing to feed my students Western epistemologies. It is important to acknowledge that as we wrestle with the project of how to decolonize our discipline, we are active players in perpetuating this continuous colonizing of our students' learning through feeding them theories that may not speak to their lives as they understand them. In her book entitled *The Psychic Life of Power: Theories in Subjection* (1997), Butler sought to explain how conformity and attachment to subjection emerged.[21] Butler's theory of subjection emerged within the context of a concern about how women, including those who have embraced feminist theories, developed an "attachment to pernicious and subordinating norms of femininity" that persists "alongside a rational critique of those very norms in and on the same self". Butler's theory is a useful one that explains the ways in which ambivalent processes of becoming a subject emerge in and through subjection to power structures and relations. It helps in explaining the emergence of interpellated subjecthood that is passionate about some of those technologies of subjection it is expected to resist and defeat. Critiquing ourselves and reflecting on the reasons for our actions might assist us as we seek to "undo" or "un-think" the taken for granted and the normative. What are the challenges we face as we seek to re-define social psychology in our local context? What is stopping us from changing the faces of theorists in our books? The stubbornness of refusing to change and sticking to the "mainstream" has to change. Some of the challenges of daring to go against the mainstream are the possibility of not getting published or being offered space to bring in alternatives.

Social psychology suffers from what Gordon[22] calls "epistemic colonization", which speaks of how ways of knowing continue to be claimed/assumed to only come from the West or Europe. To where shall people return — where does decolonizing begin? The assumption/erasure/ignoring the history of the black people (specifically in South Africa) strips them of their history. I would like to draw our attention to what Gordon[23] calls "disciplinary decadence". In his discussion of methodological assumptions, Gordon argues that "a danger emerges where the human subject is squeezed into the disciplinary presumptions by which it is studied. The discipline would, in other words, become deontological or absolute; its methodological assumptions would be presumed isomorphic with the intentional life of its subject as well as reality itself".[24] This is the disciplinary decadence presumption where inter/multidisciplinary is not offered space. As a way to offer an alternative, Mignolo[25] points us to what he calls "situated knowledges", where various methodologies are given space and embraced.

Mignolo warns that it is not about what we teach but how we teach it as well. He asserts, "I have been supporting in the past those who maintain that it is not enough to change the content of the conversation, that it is the essence to change the terms of the conversation".[26] Mignolo problematizes the notion of what he calls "the detached observer", which he says is understood as "the neutral seeker of truth and objectivity who at the same time controls the disciplinary rules and puts himself or herself in a privileged position to evaluate and dictate".[27]

The challenges of coloniality in social psychology are not only in the theorizing but in the methodologies as well. The pre-determined "scientific designs" that have been created elsewhere should be troubled and re-imagined, taking into consideration how contexts and experiences should determine how phenomena can be explained and understood. The dependent and restrictive research designs that have for a long time been taken as the norm within mainstream psychology do not only influence, if not straightjacket, what can be taught but also what can be published as well. Alternative or "different" designs are often perceived as somewhat suspect and not responding to what psychology seeks to do.

Imposing meaning or theorizing on people's experiences without acknowledging context is a form of what one of the theoretical psychologists, Thomas Teo, calls "epistemological violence".[28] This is a form of imposing/importing knowledges without regarding people's lived experience and meaning-making through their own perspective. The challenge of taking alien experiences as the human standard should be viewed as problematic as it leads to everyone else having to fit into pre-determined knowledges. In his article entitled *Indigenous Knowledge in the Decolonial Era*, Doxtater[29] argues that "the colonial-power-knowledge communicates particular cultural presupposition that elevate Western knowledge as real knowledge while ignoring other knowledge". Western knowledge has been perceived and taken as the master narrative for a long time. This master narrative has been and continues in some ways to be the well wherein the quest and thirst for knowledge can be quenched. This perception needs to be challenged by highlighting counter narratives and new alternative ecologies of knowledge that can be made possible by epistemic pluralism. It is crucial to acknowledge and offer space for the springs, dams and oceans of other knowledge, situated and multiple knowledges that exist outside the West.

In an interview on re-imagining psychology in Africa, Dr Moagi-Gulubani asserted that "it is imperative for African thought and experience to be incorporated into prevailing explanatory models of human behavior in order to acknowledge the African people and their experience." She urged African psychologists to avoid perpetuating a history of imperial psychology and exterminating the complex and dynamic contexts within which behaviours are learned.[30] There is therefore a need to put on a different epistemic lens that allows space for lived experiences of the "other" to find expression in the production of knowledge in psychology. As a discipline, psychology lends itself to multiple ways of viewing the world as influenced by contact, context and the environment within which we exist. Enculturation and socialization play a crucial role in how people will behave and react towards others in their society, and these are issues that have to be taken into consideration when theorizing.

Social psychology has for a long time studied human behavior in controlled/ enclosed environments where behavior could be observed, and from these observations, theories and generalizations were made. One of the challenges with this method of study is that people might not behave the same way as they would in their natural environment. Some of the theories that were "born" from such experiments were Henri Tajfel's theory of social identity and Stanley Milgram's theory of obedience, and the bystander effect by Latane and Darley, to name but a few. I will now briefly discuss the bystander effect:

The bystander effect theory was constructed by Latane and Darley in New York City in America in 1968. These two New York psychologists were prompted by a newspaper article that reported on a woman being killed while 38 people witnessed and did nothing to help. The two psychologists were intrigued by this report and set out to conduct a number of experiments looking at the reasons behind people choosing to assist or not assist during an emergency. They conducted a number of experiments that sought to understand helping behavior. They concluded and theorized that the bystander effect (people are less likely to provide help when they are in groups than when they are alone) influences helping behavior. This theory made its way into numerous social psychology textbooks and has been uncritically used and applied without acknowledging the history and context wherein it was constructed. There have been numerous critics of this theory (most notably Cherry,[31] and Manning, Levine and Collins[32]) highlighting how issues of gender, race and history were not taken into consideration by these psychologists when they formulated their theory. When looking at reasons why bystanders may choose to help or not, it is crucial to take into consideration their backgrounds, cultures and experiences. Such aspects are usually left outside the experiment rooms, thereby assuming that people can be stripped of their context/lived experiences in the quest for universality.

By embracing and taking on a decolonial stance, social psychology can embrace the politics of pluriversality. According to Banazak and Ceja, pluriversality is "an attempt to make visible and viable a multiplicity of knowledges, forms of being, and visions of the world. Pluriversality is equality-in-difference, the possibility that many worlds can fit in one world. It is the future alternative of modernity/coloniality".[33] For a long time psychology has focused on the individual and an assumed universal way of viewing the world. By prescribing standardized manuals such as the DSM (diagnostic statistical manual) to diagnose, categorise and label behaviour, the discipline assumes that a recipe can be used to understand people and predict behaviour in the same way in various contexts. Adopting a pluriversal view might assist the discipline to step back and not be quick to label.

What Happened to the 'Social' in Social Psychology?

> Psychology of liberation attempts to work with people in context through strategies that enhance awareness of oppression and of the ideologies and structural inequality that have kept them subjugated and oppressed, thereby collaborating with them in developing critical analyses and engaging in a transforming praxis.[34]

In one of the studies I conducted on the phenomenon of suffering, I highlight how there is minimal work in social psychology on the "social nature of suffering", which is symptomatic of the retreat from the social in social psychology. The individualizing and biologizing of pain/trauma and the refusal to look at resistance/silence/violence has contributed to the exclusion of people's social experiences of suffering. This was also noted by Billig[35] in his argument that there is depopulation within social psychology where individuals are treated as interchangeable and people's lived experience is rarely acknowledged. Billig further argues that "to understand the rhetorical meaning of discourse, it is often necessary to take into account what is left unsaid".[36] Billig asserts that relying heavily on "statistical operations" and using "averaged group score" adds to the elimination of the individual and produces a "disembodied unpopulated psychology". Involving the viewpoints of the people we study, and acknowledging their voices and language, might lead to a social psychology that does not seek only to generalize, but one that recognizes the importance of people's social experiences as they understand them. Drawing from various psychology scholars, Fine reminds us that "social psychology has a long, and often buried, tradition of research that reveals and challenges social justice, research designed to provoke action for a more just distribution for resources and dignity".[37] With this in mind, one would assume that social psychology would take on issues of individual and social suffering as crucial points to consider when theorizing, but this continues to be absent. Cherry[38] argues that in the quest to generalize, social psychology makes bold claims that are often decontextualized and disregard history. By acknowledging context and putting on the critical lens, social psychology might better critique issues of oppression and resistance.[39]

Psychology in South Africa continues to rely on theories from the West, and for this reason there is a need for re-thinking how and where knowledge is produced, and a move towards an acknowledgement of local knowledges that can assist us in theorizing from our local context. In my teaching of community psychology, for example, I incorporate issues of gender, power, class, politics and history and how these intersect with psychological issues such as poverty, homelessness, violence, HIV and AIDS. For us to be able to think of ways to deal with issues that affect people and their well-being daily it is necessary to draw from local experiences, and to look at how people define and understand their circumstances. Theory and methodologies within the sub-discipline of social psychology need a critical look and problematizing. The consistent quantifying of people's experiences and assumptions for generalizability can be perceived as tools that contribute towards the colonizing of knowledge.

It is crucial to interrogate who determines what is worthy of being included when theorizing about social issues, and people's lives in general. There is a need to acknowledge the constant relationship that exists between the personal and the social and how the two continually influence each other. Social psychology needs to venture to places where the light is a little dim and be willing to move towards uncomfortable spaces that do not have clear cut answers.[40]

Fine[41] offers an invitation to conduct critical research that does not only focus on the researched, but places the researcher in a position of accountability.

Because psychology is a discipline that tackles issues of human behavior/ interactions in social contexts and seeks to attain social justice, it therefore becomes important to think about its decolonization and how it should take seriously the fact that social issues cannot be understood in isolation as they intersect with one another. One of the steps towards decolonizing is acknowledging that "a psychology that wants to be taken seriously by the society it seeks to address cannot but be rooted in that society, yet should also avoid ingratiating itself with the powerful social groups".[42] It is critical to draw from the work of liberatory psychologists who highlight the importance of understanding people from their own point of view, and avoid 'speaking for others'.

Creating Space to Decolonize

Any social psychology must, by definition, be a psychology of a society—that is to say, to be truly social, it must be concerned with

specific contexts, contexts inhabited by real, living people; people in-
habiting bodies, living in specific communities, with particular histories,
not abstractions [...]. If social psychology has not grown out of the
social context it seeks to understand and engage with, and if it regards
itself as the psychology of every society on earth, then it cannot be a
psychology that is appropriate for any one social context.[43]

When we embark on the project of knowledge-making, we need to ask ourselves, knowledge-making for whose benefit? For the advancement of what/
whom? It is therefore critical to check why we do the work that we do and
how we do it — for whose benefit? There is a need to engage in what Mignolo
calls "epistemic disobedience", where people are offered space to be agents
of their own lives and experiences. Ratele[44] points to how:

It is perhaps worth reiterating that definitions are never entirely neutral
and innocent, because how a discipline is defined determines what it
regards as worth studying, as well as which questions it asks and
which answers it seeks. And the questions it asks and the answers it
searches for serve as lenses through which it perceives and analyses
objects, events, processes, interactions, and relationships. In general,
a definition of a discipline directs the attention and activities of those
working within in. It determines what is important to look for, where
to look for it, and how to go about looking for it. Having accepted a
definition, some aspects of objects, events, processes, and so on become salient while others do not.

Drawing from this elaborate explanation from Ratele, the definition of the discipline carries powers of inclusion and exclusion, allowing those who come
up with the definition to determine the process. Many of our disciplines continue to be stubborn as they want to be the authority voice in knowledge- and
meaning-making. There is a need for conversations across disciplines where
cross pollination of knowledge and theorizing can take place. The situation in
psychology is so chronic that even among the sub-disciplines there are hardly
any conversations taking place. With this in mind, it is critical that the work
starts from within. There is a need for an interdisciplinary lens where constructing theories and knowledge does not happen in a vacuum.

At this point I would like to join Doxtater[45] as he calls for a decolonial era
that aims to "emancipate Indigenous knowledge of governance, sovereignty,
agriculture, architecture, mathematics, astronomy, communications, medicine,
and healing". Grosfoguel[46] leaves us with a haunting thought when he argues
that "we still live in a colonial world and we need to break from the narrow

ways of thinking about colonial relations, in order to accomplish the unfinished and incomplete twentieth century dream of decolonization". I see this as a challenge to us as scholars as we contribute to knowledge production for future generations; we need to stop recycling borrowed theories and epistemologies, and move towards the dark places that many do not dare to approach in the quest for providing knowledge that is relevant and created with and in consultation with those whom we claim to represent.

In a talk given in the department of psychology at The University of South Africa (March 28, 2013), Ramose offered the analogy of a mirror and the telling of a story. He asked: what is it that reflects back at you when you look at the mirror? He linked this to knowledge and construction of theories. Do you see yourself in the story being told? Can you relate to what you are required to study or read in the books prescribed for you or that you prescribe for others? Ramose argues that there needs to be space offered for multiple and sometimes contesting paradigms. He unpacks the notion of what research is, as it is through it that methodologies and theories come to being. We have a responsibility to critique and facilitate a space for multiplicity that draws from context.

I have had the opportunity to conduct research, analyze data, and make interpretations of the findings. While this has been a useful enterprise, I cannot help but think about my role as a contributor towards epistemological violence ... how many of my participants' voices are audible in my reporting of what they shared with me? To what extent did I treat them as the "other" by speaking on their behalf? These are some of the issues I constantly battle with in my pursuit of knowledge creation. How much of our data allow space for multiple interpretations? The attempt for universality and quest for generalizability does not leave enough space for various ways of meaning-making. It is therefore important that we constantly step back and critically look at our work and who/what it speaks to.

One of the ways to move towards decolonization of knowledge is acknowledging and drawing from already existing perceptions/views of the world as people experience and understand it. We need to take seriously how people make sense of their everyday experiences, for example, their construction of identity, understanding of the notion of obedience, and their conceptualization of self in relation to others. We cannot create knowledge about people without them; we need to strive towards creating knowledge with and from people's own perspective and view of the world. Theory cannot and should not be looked at in isolation; it should be looked at within the context it is ultimately used/applied. We need to ask ... whose theory and knowledge is privileged?

Conclusion

Social psychology continues to be a critical sub-discipline of psychology which aims to interrogate and take seriously issues of social justice. In this chapter, I attempted to highlight the problematic nature of a universal voice that claims to be globally representative through theories that are deemed objective and translatable in various contexts. There is a need to critique the lenses we use when theorizing, to take seriously the voice of the *subject* (subaltern), and to acknowledge and dismantle the coloniality of knowledge that continues to be Eurocentric. There needs to be a decolonizing of knowledge so that more than one centre of knowing is realized.

References

1. Grosfoguel, R. (2007). The epistemic decolonial turn. *Cultural Studies, 21*(2–2), 211–223.

2. Ibid.

3. Chinn, P. W. U. (2006). Decolonizing methodologies and indigenous knowledge: The role of culture, place and personal experience in professional development. *Journal of Research in Science Teaching, 44*(9), 1247–1268.

4. Ibid., p. 1249.

5. Quijano, A. (2000). Coloniality of power, ethnocentrism, and Latin America. *NEPANTLA, 1*(3), 533–580.

6. Apfelbaum, E. R. (2009). Against the tide: Making waves and breaking silences. In L. P. Mos (Ed.), *History of psychology in autobiography, path in psychology* (pp. 2–35). London, England: Springer.

7. Martin-Baro, I. (1994). Writings for a liberation psychology. In A. Aron & S. Corne (Eds.), *United States of America*. Harvard College.

8. Lykes, B. (1997). Activist participatory research among the Maya of Guatemala: Constructing meanings from situated knowledge. *Journal of Social Sciences, 53*(4), 725–746.

9. Freire, P. (2004). *Pedagogy of hope*. London, England: The Continuum Publishing Company.

10. Foster, D. (2004). Liberation psychology. In D. Hook (Ed.), *Critical Psychology* (pp. 559–602). Cape Town, South Africa: UCT Press.

11. Liem, R. (2003). History, trauma, and identity: The legacy of the Korean War for Korean Americans. *Amerasia Journal, 29*(3), 1–19.

12. Doxtater, M. G. (2004). Indigenous knowledge in the decolonial era. *The American Indian Quarterly, 28*(3–4), 618–633.

13. Ibid., p. 618.

14. Ibid., p. 620.

15. Moscovici, S. (1972). Society and theory in social psychology. In J.Israel & H. Tajfel (Eds.), *The context of social psychology: Critical assessment* (pp. 17–68). London, England: Academic Press.

16. Baron, R. A., & Byrne, D. (1981). *Social psychology* (3rd ed.). Boston, MA: Allyn and Bacon, p. 7.

17. Ibid., p. 6.

18. As cited in Ratele, K., (2003). Introduction: A psychology of a society. In K. Ratele (Ed.), Social psychology: Identities and relationships. Lansdowne: UCT Press, p.12.

19. Ibid.

20. Ibid., p. 9.

21. Butler, J. (1997). *The psychic life of power: Theories in subjection.* Stanford, CA: Stanford University Press.

22. Gordon, L. R. (2007). Through the hellish zone of nonbeing: thinking through Fanon, disaster, and the damned of the earth. *Human Architecture: Journal of the Sociology of Self-Knowledge, V* [Special Double Issue], 5–12.

23. Ibid., p. 8.

24. Ibid.

25. Mignolo, W. D. (2009). Epistemic disobedience, independent thought and de-colonial freedom. *Theory, Culture & Society, 26*(7–8), 1–23.

26. Ibid., p. 4.

27. Ibid.

28. Teo, T. (2008). Empirical race psychology and the hermeneutics of epistemological violence. *Human Studies, 34*, 237–255.

29. Doxtater, p. 619.

30. As cited in Matoane & Hagen, 2011, p. 32.

31. Cherry, F. (1995). *The "stubborn particulars" of social psychology: Essays on the research process.* Florence, KY: Taylor & Frances/Routledge.

32. Manning, R., Levine, M., & Collins, A. (2007). The Kitty Genovese murder and the social psychology of helping. *American Psychologist, 62*(6), 555–562.

33. Banazak, G. A., & Ceja, L. R. (2008). The challenges and promise of decolonial thought to Biblical interpretation. *Postscripts, 4*(1), 113–127.

34. Comas-Diaz, L., Lykes, M. B., & Alacrn, R. D. (1998). Ethnic conflict and the psychology of liberation in Guatemala, Peru, and Puerto Rico. *American Psychologist, 53*(7), 778–792.

35. Billig, M. (1994). Repopulating the depopulated pages of social psychology. *Theory and Psychology, 4*(3), 307–335.

36. Ibid., p. 318, 322.

37. Fine, M. (2006). Bearing witness: Methods for researching oppression and resistance — a textbook for critical research. *Social justice Research, 19*(1), 83–108.

38. Cherry.

39. Ibid.

40. Fine, p. 84.

41. Ibid.

42. Ratele, p. 13.

43. Ibid.

44. Ibid., p. 11.

45. Doxtater, p. 629.

46. Grosfoguel, p. 221.

Part III

Methods, Methodology, and Subjectivity

Chapter 10

Decolonising African Political Science and the Question of the Relevance of the Discipline for Development

Fidelis Allen

Introduction

Since political science emerged as a field of study in the nineteenth century, there have been growing narratives on its development. There have been interesting success stories, too, with regards to research breakthroughs.[1] One concept used to describe the field's integrative tendency in an era of globalisation is 'developmental historicism'.[2] It explains the formative years in which the field, from a global sense, sought to look like a cocktail or blend of national political science. Developmental historicism was at once the point of departure for the discipline. African political science was non-existent at the time though, and like other examples of national political science, would emerge later under the influence of American political science. Worthy of note is the fact of American political science itself being heavily influenced by British political science in ways that completely blurred any distinction between them. Interestingly, it — American political science — started what can be seen as a decolonisation process from the influence of British political science after the First World War. It sought to diverge from the idealism and vigorous Marxism which defined sections of British political science to neopositivism and empiricism. These compartments, however, are not watertight, as it were. New approaches to the study of politics began to emerge after the Second World War. Besides,

American political science would ultimately emerge as a hegemonic force with visions of a universal field of study. Consequently, some scholars have simply referred to global political science as American political science.

Despite known achievements in many areas of the field, including its traditional and new sub-fields, there has been a growing intellectual dissatisfaction with political science. The field has made huge contributions in several quarters. For example, the World Bank now depends much on field work undertaken by scholars including political scientists. Alt et al.,[3] for example, argue that game theory has influenced security policies even though it may have had implications for other problems. A number of methods or approaches in political studies — such as ethnography, qualitative, historical and so on — are being utilised to test key hypotheses in the field and facilitate policymaking. Criticisms levelled against American political science have formed the bulk of what can be seen as critique of political science, in my view. It also shows the problem with the extant level of influence American political science has had on the field and on political science of countries worldwide. The most piercing knock on the discipline has come from within. Thomas Hook, for example, argues that:

> [O]bjective description and precise measurement have become their ideals. [...] The result has been at the worst a mechanistic interpretation [...] and implied a pure positivism, scientistic rather than scientific, and often including materialistic and relativist dogmas.[4]

The claim to scientific objectivity and precise measurement by definition is at once a source of criticism. It raises the old question of the superiority of positivist ontological and epistemological positions to interpretive or constructivist positions. American political science encouraged the thinking that positivism was superior to interpretive logic. Fortunately, that matter seems comfortably settled with the admittance of many that both methodologies share the same logic and do legitimately contribute to the production of knowledge on a general note. Otherwise, American political science has inspired accusations of dogma capable of calling into question the scientific status of national political science that pays less attention to positivism. The question of rigor and relevance comes out clearly.[5] To move up the ladder of relevance in the development of the continent through analysis, African political science has to be able to continue to reconcile this divide and play down the elevation of one against the other.

"Early in its development, political science established itself as part of modern secular authority, with something to say about government and politics. This achievement did not, though, lead to much noticeable impact on governance and policy, with the exception of administrative reforms," notes Kenneth Prewith.[6] The social value of political science in terms of policy impact has never been discounted. Meanwhile, American political science's transnational exchanges have had implications not only for how political scientists in other parts of the world practise the profession, but also for the type of policy impact expected—neoliberal policies and democracy. The influence is both enormously inflictive and a blessing. It has had severe implications for the type of training new entrants in the field receive by way of education, and for the structure and content of what is studied. It has caused generational transfer of Western ontological positions and epistemology, deterred originality, and enslaved some who think about political processes in the developing world only in terms of structures and practices handed down through Western political knowledge on Africa's postcoloniality. These have in turn shaped the capacity of national political science in developing countries like those in Africa to play an important role in the development of the continent through research, teaching and training.

An inferiority complex is also part of the outcome. Accepting without questioning standards or criteria set by Western scholarship for analyses of political structures and processes reflects this inferiority complex. It speaks clearly about the hegemony of American political science.[7]

The critical point in this section of the argument is that Africa is rich in traditional concepts, ideas and values for peaceful co-existence. Many African communities have rich histories of traditional peaceful approaches to resolving conflicts. The sub-field of international relations, of late, has become intensely critiqued. For example, Manuela Lavinas Picq argues that it is guilty of hegemonic tendencies and the production of knowledge detached from the world it is "supposed to understand".[8] The danger for policymaking and positive change in society can be grave. Worse, some theories in the sub-field have an unacceptable inability to adequately explain African conditions. African international relations is hardly accommodated by core international relations theories. If we accept international relations as a discipline of power relations among state actors in the global system, then we need to understand the nature of power dynamics in the discipline. We need to be able to probe the extent of power projected through knowledge on developing countries. In the words of Kate Manzo, "just how independent of imperial power relations of power is the knowledge produced by modern disciplines"?[9]

Following from this, creating empirical indicators for political concepts such as 'good governance,' for example, can be a challenging exercise if we remember that this concept emanated from Western political scholarship to explain political and governance problems in developing countries. And as part of Western aid projects using aid to bargain for democracy, the concept was implicated in the given power relations that Manzo describes as imperial. Imposition of these concepts, understood in some cases as instruments for replicating institutional practices in the developing world, spells a need for massive reconceptualisation. Therefore, until the concept of good governance is properly domesticated or decolonised via reconceptualisation, it contributes only marginal value to analysis or research into institutions and practices envisioned for the development of Africa, and serves only as a power instrument for cultural, political and economic domination.

The current global political, social and economic processes are knowledge driven. This has large-scale implications for the recruitment of new entrants and the strengthening of capacity of older members of the field. Among the need for critically considering what the individual and society actually need in a dynamic world is equipping the new entrants with the history of certain concepts and ideas that have long carried values that oppose citizens' welfare. Some of these concepts are suspect and capable of hindering good analysis. That is to say, both rigour and relevance have unique places in political science. None should be sacrificed for the other.

The point being made is that knowledge produced by scholars in the field fails to connect with reality. The hegemony of American political science results in unquestioning acceptance of Western concepts, methodologies and results of research loaded with Western materialist values. This is hindering original thinking about development in Africa. Claude Ake's thoughts ring out very clearly.[10] His thesis on the political development of Africa implicates Western social science research or analyses on Africa. He sees it as imperialism. As he argues:

> A third aspect of the imperialist character of the theory of political development and political science writings on the Third World in general is that they try to impose capitalist values. Like other Western political science writings on the Third World the theory of political development assumes a capitalist view of man and of society, and tries to pass this on as universal truth.[11]

From the above argument, Western political science is distrusted in many quarters and can hardly pass as a complete science for explaining development in Africa. Capitalism in the guise of neoliberalism is ambitiously restrictive of alternative ideas. The bulk of African political science has related comfortably with it and served as an instrument for endorsing it in practical political settings where political elites call the shots. Neoliberal policies have had a field day as a result of this trend. Political science, especially during the military eras in Africa, easily manifested this neoliberal character. It has continued un-abated even after multiparty democracy began to take root in the continent. From the foregoing, political science does have substantial value and impact, but it is at once problematic when it comes to driving development policy in the context of African conditions.

What is the implication of all this for African political science when it comes to considering the role of the field in the development of the continent? This is a crucial question for thinking about or exploring the kind of political science that Africa needs to be able to increase its role in the development of the dis-cipline and African political conditions. The question is also: what kind of po-litical science does Africa need to tackle its development challenges? Reflecting on African political science in the context of the overall character of global political science and development is necessary.

On the Question of Development

Let us examine briefly the kind of development analysis prevailing in po-litical science in relation to the type of development Africa needs. Development in the continent has been approached from a growth perspective. It can now be easily said that about seventeen countries in Africa have maintained fair or interesting growth rates in recent times. This is because these countries have hovered between 5 to 7 percent annual growth, measured in terms of gross domestic product (GDP). Growth itself is a concept that predominantly rep-resents the values and interests of Western capitalist societies and Africa's elite classes. The growth approach is deceptive and neglectful of social and eco-nomic inequality. For many countries in the developing world with an inter-esting annual growth rate, there has been increasing worry about the problem of inequality. Nigeria was mentioned recently by the Standard Chartered Bank Development Index as one of nine countries in the world with improving de-velopment records.[12]

This type of pro-growth assessment of development is hardly challenged by political scientists lucky to have found themselves in a position of power in Africa. There are inherent paradoxes such as wealth versus affluence, rich versus poor, and the fact that the lower prong of society has consistently shown signs of lacking the capacity for social mobility, which the evaluators under-mined. Sadly, rather than impact policy, the section of the political science community that dared to challenge the growth analysis of development has faced opposition from the political class or suffered in one way or another at the hands of those in this class. Incidentally this class is also at the forefront of driving neoliberal policies in the continent. Despite the positive reports of development in Nigeria, the bulk of rural populations have continued to suffer a severe lack of basic social services, even as the market trajectory increasingly dominates public service delivery.

Development is seen more or less as Westernisation of political and economic systems in developing countries. As earlier mentioned, this is the cornerstone of Claude Ake's critique of Western social science as imperialism. Western analyses or knowledge on developing countries promote the interest of capitalist values. Western cultural, social, political and economic values are projected through social science knowledge, concepts and methodologies. The imperialist characterisation speaks to the question of colonisation of the field. In this sense, modernisation theory can be viewed as a strategic formulation for the enthronement of Western models of development in developing countries, or as a prescription for the development pathway in developing countries, especially those seeking to recover from a bleak colonial past.

Rather than take into consideration the interest of the majority of citizens as well as the poor, pro-growth development has fed a liberal and neoliberal political science knowledge infrastructure which in turn has progressively driven policy in Africa. The net result has been a lack of satisfactory social character of African political science. Many political scientists who are aware of this limitation, who once professed a need for alternative models, sadly get easily co-opted away when given opportunities to serve in policymaking positions.

One aspect of the problem is the opposition of political elites to political science that focuses on alternatives to neo-liberalism. They see such proposals as radicalism and unnecessary. Even when the neoliberal order continues to reinforce and widen the gap between the rich and poor, political elites woo political scientists away with political appointments where necessary or reject them and their alternative ideas. In the circumstances, a good number of them have taken this neoliberal value to government and directed programmes driven by it. Not that this in itself constitutes any evil. The outcome has been detestable in many areas of the political and economic life of citizens. Intellectual inputs of political scientists and others in the rest of the social sciences that propped up the failed Structural Adjustment Programmes which started in the 1980s in countries of the continent remain a sound critique of political science. Worse, the pro-growth conceptualisation of development that a significant section of the African political science community has accepted is victory for American political science; efforts must be made to reverse this through extensive reconceptualisation.

The continent continues to face diverse socio-economic and political challenges. These challenges, ranging from political instability and violent conflict to climate change in many parts of the continent, are critical elements of the political science discourse on development in Africa. The lack of basic social services such as affordable healthcare and education, poor infrastructure, insecurity and so on have remained key concerns. Despite the transition to multiparty democracy which began in the 1980s, ethnic, religious and economic conflicts have not subsided in many of these countries. Only five African countries, namely, Botswana, Mauritius, Senegal, and Zimbabwe practised multiparty democracy in the '80s. Since then, beginning in the 1990s, nearly all African countries have made substantial progress in terms of transition from authoritarian political systems to multiparty democracy. Without a doubt, this ought to be a blessing. It ought to engender significant improvement in the wellbeing of citizens, political rights and consolidation of democracy. But many of these countries' political elites either did not quite embrace the democratic principles handed down by Western political science or failed to integrate African democratic elements that characterised many pre-colonial African political systems. Pre-colonial traditional political practices in some parts of Africa were driven by values that sought to promote democratic participation and the welfare of citizens. Rather than researching this in order to find a way to integrate these practices with modern democratic practices, African political science has neglected much of it. Many countries in the continent practising multiparty democracy have therefore continued to show signs of retrogression. "Severe economic stagnation and decline in most African economies served as the internal spark for political discontent," notes Peter J. Schraeder.[13] Events in West Africa, where the war on terrorism in countries like Nigeria and the Sahel have added new dimensions to the development crisis, demonstrate a need for African political science to look more into the urgency of contributing more to resolving these crisis. The point therefore is for African political science to analyse and understand what fundamentally the problem of democracy and development in Africa is. The appearance of the democratic wave of the 1990s and its reversal shortly thereafter suggest the fundamentally faulty science of Western democracy. Probing this science in order to identify what is best for the continent should be the concern of African political science.

Broader Implications of Epistemic Alienation

The point I have been making is, political science has been dominated by American political science. This incapacitates African political science in many ways, including by burdening it with values imposed through concepts, methodologies and knowledge. It has bred an inferiority complex in the developing world and continued to promote knowledge that speaks insufficiently to reality within the African context. African political science is used loosely here to mean a body of knowledge that not only seeks to understand the realm of politics on the national and international fronts, but to also influence the character of practical politics in the continent, and by so doing, help close gaps between principle and practice. Since the field provides the tool box for searching for good government and good citizens,[14] continued acceptance of this burden can only amount to sustained use of Western political science intellectual lenses that cannot always apply to the African situation. Some of these lenses are disconnected from the African socio-economic, political and cultural context.[15] Knowledge produced through them, in many instances, makes little sense and contribution to real development.

As can be inferred, a wide array of gaps between American and African socio-economic, cultural and political contexts exists. The same applies to European political science, which has equally gained steady influence on African political science. African political leaders who simply imported political ideas and political systems that prevailed in the former colonisers' countries saw that there was no foundation for these systems to easily succeed in many African countries without due consideration for what is needed. They were also not intended to succeed without these considerations. American and European political science play far-reaching roles, often not properly analysed. In other words, the European and US intellectual contexts on social, economic and political problems have continued to serve as models on which African scholarship must base analyses. Only little can be expected as gain in terms of addressing the unique African situation or environment. Richard Peet and Elaine Hartwick referred to it as intellectual dependency theory. "This intellectual dependence entails export of raw data from the Third World to the First where its surplus (generalised knowledge) is realized as theories and then exported back to the Third World as pearls of wisdom," note Peet and Hartwick.[16]

Indigenization of social science, suggested by Peet and Hartwick[17] as a solution to this problem of dependence, "means more than mere adjustment of methods and reconceptualisation of concepts to fit with non-Western environment and problems." It means an epistemic break with Western epistemic and methodological traditions. According to these scholars, indigenization means "instead, deriving scientific theories, concepts and methodologies from the histories, cultures, and consciousness of non-Western rather than Western civilizations." This by no means implies wholesale rejection of Western ideas, concepts, and methodologies merely because they are Western, but rejection of the idea that they are the only ideas, concepts and tools of analysis to be applied to understand every other situation. It is the rejection of Western social science's darker side, which Ake calls imperialism, the tendency to negate other ways of knowing in order to maintain its hegemony over ways of thinking. It simply means that it is irrational to unquestionably accept Western values paraded as concepts, methodologies and knowledge in global political science. For it only goes to show the extent to which African political science has depended intellectually on external ideas for the fixing of the continent's many problems. The idea is not necessarily to cast out one hegemony to replace it with another. Attaining an epistemic plural intellectual climate in which African political science can navigate in its own rights should be the goal.

What Is to Be Done?

Decolonise Orientation and Methodology

Education remains critical. Political science and international relations, for example, need a different orientation. The myth of scientific objectivity and its contested nature imply a need to promote methodologies and knowledge that inspire alternative models. Regarding the role of education, curriculum developers should aim to raise new entrants in the field that can theorise African international relations. To the extent that students have merely followed the path of ideas and theories passed on as universal truths by American political science, the circle of disconnection of knowledge from reality will continue. A process through education that furnishes gradual and basic historical and political analyses of the development of the field in the 21st century is not only necessary, but the discipline has to be more responsive to the needs of the African people.

This will entail systematic reconceptualisation of the language of African political science, issues and development challenges. The content of research outputs and what is studied in the field have to be addressed or reviewed regularly in line with the changing dynamics of political processes across countries in the continent. Decolonisation of political science knowledge infrastructure calls into question the validity of a political science whose concepts are irrelevant for tackling issues that affect the development role which the African extraction of global political science ought to be playing. Western neoliberal values embedded in concepts, methodologies and findings by political science researchers stand in opposition to the myth of science which the field at the same time makes claim to. A rational African approach will help in these processes. This process should begin with clarifying or reconceptualising development. The concept is erroneously seen as a process of transplanting or embracing Western models and processes of socio-economic and political change in Africa. This modernisation outlook has proved to be defective.

African political science has to be able intensify its promotion of analyses that look into the prospects of alternative proposals that speak to the poor and real needs of society while lessening its accent on the growth approach, without attaching itself to known Western radicalised and neoliberal models. In any case, existing neoliberal knowledge infrastructure has proven to be inimical to the poor in many sectors of the continent. To decolonise in this context will include indigenisation and critical assessment of global political science in the context of what is suitable or realistic for Africa.

Regular authentic analysis of political issues is needed. Politicians cannot be left to drive the process. As is generally known, societies' countless problems — for example, social, economic, political and cultural — require relevant political space to tackle. This entails deployment of politics, proper understanding of its processes and outcome matter. The seeming lack of a decolonised and established profession of political science accustomed to thinking clearly about these problems and their possible solutions in Africa is a threat to the continent's political future and serious enough to warrant concerns. Political science, right from the beginning, has been framed as a problem-solving discipline for which development in this direction should be desired. National political science communities of countries in Africa have to assume this responsibility and not wait for an external political science to drive the process.[18] This was the same path that American political science followed to diverge from British political science after the Second World War. Having traced its root to British political science, it was able to attempt creating a truly American political science to address the goals of the country's political, economic and cultural systems — American dreams and values.

African political science clearly needs to follow the path of analysis, research and knowledge production that relate practically to policy and the welfare of citizens by breaking from designs that ignore these needs. Producing socially relevant knowledge and reconceptualising concepts such as state and development are indispensable to an African political science that can support development in Africa.[19] It is not news that the state in Africa, rather than facilitating development, has continued to constrain it. Given the way development has been understood and interpreted, African political science has to promote an alternative notion that transcends the theoretical formulation of being the result of what the state can deliver to passive citizens, to building the capacity of citizens for a collective response to problems of society. This means deriving a concept of development that helps to deal practically with the welfare deficits of citizens. The more desired change should be an effort by African political scientists to begin to employ more authentic methodologies to collect the lived experiences of Africans on the ground, distil them in order to generate theoretical generalisations/postulations, so that we develop theories derived from lived experiences. So, instead of going out to prove an adopted theory, analysts should seek to draw out of data possible theoretical postulations, just like Peter Ekeh did, leading to theories on Two Publics and Social Exchange, both of which remain ignored by African political scientists and social scientists generally.[20]

Social Character

Closely related is the need for an increased social character of African political science. The field has to be seen to be playing a more social role by inspiring studies that provide people-oriented development. It can help to define societal goals and participate practically in extra-political activities in order to impact politics and policy. To achieve these, intellectual dependence on Western political science has to be checked. Concepts, methodologies and knowledge on Africa have to be interrogated in light of reality. To this end, Adcock, Bevir and Stimson argue:

> In the United States the professionalization of social science dovetailed with the rise of the large research university and its model of educating and training graduate students in specialised fields. The naturalistic model was adopted to these new conditions and to the aims of providing useful knowledge for social progress.[21]

Social progress should drive knowledge production through extensive university research and the right education of students.

Conclusion

The point made is that African political science can hardly make a substantive impact in the development of the continent because it remains an externally driven scholarship on Africa. Knowledge produced by American political science, for instance, has had impacts on political science in Africa. The core of development is research. Politics is of essence, and here a process of weeding off values imposed as knowledge and methodologies is needed to influence for good. Policy-relevant research by African political science will make more impact on development when decolonisation of the field is in process. This is because much of what is presently offered as knowledge, education and research in the field is more or less values (neoliberal) that do very little in addressing the needs of the poor.

The chapter has explained how decolonisation of African political science is important in the development of 21st century Africa, arguing that the continent faces diverse socio-political, economic and security issues that constitute a challenge to African political science. To release its full potential and play a more active role in tackling these challenges, it should not only review some of what has been handed down to it as universal truths, but it must ensure that knowledge produced is relevant for policymaking and change in society. Having been locked in years of unproductive attachment to Western traditional conceptual and ideological toolkits which often ignore the *African reality*, African political scientists must learn to practise from a more *Africa-sensitive* intellectual space. This means a break with an epistemological and methodological tradition that have hindered the renaissance of a purely African brand. This is what I have called decolonisation of African political science.

Notes and References

1. Adcock, R., Bevir, M. & Stimson, S. C. (Eds.). (2007). *Modern political science: Anglo-American exchanges since 1880*. New Jersey: Princeton University Press, p. 2.

2. Caterino, B., & and Schram, S. F. (2006). Introduction: Reframing the debate. In F.S. Sandord & B. Caterino (Eds.), *Making political science matter: Debating knowledge, research and methods* (pp. 1–17). New York, NY: New York University Press.

3. Alt, J. E., et al. (2010). Introduction. *The encyclopaedia of political science*. Washington, DC: CQ Press.

4. Cook, T. I. (1950). The method of political science in the United States. In UNESCO, *Contemporary political science: A survey of methods, research and teaching*. Paris, France: UNESCO.

5. Alt et al., p. xiv.

6. Prewith, K. (2005, July). Political ideas and a political science for policy. *The Annals of the American Academy of Political and Social Science*, *600*, 14–29.

7. Willoughby, W. W. (1906, July). Political science as a university study. *The Sewanee Review, 14*(3), 257–266.

8. Picq, M. L. (2013, September). Critics at the edge? Decolonizing methodologies. *International Political Science Review, 34*(4).

9. Nkiwane, T. C. (2001, July). Africa and international relations: Regional lessons for a global discourse. *International Political Science Review*, 279–290.

10. Ake, C. (1979). *Social science as imperialism: The theory of political development*. Ibadan, Nigeria: Ibadan.

11. Ibid.

12. Chima, O. (2013, September 23). Nigeria, 9 others lead in development index. *This Day Live*. Retrieved from http://www.thisdaylive.com/articles/nigeria-9-others-lead-in-development-index/159667/.

13. Schraeder, P. J. (2004). *African politics and society: A mosaic in transformation*. Belmont, CA: Wadsworth.

14. This refers to citizens that contribute to political, socio-economic, cultural, technological, *nonkilling* and peaceful development of society as residents, voters, analysts, politicians, administrators, diplomats, manufacturer, activists, journalists, and professors and so on.

15. Kurian, G. T. (2010). Preface. *The encyclopedia of political science.* Washington, DC: CQ Press.

16. Peet, R., & Hartwick, E. (2009). *Theories of development: Contentions, arguments, alternatives.* New York, NY: The Guilford Press, p. 213.

17. Ibid.

18. Laswell, H. D. (1963). *The future of political science.* New York, NY: Prentice-Hall International, Inc.

19. Samson, M. (2007). Post-apartheid South Africa? A feminist rethinking of the state and development in the context of neo-liberalism. *African Development, XXXii*(3), 26–57.

20. Ekeh, P. P. (1975). Colonialism and the two publics in Africa: A theoretical statement. *Comparative Studies in Society and History, 1*(1), 91–112.

21. Adcock et al., *Modern political science,* p. 2.

Chapter 11

Telling Our Own Stories: Narratology as a Decolonial Methodology

Nontyatyambo Pearl Dastile

Introduction

The neglect of narratives from African people, particularly indigenous people, in colonial and postcolonial Africa continues to misrepresent both the histories and herstories of African people. If there is one thing about people of African descent is that their past and present continue to be spoken for and about; hence, the enduring stereotypical notions about their deformed, barbaric and misrepresented identities. As a decolonial epistemic tool, narratology, presented in this chapter as a combative methodological and epistemological tool, seeks to offer an opportunity for Africans to speak for themselves, about themselves, with each other and among each other in order to vilify prevailing distortions about and erasures of peoples' lived experiences. This chapter grapples with the epistemic silences observed about African people. It then provides a conceptual framework, which underpins the concepts used throughout the chapter. We conclude with a discussion on narratology as a decolonial tool used to unmute the African subject.

Epistemic Silencing of an African Being

Ebrima Sall in a CODESRIA Bulletin titled "Extending the Frontiers of Social Science Research and Bringing Social Science Research to Public Issues" observes what I refer to in my introduction as an erasure and a negation of the African people's ability to speak for themselves and about themselves. He notes how in both colonial and arguably postcolonial Africa

> African scholarly voices were hardly audible at the global level. The geopolitical fragmentation of Africa, together with the multiplicity of boundaries of a geopolitical, linguistic and disciplinary nature, made it impossible for there to be an integrated, self-aware pan-African scholarly community that could effectively produce knowledge and interpret social realities in Africa and in the world around us from African perspectives, and inform the decision making (including at the regional level) with the research it is doing.[1]

What Sall is making reference to is a history that is repeatedly written on someone else's terms, narratives that are underpinned by different agendas which are remarkably far removed from the lived realities of the narrator and his/her needs. Indeed, the scholarly endeavours within the continent also fall into this category. Even among African scholars located within Africa and in the diaspora, the epistemic silencing of the African subject persists, largely because of heavy reliance on "borrowed methodologies". Hence Sall[2] further notes that what Mkandawire calls the "unholy trinity of poverty, ignorance and disease" equates to "hermeneutical and epistemic silences"[3] for African subjects and subjectivities. Partly this is because of the two forms of narratives which continue to exist in Africa, which are "the West narratives which are issued from the narrator's initiative and those of the South which are from listener's perspective".[4]

Both narratives accordingly constitute the epistemic and hermeneutic silences mentioned above, and not only because of the geographical location of both the narrator and the listener, but rather because of the epistemological orientation of both, which results in the mutation of the African subjective experience and lived world. Hence Mamadou Diouf[5] ponders on "which identities are formed in this process? And what are the idioms of expression and representations?" In essence, he raises the question of whose history and whose story is told, and by whom.

Fricker describes the forms of "testimonial injustice" as pre-emptive testimonial injustice and epistemic objectification.[6] According to her, pre-emptive testimonial injustice denotes a form of injustice "where the prejudice against the speaker's social type operates in advance to prevent their view even being solicited". While epistemic objectification refers to "that particular kind of silence associated with forms of objectification — 'silencing' [...] a morally bad form of epistemic objectification which is an exclusion from the practice (that of pooling information) which dramatizes the very core of the concept of knowledge". The first form of silencing, pre-emptive testimonial injustice, she argues stems from the fact that a majority of scholars initially focus on understanding the position of the knower, the informant. She describes this as the "state of the Nature's story", where primacy is given on establishing the accuracy and sincerity of the knower before he or she speaks. The aim thus is to first ascertain the "truthfulness" of the story. Thus how one then examines this truthfulness is through a pre-occupation with who "a good informant" would be. Fricker thus argues that this kind of pre-judgement about the subject's truthfulness discredits the narrator's voice, thus leading to the silencing of the subject. This is because of an assumption that there are people who, even within a similar geographical orientation, will remain silenced because of an assumption that they do not contain the mental faculties to render their stories or narratives worth listening to, thus disallowing them to speak. This is what she describes as pre-emptive testimonial injustice, which denotes the exclusions based on the assumed disqualifying subjective criteria of who can speak, what the subject knows, how they speak and what they can speak about.[7] Accordingly, Fricker is of the view that

> epistemic exclusions — barred entry to the community of inform-
> ants — is obviously also a crucial feature of the politics of epistemic
> real life. The exclusion in fact marks a commonplace form of testi-
> monial injustice: those social groups who are subject to identity prej-
> udice and are thereby susceptible to unjust credibility deficit will,
> by the same token, also tend simply not to be asked to share their
> thoughts, their judgements, their opinions. (If the word of people
> like you is generally not taken seriously, people will tend not to ask
> for it.)[8]

Because this kind of injustice is not publicly enacted, the narrator is there-fore discredited of any intellectual or moral compass. As such,

> [t]he credibility of such a person on a given subject matter is already
> sufficiently in prejudicial deficit that their potential testimony is never
> solicited; so the speaker is silenced by the identity prejudice that un-
> dermines her credibility in advance. Thus purely structural operations
> of identity power can control whose would-be contributions become
> public, and whose do not.[9]

This form of pre-emptive epistemic injustice is observed among African subjects, particularly, indigenous African people, who have been excluded from telling their stories because of the exclusionary practices in the colonial and postcolonial eras. Exclusion on the basis of misconceived illiteracy has been used to exclude indigenous people in telling their own stories, thus leading to "internalised othering" and inferiority of mostly African people regarding their abilities to articulate and re-articulate their own life worlds. As Fricker[10] argues, "[T]estimonial injustice, then, can silence you by prejudicially pre-empting your word".

The second form of testimonial injustice results from the epistemic objectification of an informant. Thus while pre-emptive testimonial injustice presumes a subject as unknowing and thus not deserving of any consideration, epistemic objectification rests on the premise that since there are subjects who are credited with an ability of knowing, such subjects face exclusion. Exclusion manifests itself in the way that as a "trusted informant" he may be expected to withhold information from the very community members who had been excluded by virtue of their lack of credibility.

> [H]e is thus demoted from subject to object, relegated from the role of active epistemic agent, and confined to the role of passive state of affairs from which knowledge might be gleaned. He is ousted from the role of participant in the co-operative exercise of the capacity for knowledge and recast in the role of passive.[11]

Within this context, the subject therefore may lose his sense of belonging from within and among communities members. But more so, the onus may be on the subject to speak on behalf of others, which Linda Martin Alcoff bemoans as "arrogant, vain, unethical, and politically illegitimate".[12] This is because it allows a disconfiguration of an individual's identity while at the same time allowing fragmentations within communities. Both forms of epistemic silences lead to what Fricker[13] calls hermeneutic injustice and hermeneutic marginalization.

Hermeneutic injustice is observed when "someone has a significant area of their social experience obscured from understanding owing to prejudicial flaws in shared resources for social interpretation". Hermeneutical injustice is thus "the injustice of having some significant area of one's social experience obscured from collective understanding owing to a structural identity prejudice in the collective hermeneutical resource".[14]

Hermeneutic marginalisation refers to "unequal hermeneutical participation with respect to some significant area(s) of social experience".[15] These forms which emanate from epistemic injustice may occur conspicuously and thus may not be easily detected. The way they occur may also be intertwined with other forms of subjectivation, which may mask the epistemic silencing a subject may be exposed and subjected to. However, even within these undercover or undetected formations, narratology underpinned by a decolonial mediation aims to unmask the various forms of interweaving colonial practices within which are embedded forms of colonial tools to reinforce othering and inferiorisation. And because the decolonial epistemic perspective aims to unmask the hidden forms of prejudicial practises, it thus aids in detecting hermeneutical injustice as a "form of powerlessness". It is also important to note how these forms of injustices may coalesce into a deformation of the subjects' ontological and reasoning ability, thus affecting one's social identity. As identities are complex and thus may not be subsumed under one hydra-headed epistemic location, narratology provides a tool which may be used from a decolonial vantage point to give credence and epistemic justice to an otherwise silenced subject.

Narratology as Decoloniality

In order to restore African subjects' identities and imagery it is crucial to "restructure the way we study Africa", as observed by Diouf.[16] Similarly El Amin[17] proposes that what is essential is to

> place emphasis on micro-level empirical field research that captures Africa's complex reality and the diverse forms in which the same development problems manifest themselves in different parts of the continent. The necessity of micro-level field research is imposed by the complexity and heterogeneity of forms that defy generalisation and perceived conceptions.

Narratology as a decolonial tool seeks to achieve this by foregrounding its epistemic location against the coloniality of knowledge. In narrating one's story what may emerge is a discursive methodological tool that provides context into people's everyday worlds. This is more applicable for subjects whose experience and ways of knowing have been silenced and relegated to the margins. Narratology therefore seeks to restore the truth, place and identity of the African subject by giving voice to a muted subject.

Coloniality of knowledge seeks to redress and identify the discursive forms of colonization that privilege the Cartesian way of understanding and viewing the world. Such include the Anglo-Eurocentered practices whereby the only "discourse for articulating" Third World (and specifically women's) lives is the norming and normative Anglo-European one. That is, the subject is approached only in terms of the concept of rationality constructed by modern Western epistemology. Rationality's research methodologies dictate that the only agents are presumed to be the knowing (authorized) subjects, and within authorizing institutions, theirs is the prerogative to interpret and package information. The whole of other subjects involved in this encounter are thus muted and silenced. Western scientific practice thus positions the researcher as a judge of credibility and a gatekeeper for authority.[18]

As one of the contours of decoloniliaty which is predicated on the domineering practice of coloniality, which "makes reference to race, and thus, to space and experience",[19] narratology as decoloniality therefore seeks to disrupt prevailing silences among and about the African subject and subjectivities. This is achieved through what Mignolo[20] regards as a "process of translating and rewriting other knowledge, other cultures, other ways of being, presuming commensurability through Western rationality". The aim of narratology is to act and work with the self and the recognition of the centrality and particularity of individual experiences, particularly those of the "poor and marginalised, with whom partnerships can be forged to better serve the continent and its people".[21] In that way the African scholarly community would, as El Amin[22] sees it,

> restructure the way we study Africa [...] in order to re-create the marginalisation of Africa from the rest of the world. To reverse seeing Africa as a continent of absent history and to privilege Africa's narratives and locating it within the African diaspora which in turn will be re-inventing the study of pan-Africanism.

Narratology thus would seek to "theorise the African experience especially where it seems to contradict conventional wisdom".[23] How can narratology be used to decolonise knowledge production in Africa in order to shift the geography of reason and thus re-incarnate the African subject as an ontological being? To put the theory into practise one has to identify what methodological approaches can best be adopted to allow people to tell their stories.

Narratology and African Centeredness

Wilson[24] argues that within the colonised world, Frantz Fanon advocated for oral histories when he argued that literature from the Third World relies heavily on oral traditions. Fanon described this as a "literature of combat" in that it is premised on "oral traditions to shape a trajectory that moves the tribal nation toward a pre-colonial, indigenous form of governance". Oral history as a form of re-telling the story enables the subject to occupy a central space in the story. Hence it "necessitates that characters undergo a change in order to return to the settlement and to achieve a previously elusive wholeness".[25] Wilson concludes that "in *Ceremony* [...] the oral tradition is not a metaphoric sign, or even a unitary sign for authenticity or truth, but is instead the possibility of truth itself, the possibility of a future for indigenous peoples".

Oral history therefore becomes a form of narratology that is epistemologically related to a large part of indigenous knowledge, cultural transmission and community engagement.[26] Without simply accepting life story data as "unmediated representations of social realities", as Atkinson and Delamont[27] caution against doing, the researcher engages in a reflexive process to demonstrate how narrative realities encountered through life story research coincide with historical truths. In the words of Plummer, use of documents of life such as narrative/biographical studies implies "getting close to living human beings, accurately yet imaginatively picking up the way they express their understandings of the world around them, perhaps providing an analysis of such expressions, presenting them in interesting ways, and being self critically aware of the immense difficulties such tasks bring".[28]

Within the particularities of the African context, narratology finds its relevance and applicability within the Africa-centred decolonial paradigmatic discourse, which seeks to analyse and explain Africa from within. This paradigm posits that the primary site of studying African realities cannot be located outside the context of Africa. And as such, because Africa and African subjects remain a contested terrain, which has endured numerous forms of misrepresentation, intellectual and ideological terrains can no longer be imported from the West. This is because African philosophers have paved the way for Africanists and Africans to reinvent, reclaim and reassert the imagery of Africa and Africans from the neocolonial impositions and related condemnations. The apparatus for rebirth includes African decolonisation of prevailing paradigms. Nabudere[29] defines African decolonisation as a reclamation of African voices through recognition of heritage and knowledge systems brought about by oral tradition. Oral histories and herstories would thus enable African scholars to "unlearn, to rethink, to reconceptualise and deconstruct the hegemonic discourses".[30] Centring and giving primacy to African stories is also advocated by scholars such as Molefe Kete Asante (Afrocentricity), Archie Mafeje (Africanity and combative ontology), and Keto Tshehloane (African-centred paradigm). The central argument running through these paradigms is the call to centre studies on Africa and African communities and the diaspora, within Africa. The call for centring is premised on the fact that when one is centred in his or her intellectual corpus, any solutions proposed will be culturally relevant to local communities and may result in sustainable problem solving in line with pan-African ideals.

Democratising Knowledge through Narratology

Within the South African landscape, Coetzee *et al.* argue that there exists a fertile ground from which a country undergoing the post-democracy phase can begin to "democratise knowledge".[31] These authors argue that such knowledge transformation would seek to answer the pertinent questions relating to Africa's memory of the past and how this history remains a part of the present. But such democratisation cannot be achieved if knowledge remains a terrain which is only reserved for the privileged few in any part of the community. Both Mafeje[32] and Nabudere[33] demonstrate to us that only when the "uncertificated communities" are included in the knowledge-generating and knowledge-producing cohort will the process of decolonising knowledge succeed. Therefore the narrative discourse, through the telling and retelling of life stories, can serve to bring the politically excluded,[34] the wretched of the earth (Franz Fanon) to "express their feelings, thoughts and daily experiences of victims of oppression will give substance and resonance to human suffering […] to lay open the deep roots of institutionalised racism, oppression and imperialism in South African society—not only the remnants of the apartheid regime but also those underlying a new wave of domination, corruption and self-enrichment …".[35]

Narratology thus enables testimonial knowledge to allow the narrator to speak and reveal his or her own truths. However, Hougland argues that while giving testimony may be hailed as a tool for allowing marginalised voices oralcy, one needs to be cautious of the actors and the power relations embedded among different players engaged in the process of giving and receiving testimony. Hougland[36] in a paper subtitled "Giving testimony and coloniality of knowledge" raises several concerns which are pertinent while giving testimony. These include "When does a subject of knowing become a knowing subject? How can a (marginalized) subject of knowing be acknowledged by discourse as a knowing subject?"

Her concern reverts back to the epistemic silences observed in, amongst others, Western scientific practices, which tend to "position the researcher as a judge of credibility and a gatekeeper for its authority".[37] Indeed, these pertinent questions dominate scholarly engagements, particularly among scholars engaged in the project of decoloniality. Walter Mignolo[38] cites Anibal Quijano[39] opinion that "the coloniality of knowledge keeps us from accepting the idea of knowing subjects outside the confines of modern epistemic rationality".

When scholars remain epistemically ignorant or blinded by the Western promise of modernity, they remain decentered and thus occupy opposite polar ends, which reinforces the colonial structures of producing and generating knowledge. Hence there continues to exist hegemonic assumptions about African subjects and subjective experiences. What the coloniality of knowledge specifically allows us to do, therefore, is to acknowledge the different positionalities that people occupy in society. For instance, even among the marginalised groups there are different classes, genders, and sexual and religious orientations which determine the ontological locations people occupy.

As such it is imperative for African scholars to find ways of hearing the pluralities of voices within the marginalised groups. One way of hearing such testimonies has been addressed by scholars such as Linda Tuhiwai Smith (on decolonising methodologies) as well as Bagele Chilisa (indigenous research methodologies). Both bodies of work seek to bring to the forefront of scholarly endeavours indigenous epistemologies through deploying indigenous African proverbs and songs[40] as well as indigenous story-telling and indigenized Euro-Western approaches.[41] The value of "oral transmission of knowledge, values, customs and beliefs" in African culture, particularly among indigenous populations, holds significance for communal survival.[42] Passed across generations through songs and folklore, these indigenous knowledge transmitters enabled the sustainability of the use of indigenous languages, the folk wisdom and mores whose meaning may be lost when translated into colonial languages such as English, as well as the codes of conduct, which not only impart formal education but spiritual wisdom passed from one generation to the other. What is interesting is that these forms of indigenous knowledge systems crossed boundaries and cultures and fostered a culture of nationhood, neighbourliness as well as a spirit of communalism. Regrettably, modern education systems relegate these into the periphery as modern science privileges and universalises Western thought. To illustrate this point, I make reference to one of the conversations I had when I was conducting interviews with incarcerated women in correctional centres. My conversation with 57-year-old Matlou about her pre-incarceration role within the community versus the one since her incarceration reveals the persistent relegation of indigenous ways of being as inferior.

NP: What did your job at home entail before you were incarcerated?

M: There is a group of traditional dancers who put on our traditional clothes. So if something, a necklace, is broken, I am the one who mends it and replaces it. I want to go back to restart my project because there I have my project, where I train chiefs, to also conduct vaginal testing (to teach children not to have sex when they are still young), and by the time when I was arrested I had a project. I had to train the chiefs about their language.

NP: Let's go through these one by one, when you train chiefs, what do you do?

M: I teach them their language and how to conduct themselves and the process of picking a new chief. And also train them how the burial of a chief should be conducted. I show them that when a chief is deceased, his casket or coffin cannot be carried like that of a commoner, they have their own way of doing this.

NP: How do you train girls to abstain?

M: We do the dhomba and we do the snake dance. We check them first [vaginal testing] so that you cannot be part of the snake dance if you are not a virgin.

M: And the project?

Noria: I make the traditional beads and the traditional Venda dress (Mwenda).

NP: Besides your training the inmates how to dance, do you also train the inmates on how to conduct themselves, that is, the vaginal testing and how to behave?

M: I was about to the start but the police limited me.

NP: Why?

M: The police said they don't want the traditional things to be done here, but they only want Christian things.

NP: Were you a Christian before coming to prison?

Noria: No, but now I have to be because of the traditional things that I was doing, they don't go hand in hand.

The conversation illustrates the hegemony of correctional service programmes as well as the Eurocentric orientation of correctional service personnel and policies that remain entrenched in the geo and body politics associated with Christianity. Matlou is thus conditioned into Christianity, disavowing her pre-incarceration role and traditional duties as barbaric and demonic. Interestingly, even the sangomas (traditional healers) incarcerated in one of the correctional centres explained how a group of five women are prohibited from practising their respective traditional rituals that would avert any form of relapsing to illnesses that enabled their diagnosis as traditional healers. Mampho (M1), 58, and Mambongo (M2), 43, two of the sangomas, say:

> NP: Are you allowed to, for example, use your gift and appease to your ancestors here?

> M1: It is bad. But right now I don't use it.... I can't use it here because if I use it and someone reports me to the office, then the police will ask if I am here to serve a sentence or to practice sangoma. It's difficult to be talked by somebody like that. I am afraid to practice.

> M2: I can only do it spiritually because to just drop everything is going to be difficult. This sangoma thing comes from the ancestors. I cannot just stop it.

> M1: I became ill. I had swollen feet, a headache.

> NP: What did the prison do?

> M1: They took me to the hospital. They [hospital staff] told me that it is the ancestor thing and did not help me. The problem just disappeared without any medication.

While the project of indigenisation has been fraught with rampant criticisms such as violent appropriation and enduring questions of the legitimacy of some groups claiming authentic indigenous blood lines over others, it remains a pertinent and important concern. Thus indigenous voices are brought into the mainstream of academic scholarly work in order to redress what Linda Tuhiwai Smith observes as being that "research" is probably one of "the dirtiest words in the indigenous world's vocabulary".[43]

These observations are bolstered by Hoagland,[44] who observes that among indigenous communities there lies a question which scholars from a decolonial epistemic approach need to contend with: "how do they engage with each other?" And how do both the participants (narrator and listener) position themselves? These questions are pertinent in the decolonising project as the use of narratives may in itself be silencing. In this instance, then, a decolonially positioned scholar has to do what Motsemme[45] proposes:

> To read these silences, just as we invest in reading speech and action in the social sciences. Reinterpreting silence as another language through which women speak volumes, allows us to then explore other, perhaps hidden meanings regarding the struggle to live under apartheid.

Through reading not only spoken language or voices, those who are silenced and seem inaudible may be read as well because such silence may represent forms of resistance and agency. Silence therefore may be a form of protest, a reclamation and self-assertion for one to remain and retain his or her story as theirs. This is particularly common among indigenous communities who have been subjected to appropriation of knowledge by donor-driven scholarly work. Narratology therefore seeks to be an all-inclusive paradigm that reaffirms individual agency and humanism, thus giving hermeneutical justice. As Michael Horswell[46] advises, "The issue should not be, 'Can the Subaltern Speak?' but, in the colonial or any historical context, how to decipher his or her voice from the multiple utterances that form hegemonic discourse".[47] Hermeneutical justice, according to Hougland, makes reference to "an alertness or sensitivity to the possibility that the difficulty one's interlocutor is having as she tries to render something communicatively intelligible is due not to its being a nonsense or her being a fool, but rather to some sort of gap in collective hermeneutical resources".[48]

The restoration of an individual's identity requires the listener in narrative contexts to refrain from epistemic ignorance. It requires reflexivity informed by decolonial epistemic approaches that addresses each person as an individual, human being whose humanity and humanism may be reclaimed by being given space to talk and be listened to. Such enables the forms of power, being, and gendered, racialised and ethnicised identities to emerge and form part of scholarly debate. And as Hoagland[49] states:

> In practical contexts where there is enough time and the matter is sufficiently important, the virtuous hearer may effectively be able to help generate a more inclusive hermeneutical micro-climate through the appropriate kind of dialogue with the speaker. In particular, such dialogue involves a more pro-active and more socially aware kind of listening than is usually required in more straightforward communicative exchanges. This sort of listening involves listening as much to what is *not* said as to what is said. […] *[I]n order to create a more inclusive hermeneutical micro-climate shared by hearer and speaker, its general exercise is obviously conducive to the generation of new meanings to fill in the offending hermeneutical gaps, and it is thereby conducive to reducing the effects of hermeneutical marginalization.*
> [My emphasis]

In addition to hermeneutic justice, narratology as decoloniliaty also seeks to offer epistemic justice to subjects. Fricker[50] suggests that one of the conditions of epistemic justice is to adopt an inclusive restoration.

What the citizens rightly want is justice proper—that is, *just* outcomes achieved for the right reasons [...]. The point is rather that *justice* isn't merely an outcome; it is something that can only be delivered in the right spirit, done for reasons of justice.

Fanon in *Black Skin, White Masks* also argues,

The desire itself is grounded in self-consciousness: *when it encounters resistance from the other, self-consciousness undergoes the experience of desire—the first milestone on the road that leads to dignity. Black Skin, White Masks* offers a very particular definition of dignity. Dignity is not located in seeking equality with the white man and his civilization: it is not about assuming the attitudes of the master *who has allowed his slaves to eat at his table.* It is about being oneself with all the multiplicities, systems and contradictions of one's own ways of being, doing and knowing. It is about being true to one's Self.[51]

Narratology as a Tool to Liberate Knowledge: A Case Study of Incarcerated Women in South African Correctional Centres

If there is one population that has been relegated to the margins, epistemologically, aesthetically, it is the female inmate population in correctional centres. Numerous justifications have been used, including the numerically smaller numbers of this group compared to the male population, as an attempt to make stories about them. The women's profiles, histories and explanations about their offending have often been manufactured using similar methodologies and approaches as for the dominant male group. Such an approach, which is not only male-centred but also deeply entrenched in Euro-Western paradigms, has thus resulted in mutations and distortions about who and what a female offender is. A female offender within the South African context continues to be profiled as more of a victim than an active participant in the crime. While this does not suggest that women's victim experiences should be idolised because of an overemphasis on women's agency, it remains an epistemic injustice to make assumptions about the women's trajectories or journeys to incarceration without seeking hermeneutic justice, through giving voice to women.

In ongoing research that I conducted whose focus delved into rethinking female offending within the South African context, conversations with women revealed how allowing women to tell their stories reinscribes and liberates the women's sense of selfhood and humanity. Through telling their life stories, women engaged in "re-building an archive that has previously silenced, muted and demonised their being and self of humanism". Allowing the voices of women to speak during the research process enabled women to reveal, amongst other things, the silencing during the legal processes as well as the methodological injustices of relying on Euro-Western methodological paradigms (e.g., questionnaires) in collecting data, which result in mutations and defacing the voices of women:

> "*I could have said this in court, had I been granted an opportunity to speak and even speak freely without judgement.*" [Nomsa, not her real name]
> Gugu [not her real name] said, "*Even we are very happy that someone comes here and just talks like this. We don't usually have visits like this. Since 2005 there has never been anyone who came here to visit us like this, no one, no one. I just wish people can come here so that we can talk. I just want to realise my dreams when I leave here. Love yourself, love your child. One day I will wave at you from a car stopped in the robots and I will realise my dream.*"

This is even more so for indigenous populations whose competence in speaking and articulating in the dominant language in which such questionnaires are usually designed precludes their ability to tell their stories. Thus epistemic ignorance of the aesthetics of language amounts to both an epistemic and hermeneutical injustice when researchers adhere to colonially embedded methodologies and frameworks.

It is, therefore, on the basis of these aforementioned observations that this paper, through the presentation of women's narratives on incarceration, argues for decolonizing existing methodological discourses applied in criminological studies. In practice this implies activism and social justice so that "justice for all" can be translated into practice. The life stories suggest a move towards humanistic, emancipatory, liberatory methodologies and approaches to research. This may serve to ensure that the stereotypical social imagery of offenders depicts the lived circumstances informed by the social formations and structures within which women emerge. This enables relevance to the dreams of the "African Renaissance" and, most poignantly, leads to scholarship that is not only effective but also affective and decolonised. These mental detours are long past their sell-by date, but the social relevance of African criminologists and criminology in particular needs to be informed by these existential conditions. Furthermore, the conversations with women incarcerated in prisons reveal the importance of drawing information from "the source". This stresses local relevance while forming cultural specificity to reveal the multiplicity of meanings inherent in social lives. Therefore, as opposed to polarizing discourses, I am located within the lived and embodied experiences and life worlds of women incarcerated in South African correctional centers to influence policy and theoretical formulations which are relevant for rehabilitative programming.

However, it should be noted that among the group of 55 women who participated in this research, there were also noted silences about some specificities of their experiences. For instance for Namhla, 58, narrating her story of domestic abuse, particularly about the sexual challenges she experienced in her marriage, also allowed women to regain their sense of agency and power. While they are at times forced to reveal private nuances of their lives, especially during assessment and court processes, conversations with women enable them to narrate that which they want to narrate. Although this has often been cited as one of the flaws in personal interviewing, for instance, refusal to share information should also be seen as a source of reclaiming one's self. As Motsemme suggests, within the narrative context when women become silent,

> we begin to read these silences, just as we invest in reading speech and action in the social sciences. Silences [...] should then be viewed as part of a range of 'languages of pain and grief' to narrate often hidden but troubled elements of their recent past.[52]

Narratology as a decolonial tool for recovering the voice and re-reading silences requires epistemic disobedience. This implies neglecting taken for granted and audible voices and thinking beyond methodological and epistemologically established frameworks, which would allow academicians, scientists to speak with subaltern groups. As such, the approach does not simply regard human beings as participants or observers in the generation of knowledge, but rather as equal subjects actively participating in re-writing, re-inscribing and re-articulating subjectivities and writing a new decolonial archive which aims at liberating indigenous and sustainable knowledge.

Narratology as a decolonial tool seeks to offer both epistemic and hermeneutical justice to restore, recover, and lead to the rebirth and reincarnation of an African being. It serves as a key to destabilising existing hegemonic assumptions about African subjectivities and a buffer against enduring misrepresentations of African people. Diouf[53] supports the decolonial moves and denotes that any form of rebirth should include an enquiry into "how 'modern' (for lack of a better word) and/or the contemporary is being (re)articulated in a time of African Renaissance (what period?), a time of crisis, expectations and hopes of flourishing in pluralistic identities and manifestations". Through narratology it is important to retell and rewrite our stories within a decolonial epistemic paradigmatic discourse, to reconstruct and reshape the African scholarly discourse. As Hougland[54] observes,

> [m]any people not framed as the center are embedded in different locations, indeed often in different cosmologies, which fertilize them, give them their possibilities and from which they think and speak complexly.

Narratology unearths and retraces such diverse locations thus giving primacy to the superdiverse structures and locations from which people speak. As McFarlane rightly points out, "[I]t is time to get serious—to listen to culture".[55]

Conclusion

By implication this chapter demonstrates a call to return to the source, to the cradle of humankind, to generate and engender equitable knowledge that seeks to restore the dignity of human, and particularly indigenous, communities. The chapter, through narratives of and conversations with women incarcerated in correctional centres, argues for narratology through story-telling, oral histories and testimonies as an attempt to avert epistemic and hermeneutic injustices suffered by colonised groups. It argues for scholars to remain culturally relevant. This requires academic detours and ruptures that demand a move beyond reticence and resistance in the face of failing and dehumanising forms of knowledge production. For the African continent, narratology, a combative decolonial tool, encourages stories, histories and herstories to originate from and be rooted in the cultural assimilations and aesthetics of Africa. This requires a deeper engagement and commitment to actively engage with communities and sites of knowledge and enable the reading of Africa from within. Indigenisation through folklore and mores, revaluing African languages and ways of being, telling and retelling stories and the embedded silences within these narrations, is a form of reinventing ourselves and thus creating a space for existence through mutual dialogue in knowledge production.

Notes and References

1. Sall, E. (2012). Extending the frontiers of social science research and bringing social research to public issues. *CODESRIA Bulletin*, (3 & 4), 3–6.

2. Ibid., p. 3.

3. Fricker, M. (2007). *Epistemic injustice: Power and the ethics of knowing*. Oxford Online.

4. Guha, R. (2002). History at the limit of world-history [Italian Academy Lectures]. New York, NY: Columbia University Press.

5. Diouf, M. (2012). African history/history in Africa: Academic, vernacular histories and area studies. *CODESRIA Bulletin*, (3 & 4), 8–11.

6. Fricker, *Epistemic injustice.*

7. Ibid.

8. Ibid.

9. Ibid.

10. Ibid.

11. Ibid.

12. Alcoff, L. M. (1991). The problem of speaking for others. *Cultural Critique, 20,* 5–32.

13. Fricker, *Epistemic injustice.*

14. Ibid.

15. Ibid.

16. Diouf, p. 10.

17. El Amin, A. K. (2012). Challenges facing Africa and those facing the social sciences. *CODESRIA Bulletin*, (3 & 4), 14–16.

18. Maldonado-Torres, N. (2004). The topology of being and the geopolitics of knowledge: Modernity, empire, coloniality. *City, 8*(1), 29–52.

19. Ibid., p. 42.

20. Mignolo, W. D. (1995). *The darker side of the renaissance.* Ann Arbor, MI: The University of Michigan Press.

21. El Amin, p. 16.

22. Ibid., p. 14.

23. Mamdani, M. (2012). Historical research with historical depth: Africa, human rights and citizenship. *CODESRIA Bulletin*, (3 & 4), 7–11.

24. Wilson, M. (2008). *Writing home: Indigenous narratives of resistance.* East Lansing: Michigan State University Press.

25. Ibid., p. 124.

26. Coetzee, J. K., Elliker, F. & Rau, A. (2013). Training for advanced research in the narrative study of lives within the context of political and educational transformation: A case study in South Africa. *Qualitative Social Research, 14*(2), 1–18.

27. Coetzee et al.

28. Ibid.

29. Nabudere, W. D. (2006). Towards an Afrikology of knowledge production and African regeneration. *International Journal of African Renaissance, 1*(1), 7–32.

30. Gibson, C. (2000). Afrocentric organisation development? Shifting the paradigm from Eurocentricity to Afrocentricity. Unpublished Master of Arts Thesis, University of Toronto, Canada.

31. Coetzee, et al.

32. Mafeje, A. (2000). Africanity: A combative ontology. *CODESRIA Bulletin,* (1 & 4), 66–71.

33. Nabudere, W. D. (2011a). *Afrikology, philosophy and wholeness: An epistemology.* Pretoria, South Africa: Africa Institute of South Africa.

34. Coetzee et al.

35. Ibid., p. 14.

36. Hoagland, S. L. (2010). Giving testimony and the coloniality of knowledge. Retrieved from http://www.cavehill.uwi.edu/fhe.

37. Ibid.

38. Mignolo, W. D. (2000). *Local histories/global designs.* Princeton, NJ: Princeton University Press.

39. Quijano, A. (2000). Coloniality of power, Eurocentrism, and Latin America. *Neplanta: Views from South, 1*(3), 533–580.

40. Chilisa, B. (2012). *Indigenous research methodologies.* Los Angeles, CA: Sage.

41. Smith, T. L. (1999). *Decolonizing methodologies: Research and indigenous peoples.* London, England: Zed Books.

42. McFarlane, A. H. (2012). "Other" Education down-under: Indigenising the discipline for psychologists and special educators. *Other Education: The Journal of Educational Alternatives, 1*, 205–225.

43. Ibid., p. 1.

44. Hoagland.

45. Motsemme, N. (2004). The mute always speak: On women's silences at the truth and reconciliation commission. *Current Sociology, 52*, 909–932.

46. Hoagland.

47. Ibid., p. 234

48. Ibid.

49. Ibid.

50. Fricker, M. (2013). Epistemic justice as a condition of political freedom? *Synthese, 190*, 1317–1332.

51. Fanon, F. (1967). *Black skin, white masks.* Pluto Press: Grove Press Inc.

52. Motsemme, p. 911.

53. Diouf, p. 10.

54. Hoagland.

55. Ibid.

Chapter 12

Researching the African
Subject in African Politics

Tendayi Sithole

Introduction

This chapter attempts to centre the African subject *qua* epistemology from
the limits of being in the discipline of African politics. The contention is that
the notion of the method, and, by extension, methodology, is difficult to reconcile when it comes to the African subject whose existential conditions are
ontologically void and there is no effort in African politics to raise ontological
questions. The chapter first introduces decolonial mediation as a methodological tool of researching the African subject, and also to serve as a critique of
the Euro-American methodological canon, namely, qualitative, quantitative
and triangulation, which are foundational in African politics and tend to negate
the subjectivity of the African subject. Secondly, the notion of method will be
engaged as it relates to the African subject by introducing the notion of method
against method. This means to critique method, which of course will not be
accepted in the convention of method as is. The argument is made that researching the African subject by means of decolonial mediation requires a shift
in the geography of reason and to open new vistas of reconfiguring African
politics and by positioning the African subject as the agent of politics. The
African subject and the research should root epistemology from the ontological
site — the positionality of the African subject from its existential conditions.

The chapter unravels the positionality of the African subject as a subject
that has been classified, labelled and represented as a lacking subject and shows
how Euro-American methodology has been a useful tool of subjection. Finally,
the chapter argues for a decolonial turn and options instead of alternatives.

Decolonial turns and options are liberatory in stature, and they solidify decolonial meditations in order for the African subject to emerge and open up more sites of epistemological intervention by means of epistemic breaks, more specifically in the field of African politics, rather than one replacing another.

The Problem of the Problematic People

What is the problem of the problematic people? To try to respond to this difficult question, what can be said is: being the African subject (as people) is a problem and to be a problem is to be the African subject, more so if the subjectivity of the subject is something considered exterior to it, by means of being methodologised outside its own existential realities. This has been of convenience in that the exteriorisation of the African subject is not even seen as problematic as knowledge practices *qua* method are instruments externally invented to study the other and its socio-political milieu. The African subject is often a problem in the sense that it is a subject, as Gordon notes, which is faced by the problem of existence.[1] The problem of existence is one that is key in its attempt to deal with and confront the questions of freedom, alienation and degradation.[2] The existence of the African subject is problematic since the subject is militated against by being positioned as an aberration from the norm and the thinghood of the living, an entity that is substituted dead and whose life is not worth being accounted for. It is the subject which stands out as an existential enigma erased from the foundational base of epistemology in that the deployment of continental reality — Africa and its subjects in the discipline of African politics — is dictated from outside, and yet what stands out is the problem in the pathological sense.

The African people are problematic as subjects because they are racialised, the very characterisation that puts them at the receiving end of epistemic racism. Epistemic racism is the exclusion of other knowledges, local/public histories, epistemologies and subjectivities which are said to fall outside the epistemological grid of universalism. The origin and thought of African politics as a discipline does not of course originate from the African subjects themselves but from the Euro-American canon, which of course, like anthropology, is the study of the other, and by extension in relation to African politics the study of the geo-political nature of where the African subject is located. Of course, the emphasis is more on the geo-political nature of the subject, political institutions, regional issues, political thought, and the political dynamics which are affected by the subject. What is often not present is the agency of the African subject and the existential nature of the subject in trying to combat all modes of oppression and remnants of colonisation as an ongoing project. The content of African politics has been the matter of presentation and representation that signifies African subjects outside the ontological landscape, and what emerges from African subjects is considered a debased form of epistemic intervention which seems to be locked in 'a mute, fixed and stable world'.[3] This then suggests that African politics, if it came from the geo-political reason of African subjects themselves, is something that will be questioned on the basis of it not being epistemologically privileged. As such, there cannot be claims and propositions that are worth taking seriously, and of course, the case of epistemic ignorance sets in, in which African modes of criticism and epistemological interventions are said to not to exist, not being epistemological at all. In a nutshell, African politics from the margins of the Euro-American canon is said to be no knowledge at all, and for it to be knowledge it must first be disciplined by the Euro-American canon.

It is in the existential condition fraught with exclusion that the Africa subject does not even make the figure of what Savransky calls epistemological exclusion.[4] This stems from the logic that what is regarded as a problem is something to be rendered invisible, and exclusionary practices take the centre stage. Thus, African politics, more so in relation to pronouncing the political project that does not see Africa from the canonical gaze of the Euro-American lens, faces epistemological exclusion largely because the censure of the universal will be evoked, as if the lived experiences are the same and must be conceived from the Euro-American canon. The nature of African politics is one to be configured, which dwells on the neglected existential question of what does it mean to be a problem and specifically linked to the African subject? By addressing the concerns of the African subject and as a way to untangle itself from the complex web of canonical subjection—that is, the study of Africa by means of epistemological exclusion—the fundamental question should be what is African about African politics? It is therefore imperative to engage in decolonial meditations in order to foreground decolonial epistemic perspective in African politics.

On Decolonial Meditations

Decolonial meditations are rooted in decolonial epistemic perspective, and they are intended to confront and grapple with power issues in their sense of complexity. At the nerve centre of decolonial meditations is the concerted effort to engage in the process of liberating the African subject and, of course, the study of the African subject, being the one that opens the possibility of liberation since the Africa subject is at the receiving end of subjection. It is, therefore, important to point out that decolonial meditations are informed by the continued pursuit of liberation. In their application, decolonial meditations disrupt, question, displace, rattle and unsettle the guardian of the status quo — that is, qualitative, quantitative and triangulation methodologies.

The Euro-American canon methodologies — that is, qualitative, quantitative and triangulation — ran out of steam in terms of understanding the African subject, and as such they have become constrictions rather than sites that open multiplicity, even though combined by means of triangulation. They are often rigidly followed for the basis of scientific merit, but little is considered in terms of their suitability in studying the African subject. What is the bone of contention is that the African subject should be interrogated also from the location of decolonial meditations to bring to existence the African subject. The Euro-American canon methodologies have not yet given the African subject subjectivity, but subjection which makes objecthood out of the African subject.

There is no need to actually outwardly dismiss the Euro-American canon methodologies; rather they should be challenged as being ineffective in revealing how the power structures tamper with the contribution to the body of knowledge by the African subject. Adding on this, Louis asserts that research on the African subject is a contribution to the body of knowledge for it is a research different from that originating from the Euro-American canon.[5] The dominant methodologies serve as testimony to the fact that research in Africa and about Africa has been from the domination of the Euro-American canon.

As Ake posits, these methodologies are contaminated with the 'ideological bias of the mainstream Western social science'.[6] These are known methodologies that are part of the project of modernity — the latter is even tired due to its inability to deal with socio-political phenomena pertaining to the African subject and the problems that feature in the present. Out of their resilience and their paranoia of censure, they engage in what Ake refers to as sciences of equilibrium, which shows that they are in opposition to change. According to Ake, sciences of equilibrium negatively refer to other methodologies as inferior, deviant, unscientific, mythological and in crisis, to name a few.[7] This is the methodological and ideological bias loaded with negative connotations that justifies the status quo. Decolonial meditations risk being admired to be disqualified, only to be celebrated while liquidated — at worse, mutilated.

Decolonial meditations call for the decolonisation of research methodologies, but such decolonisation does not suggest they must be reformed, but wholly transformed if they are to be used to study the African subject. Decolonial meditations call for new ways of researching the African subject, and this is only possible if the African subject is studied from within, and of course, as a subject and not an object to be ethnographically extracted and hypothetically tested. This has been perversely done and even is still done by the route of methodology that supposes the African subject is mute since it is an object. Decolonising research methodologies are linked to research agendas of, about, and by the African subject, which Brun and Lund call linking theory and practice — praxis.[8] 'Linking theory and practice means getting closer to the society that independent research is supposed to critically explore'.[9] But then, this does not account for the fact that getting closer to the communities can indeed not yield the desired result of decolonising methodologies. Sklar is correct to say, 'The quest for new agenda-setting propositions may have to transcend research horizons that are familiar to political scientists in most, if not all, parts of the world'.[10]

Decolonial meditations have to be engaged with seriously at their moment of rapture and emergence. As Mignolo posits, all thinking is located, and it is important to understand the African subject in its location and the location of the articulation of subjectivity and the location which points to the direction which subjection comes from.[11] The African subject has to struggle to (re)present the self. The subjectivity of the African subject has been that of double-consciousness and bad faith.[12] The African subject has always attempted to emerge in his or her own terms, but for this emergence to emerge there must be some paternalism where the African subject is the appendage of the Euro-American canon. The subjection of the African subject has been that of power relations where the Euro-American power has the epistemological upper hand.

Decolonial meditations are necessary as they offer other modalities of understanding the African subject and its subjectivity. It is informed by what Mignolo refers to as 'a constant and coherent ethical-political critique'.[13] This is because it confronts Euro-American epistemology, which is negative to the African subject. As Mignolo argues, '[T]he starting point of epistemology founds and sustains imperial reasons (theo- and geo-politically)'.[14] This is the fertile ground, which 'others' the African subject to the point of objecthood.

Comaroff and Comaroff introduce three decolonial meditation operations.[15] The first is the mapping of the substance of the phenomenal landscape that grounds any discursive flows and following the traces of that flow to whatever direction they might lead. The second involves the extensions of the phenomenological landscape through geographical dimensions which the discursive flow constitutes itself. Such mapping is multi-sided or multi-dimensional. The third and final methodological operation involves tracing the passage of the discursive flow in terms of its nature, rapture and continuity to ascertain the local genealogy and comparative archaeology of its locality within a wider phenomenon. Smith states, 'Negotiating and transforming institutional practices and research frameworks is as significant as the carrying out of actual research programmes'.[16]

Bates et al. write, 'We seek to create such tensions in order that the contribution of African scholarship be valued, recorded and institutionalized *by the African subjects and through their own modes of methodological subjectivity*'.[17] As the methodology of the alternative knowledges, in confrontation with epistemicide permitted and perpetuated by the mainstream methodologies in studying the socio-political phenomena of the African subject, combative methodology is by its very nature disobedient. As such, it is what the status quo does not want, exposing what is hidden in modernity, hence the quick dismissal without understanding it. As Moore points out, the African subject has suffered ahistorical and selective constructions.[18] Moore adds that the African subject has been the 'exotic Other' — the figure of attraction and fascination. It is not enough for Moore to state that the African subject is transforming and should be studied in the dynamic of the transformed nature. This is because it is not clear in whose interests that transformation is. In order to study the African subject, it is not necessary to subject such a subject to methods as if methods in themselves are devises that are beyond criticism.

Method against Method

Methods are 'epistemic and social constructs whose intellectual, institutional, and ideological configurations are mediated and mapped by the unyielding demands of historical geography'.[19] Method is restrictive and contextual. It cannot be universal as it disconnects, excludes and silences. Method should not be de-contextualised and should be attentive to the lived experiences of the African subject. Subjectivity of the African subject should be that of centredness, which means self-assertion and self-presentation, to understand the discourses central to the African subject.

Gordon refers to it as 'the paradox of a method against method'.[20] This is a paradox not just in the puzzling sense, but a paradox which takes the existential conditions of the African subject seriously. The African subject is not a raw material for extraction to be made sense of, but rather, the subject to be engaged with on its own terms. According to Gordon, this paradox of method against method is performed in any act of reflection.[21] This means the lived experience of the black subject is essential in method, since it is a method which does not instrumentalise, but conscientises the African subject to make sense in the world.

So, the paradox of a method against method is actually the authorisation of the disruption of method. The disruption of the method in Fanon's philosophy of existence is a means of introducing the black subject, who has been an object, to become a subject. That is, the black subject is the one that is in charge of method, and this is the crux of Fanon's philosophy, in which antagonisms are created within method. Method against method is a 'position of embodied interrogatives, of human being[s] re-entering a relationship of questioning'.[22] This should expose the hidden within method which creates the justification of subjection and the hellish existential conditions for the African subjects.

According to Smith, exclusionary devises such as not vigorous, not theorised, not valid, not reliable, and not real are deployed as a template of judgment.[23] To amplify this, Porsanger argues that the mode of knowing is alternative since the methods call for decolonisation.[24] This is often rejected as irrelevant, primitive, subjective, essentialist and unscientific, to name but a few. Imported methodological tools ranging from normative neo-liberal through neo-Marxist to poststructuralist paradigms have dominated the field of African politics.[25] What is needed are methods that can explicate hidden and complex phenomena in a profound manner and which in a way provide the understanding of power relations—that is, the industrial complex of epistemic power hidden in dominant methodologies. Necessary methodological tools are needed for creating and recreating decolonised methodologies. Thus, this will minimise what Vaughan refers to as 'the cult of scientific prediction', which pervades the study of the African subject.[26] It is this cult, as Vaughan argues, that limits the understanding of the complex African social world and the African subject.

When confronted with methodological tools questioning and challenging convention, fierce opposition from the status quo emerges to the point of calling to halt that which is seen as a threat. 'Research contributed to, and draws from, these systems of classification, representation and evaluation'.[27] To add on this, this is what Porsanger has to say:

> In the Western understanding, research in general may be defined as an investigation or experiment aimed at the discovery and interpretation of facts. Research includes collecting information about a particular subject, revising accepted theories or laws in the light of new facts, and the practical application of such new or revised theories or laws.[28]

The African subject has been static and dynamic at the same time. The dynamism has, however, been caught—and has resulted in bondage discourses. Louis suggests that the voice of those who are racially constructed as the other and subject to research may have started out as a low murmur from the margin, but it has now become a distinct and unified cacophony of resistance and distrust as a way of subjectivity.[29] Comaroff and Comaroff call it 'an endemically colonizing enterprise' which entails 'a pre-emptive seizure of authority, of voice, of the right to represent and, incidentally, to profit — or, worse yet, an activity, founded, voyeuristically, on the violation of "the" other'.[30] The subject position of the African subject, subjectivity and subjection can be understood in terms of this colonising enterprise that Comaroff and Comaroff alluded to.[31] The African subject, they contend, does not inhabit social contexts; but it has livelihoods that justify subjection, making the African subject an object.

The methodological issues, being rigid, and the instruments through which the African subject is understood need not only to be rethought, but unthought. The positionality of the unthought exposes the scandal of subjection hidden in the Euro-American methodological canon. The positionality of the unthought can only be imagined through its affective dimension by those who are at the receiving end of subjection.[32] It is against the notion of politics of consensus which is propagated by the canon of methodology. Since existential questions pertaining to African subjects as beings, not objects, are not in the register of these politics, then the whole applicability is a collapsible scandal. In adopting this form of subjectivity, that is, the positionality of the unthought *qua* decolonial meditations, African subjects are charting new terrain in the struggle for liberation. For this struggle to materialise, African subjects should engage in ways of thinking, knowing and doing that are rooted in their own socio-historical experience.

On the Locus of Enunciation

What is essential in researching the African subject is the emphasis of the locus of enunciation, which Mignolo coins as 'I think from where I am'.[33] This is the location of the subject in terms of being, power and knowledge, and so to speak, from the limits of such, since the African subject is located in the zone of non-being. Being located in the zone of non-being, the African subject should, in relation to the locus of enunciation, shift the geography of reason. The need for the shift of the geography of reason stems from the fact that even if people occupy the same space, they do not occupy the same life. The canon of methodology as we know hides its locus of enunciation by claiming to be objective, totalising and universal.

The locus of enunciation positions the African subject to oppose the fundamentalist position of comparing, measuring, evaluating and judging human experiences.[34] This opens up the possibility to 'search for other possible knowledges and worlds'.[35] This search by the African subject is one which informs subjectivity to counter subjection, as it is directed at the African subject. The world inhabited by the African subject is a place which is on the receiving end of the darker side of modernity. It is then important to explore what this system called modernity produces in terms of its darker side. It produces weaker governments which produce corruption, authoritarianism and disabled history. The shift of the geography of reason is necessary for the African subject who is denied of ontology to think from the limits of being in order to allow the emergence of the being, the full subject in its own making.

The self-defining subject is that of self-creation and subject in the making. These aspects mean different things to the Western subject, the self-defining subject, and the African subject. The African subject is in the worst condition when it comes to the level of identity, as such an identity is imposed, because the African subject is the product of the Western subject's construction and definition. The subjectivity of the African subject is important in understanding coloniality of knowledge. Mignolo suggests that the subject position is important in terms of understanding subjection.[36] Mignolo further suggests that the knower should be questioned rather than the known to understand the very epistemic foundation of subjection. This means questioning the very apparatus and the locus of enunciation of the knower in relation to the known.

The subject is the very basis of maintaining the locus of enunciation.[37] This unveils the concealment of the Western epistemology, which suggests the knower in contrast with the unknower, who happens to be the African subject. For Mignolo, the subject controls and dictates the rules of knowledge—so be it if such a figure is implicated and there is no objective or detached being from knowledge. Adding the African subject in this explanation suggests the problematics of a subject which constitutes deprivation and bears no form of epistemic privilege.

Knowledge is always situated, and Grosfoguel articulates the notion of the locus of enunciation.[38] In terms of the locus of enunciation what matters is the enunciation, not the enunciated. The African subject's vantage point is enunciated to understand its subjectivity in relation to the subjection that comes into effect through the manner in which knowledge is used as an instrument of subjection. For this to be framed properly, it is important to state that the locus of enunciation of the African subject can be problematic if the subject is geographically located in Africa but engages Africa from the loci of the empire. This is what strengthens coloniality of knowledge, which often hides its locus of enunciation to normalise subjection.

The locus of enunciation of the African subject thinks with the African subject and from the African subject's subjectivity. It is not thinking for the African, where 'theory was still located in the North while the subject [or object] are located in the South'. The locus of enunciation, as Walsh articulates, is about thinking and speaking from the geopolitical and historical location.[39] This affirms the importance of the subjectivity of the African subject, being at the centre of the modes of self-understanding. This is informed by colonial difference, which guides the reflection and offers a lens through which to view the world. The locus of enunciation, as Walsh articulates, is also 'epistemo-logically diagrammed spaces' which offer a possibility where other knowledges exist—pluriversity and regimes of truth.[40] In amplification of this, Mignolo states:

> The enunciator doesn't name an existing entity but invents it. The enunciation needs an enunciator (agent), an institution, for not every-one can invent the anthropos, but to impose the anthropos as the other in the collective imaginary it is necessary to be in a position to manage the discourse (verbal, visual, sound) by which you name and describe an entity (the anthropos or the other) and succeed in making believe that it exists.[41]

In addition to this, Grosfoguel also states that:

> The fact that one is socially located in the oppressed side of power re-lations, does not automatically mean that he/she is epistemically thinking from the subaltern epistemic location. Precisely, the success of the mod-ern/colonial world-system consists in making subjects that are socially located in the oppressed side of the colonial difference, to think epis-temically like the one on the dominant position. Subaltern epistemic perspective are knowledges coming from below that to produce a critical perspective of hegemonic knowledge in the power relations involved.[42]

This clearly demonstrates the fact that there is no such thing as objectivity, the Western myth that knowledge is divorced from its detached subject, who aims to gain truthful knowledge. Everything is situational and embedded, and the locus of enunciation determines from which side of the global system or formation the knowledge is situated. Coloniality of knowledge should be un-derstood geopolitically.

Euro-American global design strategy is informed by binarism and hierar-chization which keep the imbalances of power and the colonial legacy intact. These are the very forms of epistemic violence which exclude, marginalise, demonise and even eliminate forms of episteme that differ from modernity.[43] Knowledge distinction has been that global history has not changed, but remains a narrative in favour of modernity and maintains the silences on its darker side.

Coloniality of knowledge creates mechanistic narratives which are informed by dominant tendencies informed by subjection, which discards other subjec-tivities differing from its own. As Walsh points out, 'To speak of the geopolitics of knowledge and geopolitical locations of critical thought is to recognize the persistence of a Western hegemony, that positions Eurocentric thought as "universal", while localising other forms of thought as at best folklore'.[44] Coloniality of knowledge originates from epistemic violence and racism which dates back 500 centuries. To add to this view, Lander has it that coloniality of knowledge 'legitimizes ongoing practices involving the colonization of people, culture, and the environment'.[45] This clearly shows the multitude of forces involved to make subjection possible in so far as knowledge is concerned. Grosfoguel puts it in these simpler historical terms:

> We went from the sixteenth century characterization of 'people without writing' to the eighteenth and nineteenth century characterization of 'people without history' to the twentieth century characterization of 'people without development' and more recently, to the early twenty-first century of 'people without democracy'.[46]

These characterisations are part of the Euro-America global design system, the forms of coloniality of knowledge to which the African subject is subjected. Knowledge has been that of the Western canon, which is in need of transplants and appendages which reproduce such knowledge. The subjectivity of the African subject has been at the margins of Western civilisation as the sole purpose of this civilisation was to engage in epistemicide. Knowledge-making in the modern/colonial world is at once knowledge in which the very concept of "modernity" rests and the judge and warrantor of legitimate and sustainable knowledge while erasing other knowledges.[47] For Mignolo, knowledge-making entrenched modernity with its imperialist purposes largely informed by subjection.

Coloniality of knowledge creates a situation where epistemic members in the colonies reproduce information from the empire's locus of enunciation. It is in this schema that the African subject is reduced to an agent of docility who defines and dictates what constitutes knowledge and what does not through a subjectivity alien to itself. This is done in the hidden locus of enunciation, where claims of objectivity and detachment from the empire will be advocated, whereas the reverse is true.

The subjectivity of the African subject rests in a state of lacking, void and deficiency, which justify subjection on the basis of marginality and racialisation. The knowledge that comes from the African subject is stigmatised, since the subjectivity of such a subject is framed similar to the subject. That is to say that the African subject is stigmatised as lacking, void and deficient, and its knowledge will be treated as lacking, void and deficient. According to Mignolo, '[C]oloniality of knowledge rests in the depositor, warrantor, creator and distributor of universal knowledge'.[48] The sole purpose of modernity is to serve the interests of the empire. As Walsh states, the sites of knowledge which are necessary for other regimes of truth are repressed, marginalised, disciplined and destroyed.[49]

The epistemic decolonial shift, which is the movement of the geography of reason, clearly indicates that knowledge about Africa should be looked at through the locus of enunciation of Africa, not that of the empire—that is, Euro-American imperial global designs which are the constitutive parts of modernity, modernity which is also the constitutive part of coloniality, since each cannot survive without the other. Modernity is informed by the expansionism of Western civilisation, which is seen as the absolute civilisation, which is the only process compared to other forms of civilisations. This goes hand in hand with hegemonic narratives projected as absolute to mask the injustices that come with subjection. Such a condescending attitude is informed by the logic of coloniality of power, which sees other forms of knowledge as not being capable of producing knowledge, as they are outside the bounds of Western modernity. So, this means for them to be knowledge, they must be within Western modernity to qualify as knowledge.

'Coloniality of knowledge is precisely the affirmation of the zero-point and the success in silencing or relegating other epistemologies to a barbarian margins, a primitive past'.[50] Maldonado-Torres calls for knowledges which are the very anti-thesis of modernity.[51] Such knowledges of cause put the African subject at the centre and take cognisance of the subjectivity of said subject to counter subjection. For Maldonado-Torres, these are alternative knowledges which find their locus in the cracks of the continent, in borders, in the Global South, in the diaspora, in movements of people, as well in the death and suffering that they may face at the violent hands of the defenders of violent states.

The Western epistemology *qua* methodology identity of the self as a self-defined subject seems to suggest that he has the power, just like the Western subject, to define and to assert himself in the world, the world of the Western subject. The Western subject transforms itself into a master subject. It completes itself by imposing the lacking and void on the 'other', the very basis that explains the subject and the subjectivity that emerges through imposing subjection on the 'other'. In Lacanian terms, the Western subject develops fantasy, it develops imagery, it develops symbolism and it develops the *Real*.[52] This is made operational in the high proportion of signification of the Western subject.

Consequently, the subject position is constituted, shaped, and positioned in relation to the lived experience of subject.[53] If this intervention was to be located in the lived experience the explanation would have been different because it is clear that the subject position of the African subject is determined without or from outside.[54] The subject position of the African subject is that of structural positionality, where the African subject is at the receiving end of the self; the self is thus given and determined for it from outside. It is this self which is under constant surveillance at the level of the body—that is, the body of criminality, because it is raced and finds itself in the anti-black world.

Essentially, subjects comply with demands defined and imposed by the subjectivity of creating the world.[55] These demands are results of oppressive sociopolitical norms embedded in structure—that is, subjection. It seems that the notion of the self should comply with the demands of such a world to fit into the notion of 'ideal proper'. The ideal proper can be seen at the level of the African subject as the starting point of subjection, as it works through the logic of imposition. The self in this process is part of political activity, and the subject position, by and large, is a political project which is intrinsically linked to the identity and being of the African subject. The identity and being of the African subject has and continues to be subjected to epistemological attack, to have its very own being subjected to question and be given the ontological status of being a lacking subject.

Ontology and the Lacking African Subject

The self, in the form of the figure of the Western subject, is in the *imaginaire* of the power structure that created it, its face and physicality, and thinks and acts in that image. In this form, this creates the basis of subjection, a technology in multitudinal terms. The ontology of the Western subject is benchmarked on the basis of the African subject being lacking, inferior, the appendage of the universal—that is, the other. Being the appendage, the African subject is supposed to gravitate towards the universal, to become part of the universal. The African subject is that which has no ontology. As such, being alien to the idea of the universal, this means that there is exclusion of humanity.

The point, therefore, is that of the positionality of the Western subject. It is important to understand the Western subject and not to reject such a subject and its subjectivity outright, since this will not permit understanding of the African subject in the point of its emergence and existence in the postcolony. So, the construction of the African subject at the level of subjectivity is key to understanding its positionality. So then, the subject position of both the Western and African subjects can provide a conflicting interpretation of the material and existential conditions which exist. The Western subject assumes the ego ideal of the 'I'—the autonomous self, the hybrid self in contact with the primitive, static, backward, deviant and so forth—the other self, which is not the self in full essence since it constitutes lack; it considers it to be an incomplete subject, so to speak. All these create the African subject, and such a subject should be understood in relation to the Western subject in the point of emergence.

The Lacanian intervention is not cogito but thought as the self and social.[56] The thinking transcends Descartes because the Western subject thinks with the 'other'. It is asserted by Neill that Lacan had the colonial encounter in mind, though not of the Western subject and the African subject—but the class antagonism of Western subjects. The African subject is that which constitutes a lacking and void existence, an existence incomplete. Lacan's ego identification can be stretched to suggest the misrecognition of the 'other'—that is, the African subject at the receiving end of degrading comparison. The state of comparison is ego-identification—the Western subject inferiorising the African subject to fill its incompleteness and void. Neill argues that in Lacanian terms, the subject constitutes lack and void.[57] As these are constitutive features of the Western subject, they get transposed to the African subject to negate its subjecthood, rendering such a subject that constitutes lack and void to the point of cause of its objectification.

The Western subject is the subject of self-mastery, discovery of the world and mastering the 'other'—that is, that which differs from the Western subject. The Western subject stands in the positionality of mastery *qua* the broader terrains of ontology and epistemology, which constitutes the grounds for constructing the African subject. The Western subject masters the world through colonising and changing the terms of engagement, by having the arbitrary fashion of defining, naming, categorising, labeling, identifying and mapping.[58] This is because he has his own laws, which he imposes through subjection in degrees of being direct and indirect. The idea of the Western subject means the sovereign subject who invades in arbitrary fashion, hence the Western subject's privilege to construct the African subject.

Where does the African subject fit in all of this? Three answers are essential in explaining this phenomenon, which is essentially that of subjection. The first is the filling of the void and lack of the 'other', the African subject. The representation and conception of the African subject as the lacking subject continue to stigmatise it as such. Dunst calls for the 'reconceptualisation of the subject' to say that the constitutiveness and contestation of the subject explains how the subject formation takes place.[59] This of course is different when taking the African subject into account, hence the concern of the study to understand the emergence of the African subject. This is how Said echoes this point:

> Thus the status of colonized people has been fixed in zones of dependency and peripherality, stigmatized in the designation of underdeveloped, less developed, developing state, ruled by a superior, developed, or metropolitan colonizer who was theoretically posited as a categorically antithetical overlord.[60]

The notion of the lack, void and deficiency of the African subject means the category of lesser beings, inferior things, in many different places and in different times. The conception of the world is that the Western subject is complete and the African subject is incomplete. What the African subject is said to lack, among other things, is morals, civilisation, epistemologies, peace, cognitive strength, Christianity, industrialisation, sexual mores, democracy, and human rights, to name but a few. This laid the justification of colonialism, to absolve it and to humanise it, to say that its purpose was to transform and bring salvation to the African subject, who was on the brink of self-mutilation and depletion. In short, to transform the African subject from the barbarian to a citizen and that would then make the African subject to be a complete subject.

Secondly, the Western subject creates a split consciousness in the process of subjection directed at the African subject. In this instance, there is a total rejection of the self and an embracing of the Western. This becomes useful in understanding the discourse of alterity. This is where the African subject rejects itself and aims to collapse itself into the totality of being of the Western subject. If the African subject experiences the lack and void as imposed by the Western subject, the African subject fails to recognise the fact that the Western subject is incomplete itself. Thirdly and finally, the African subject responds to subjection by resisting the discourses of extroversion and alterity. The romanticist idea which is rejectionist and nostalgic becomes nonsensical. With these discourses, the void still cannot be closed and the lack cannot be filled. The predicament in this commonality, though, is that power relations are not the same, but asymmetrical. The Western subject innovates to try to close the void and fill the lack in order to realise completeness. On the other hand, the African subject is told by the Western subject what its lack and void are and how they are impossible to close and fill, subjection.

In relation to the above, it is clear that the colonial encounter is important in understanding the structural positionality and the emergence of the African subject. The colonial encounter is also related to the process of self-mastery by the Western subject. The African subject is excluded from and also harassed to not tamper with the pleasure that is pursued by the Western subject. According to Zizek, to strive for pleasure is to engage in the pathological, so the super-ego of pleasure, its surplus, goes hand in hand with the cult of self-sacrifice.[61] As Zizek remarks, '[D]uty is my pleasure, and doing my duty, is located in the formal space of the "pathological satisfactions"'.[62] This means, as Said has stated, the 'Othering' of Africa and, for that matter, the African subject.[63] It is the externalisation which leads to the ruination of subjectivity of the African subject, or what Fanon refers to as the damned of the earth.[64]

Political (re)presentation is done by the Western subject. The African subject is left in the predicament of incompleteness, the subject, which constitutes lack and void. It is the ontologically obsolete subject as it is rooted out of the logic of the subject. The very definitive conditions of existence assume the differences of existential conditions for both the Western subject and the African subject. Zizek notes, 'At the level of the law, the state power merely represents the interests of its subjects; it serves them, is responsive to them, and is itself subject to their control'.[65] Even if this proposition would be true and valid in a political community, it is entirely different when it comes to the African subject. Mouffe (1993) points out that the political is inherent in any human society and part of the ontological condition.[66] Even though the gains of democratic revolution are hard won and must be defended, as Mouffe states, they apply to the Western subject more than they are relevant to the African subject.

The relationality of the Western subject towards the African subject is that which Zizek refers to as 'obscene excess'.[67] The obscene excess symbolises and actualises the structural asymmetry between the Western subject and the African subject. It suggests, as Zizek notes, 'a series of catastrophes which precipitated disastrous violence on an unprecedented scale'.[68] Taking the distinction of 'enemy' and 'adversary', as espoused by Mouffe, the opponent should not be regarded as the enemy to be destroyed, but the adversary.[69] According to Mouffe, the adversary is of good importance 'whose existence is legitimate and must be tolerated'.[70] This is problematic in two senses as far as the African subject is concerned. In the first sense, the African subject in the sense of ontology is non-existent. So, therefore, that which is non-existent cannot be tolerated, hence the subjection of the African subject. In the second and at least the final sense, if the African subject engages in the act of emergence, this suggests subjection—the enemy to be destroyed. Therefore, it is clear that the African subject is not the adversary, but the enemy. The idea of political community is not applicable in either the colony or the postcolony. Mouffe's remarks are revealing thus:

> When there is a lack of democratic political struggle with which to identify, their place is taken by other forms of identification, of ethnic, nationalist or religious nature, and the opponent is defined in those terms too. In such conditions, the opponent cannot be perceived as an adversary to content with, but only the enemy to be destroyed. This is what pluralist democracy should avoid; yet it can only protect itself against such a situation by recognizing the nature of the political instead of denying its existence.[71]

Even if the idea of the political is acknowledged in its complexity, as Mouffe suggests, the African subject is not part of the political, for this subject is in the space of subjection, which makes it the enemy to be destroyed. This is largely based on the fact that it is a subject which constitutes lack and void—the object. When it comes to the African subject, there is none of what Mouffe calls 'the ethical nature of the political association'.[72] The political is the absence of ethics, the very nature of subjection. As the African subject is preoccupied with the question of emerging from the clutches of repression, its ultimate desire is that of liberation. The form of subjectivity that will come into being is to have a stance against repression and to fight for emergence.

Against the Repressive and the Case for the Emergent

The discourses of justice, equality and liberty, the very ideals of the universal, fall along the wayside as soon as the African subject emerges. This is simply because what informs the subjectivity of the metropolis is its relation to the African subject, hence the idea of racial superiority, which stamps in the colonial practice of racism. As Thomas states, 'The voluntary or forced displacement of the African subjects has a long history'.[73] The notion of methodology, in its traditional sense, and persisting as it is, suggests the complicity of subjection. The African subject has not been allowed to emerge in the annals of methodology; it has been the raw material to be subjected to the economy of extraction.

Linked also to the above is the horizontal conversation approach, which advocates the empowerment of the African subject to be high in its own approach to epistemology. On the basis of this approach, the location is determined from the standpoint of the researcher. This entails a combination of deconstructivism, textual analysis, interpretive analysis and genealogies—part of which forms decolonisation of methodologies from the lens of the researcher's lived experience and not some external methodologies which constrict. The horizontal conversation approach as decolonisation has a vast array and purpose. Smith has always cautioned that problematising the African subject through the Euro-American lens, the very lens of obsession, has been the imperial history that is struck with the reality of the African subject.[74] The horizontal conversation approach is based on the epistemology and ontology of the African subject by the African subject and from the standpoint of the African subject.

The process of decolonisation requires new, critically evaluated methodologies and new ethically and culturally acceptable approaches to the study of the African subject.[75] The African subject's desire to be a subject in the real sense of the term, not the subject of lack—or worse, an object in the Euro-American canonical imaginary and stereotype—the so-called objective reality. Porsanger argues for the African subject 'to decide about their present and future, and to determine their place in the world'.[76] Louis calls for the beginning of continuing conversation,[77] that is, a research agenda which advocates decolonisation of methodologies. For Louis, the locus of research of the African subject is colonised existentially and materially, hence the need for decolonisation. The horizontal conversation approach is the confrontation of oppression and its effects at the epistemic as well as ontological levels.

The horizontal conversation approach is 'both reflective and reflexive, both imaginative and empirical'.[78] It is in the context of the mode of presentation, and representation of the African subject is in its own terms, and not inferiority and otherisation. Since the conventional Euro-American approach is a fixed design, or flexible but to a certain degree for the African subject, the horizontal conversation approach advocates a redesign for the African subject and subjectivity. The Euro-American approach needs to be decolonised when studying the African subject because they have been used as a colonising tool. The kind of methodological operation has to change when it comes to the African subject. The horizontal conversation approach has it that research itself is a site of struggle against epistemic and ontological colonisation and imperialism. The method of conversation means that the African subject is able to speak. Such speaking is indeed the mode of presentation, and representation of the African subject is located within the ambit of resistance and dissent. The purpose to be served is indeed that of opening various sites of interrogation and understanding of the African subject, its subjectivity, and how to understand and confront its subjection.

The horizontal conversation approach seeks to dehegemonise the Euro-American epistemic and ontological projects that propagate the idea of universality as if it included the African subject, whereas it marginalises it to the point of non-existence—objecthood. The idea of the universal is rooted in the Euro-American method, which does not allow contested narratives and multiple discourses. Even if these do exist, they exist within the loci of the Euro-American method. It needs to be highlighted that the idea of the universal is exterior to the African subject, since the universal is the Euro-American locality. Against this backdrop, there cannot be any conversation since the very terms of political engagement and possibility are located outside the existence and the lived experience of the African subject. So this means the very act of the universal is a totalising discourse—the very impulse of colonisation. 'Just as the method is always profoundly theoretical in its provenance, so its substance ought, always to be practice-base and context-sensitive.'[79] Mustapha concludes by saying, 'The task before the Africanist political science is to bring social transformation back on the agenda'.[80]

Almost invariably, the construction and conceptualisation of knowledge have social, spatial and temporal contest and referents. Few would disagree that knowledge, whatever the prevailing disciplinary labels, is produced through specific paradigms that are developed by certain people in particular places and periods.[81]

The horizontal conversation approach enables 'dialogue and collaboration on shared concerns'.[82] It seeks to (re)package the African subject as the self which destructs the whole architecture of the Euro-American gaze—that is, objecthood which packages methods of understanding the African subject to the point of objecthood. Since conversation is decolonised, it is a reversal discourse but not in the sense of a response, but of self-assertion and representation—the emergence of the African subject.

Conversation engages the terms of epistemic power relations, not its content. As Mignolo states, conversation is a moment of fracture and breakage, a moment of opening.[83] This is informed by impulses of freedom and liberation where in 'a world in which many worlds fit' and 'another world is possible'.[84] According to Comaroff and Comaroff, 'Discursive flows, although having focal centres, are inherently open, flexible in scope and shifting in both their content and their constituent'.[85] The universal when it comes to the African subject erects strictures. This is such that the African subject should be constantly being under the subjection of surveillance, which ultimately means the continued assault of the African subject. It denies co-presence which the African subject in the state of emergence seeks to advocate. The emergence will come into being through the continued praxis pitched at the level of the epistemological, existential and ontological. This will take the form of a decolonial turn and option, which is the path determined by African subjects as the route to liberation is in their own terms.

The Decolonial Turn and Options

The decolonial option approach embraces the 'wider framework of self-determination, decolonization and social justice'.[86] It names those who are in the margins of the universal and 'relocates and regionalizes categories framed by other historical experiences'.[87] This is to confront the hegemonic construction and power of knowledge, which justify the subjection of the African subject in African politics, in which African subjects are just atomic objects with no sense of political action informed by subjectivity. The decolonial option approach means not conforming to the methodologies provided. On this note, it should be stressed that research is a highly political activity.[88] It being a highly political activity suggests that it can be used to oppress or to liberate the African subject. The concern here is that the most dismissed political nature of research is that which advocates the emergence of the African subject and the one that is the alternative, based in the options being made available to the dominant research methodologies and its approaches. Sklar is correct to argue that '[t]he formulation of questions for research is a subjective exercise. Those who dislike the existing choice of questions are at liberty to formulate and display their own'.[89]

The decolonial option approach points out that research depends on the location of the researcher and also the political desires of the researcher.[90] According to Smith, 'Social science research is based upon ideas, beliefs and theories about the social world'.[91] Therefore, this means that research is a matter of options, not constrictions. What plagues the study of the African subject is the epistemic, ethical and political aspects rooted in colonialism.[92] It should be clarified from the onset that '[d]ecolonization, however, does not mean and has not meant a total rejection of all theory and research or Western knowledge'.[93] Porsanger states, 'These perspectives represent alternative ways of thinking about research process[es]'.[94] Hence there should be the availability of options, which the decolonial option approach requires. This means, therefore, to study African politics 'may well require a more expansive, eclectic, and imaginative approach'.[95]

The decolonial option approach as a tool 'arose "naturally" as a consequence of the formation and implementation of structures of domination'.[96] Decolonial options also arose from the epistemic domination which reappears in the metamorphosis-like form of changes, adaptations and new modalities. This opens vistas for a new paradigm or new paradigms. The decolonial option approach 'is an opening towards another thing, on the march, searching for itself in the difference'.[97] Epistemic political freedom will mean the opening and freedom of another way of thinking. The decolonial options approach is likely to face the possibility of what Mignolo calls 'silence by official interpretations'.[98]

Linked to the decolonial option approach is the epistemic disobedience approach. According to Mignolo, 'Epistemic disobedience takes us to a different place, to a "different beginning", to spatial sites of struggles and building rather than a new temporality within the same space'.[99] It confronts colonial knowledges for the sole aim of the emergence of the African subject. The epistemic disobedience approach focuses on possibilities hidden for the subjectivity of the African subject, the possibility that will liquidate the state subjection which plagues the African subject. Epistemic disobedience is the counterpoint of the Euro-American episteme and the idea of the universal. The epistemic disobedience approach is rooted in 'the dense history of planetary decolonial thinking'.[100]

> In the *faux* egalitarianism of these neoliberal times, it is easy to become mired in trivial arguments over whether "meta-narratives of modernity", or Theory, removes from "others" the capacity to present themselves or to determine their own futures. All this while the masters of the market, and powerful political pragmatists, fashion new modes of extraction, and explanation.[101]

What informs the epistemic disobedience approach is that criticism of Euro-American modernity and its technologies of subject is more urgent than ever before. This is not disobedience for its own sake, but for the emergence of the African subject. The mere fact that the African subject emerges means disobedience, because this subject must be silenced in objecthood. The epistemic disobedience approach seeks to create its own terms of freedom to criticise, choose, (re)define, create, change and exchange. As such, it is the approach which even confronts the constrictions of Euro-American methodology informed by objectivity, universalism and truth. What informs this disobedience is the danger to conform, which will lead to appropriation and adaptation, and as a result being reduced to the mechanistic thinking of the African subject. The turns and option of decoloniality are constitutive parts of decolonial meditations more so in relation to the positionality of the African subject in African politics.

Conclusion

The strength of decolonial meditations is the exposure of the hidden scandal inherent in the Euro-American canonical methodologies. It is in this study that the emphasis is placed on understanding the African subject on the basis of locating its beginning to the colonial encounter and also in the postcolony. Decolonial meditations confront the subject matter of the Euro-American episteme and advocate the centredness and emergence of the African subject. African politics needs to be understood, if it is African politics, one that is enunciated from the subjectivity of the African subject as having the epistemic privilege and, of course, not being at the receiving end of epistemological exclusion. African politics, for it to be reconfigured, should continue to be deepened in relation to decolonial meditations that aim to untangle African politics from the clutches of the Euro-American canon. The positioning of the African subject in African politics is the epistemic rupture and also the suture of subjectivities, which is essential for decolonial meditations which show that other ways of knowing and worlds are possible.

Notes and References

1. Gordon, L. R. (2000). *Existentia Africana: Understanding Africana existential thought.* New York, NY: Routledge.

2. Ibid.

3. Savransky, M. (2012). Worlds in the making: Social sciences and the ontopolitics of knowledge. *Postcolonial Studies, 15*(3): 351–368.

4. Ibid.

5. Louis, R. P. (2007). Can you hear us now? Voices from the margins: Using indigenous methodologies in geographic research. *Geographic Research, 45*(2), 130–139.

6. Ake, C. (1982). *Social science as imperialism: The theory of political development.* Ibadan, Nigeria: Ibadan University Press, p. 125.

7. Ibid.

8. Brun, C., & Lund, R. (2010). Real-time research: Decolonising research practices— or just another spectacle of researcher-practitioner collaboration? *Development in Practice, 20*(7), 812–826.

9. Ibid., p. 825.

10. Sklar, L. S. (1993). The African frontier for political science. In R. H. Bates, V. Y. Mudimbe and J. O'Bar, (Eds.), *Africa and the disciplines: The contributions of research in Africa and to the social sciences and humanities* (pp. 83–110). Chicago, IL: University of Chicago Press.

11. Mignolo, W. D. (2011). Epistemic disobedience and the decolonial option: A manifesto. *Transmodernity, 1*(2), 44–66.

12. Gordon, L. (2010). Theory in black: Teleological suspensions in philosophy of culture. *Qui Parle, 18*(2), 193–214.

13. Mignolo, Epistemic disobedience and the decolonial option, p. 55.

14. Ibid., p. 56.

15. Comaroff, J., & Comaroff, J. (2006). Ethnography on an awkward scale: Postcolonial anthropology and the violence of abstraction. In P. T. Zeleza (Ed.), *The study of Africa: disciplinary and interdisciplinary encounters* [Vol. 1] (pp. 75–100). Dakar, Senegal: CODESRIA Books. See pp. 92–93.

16. Smith, L. T. (1999). *Decolonizing methodologies: Research and indigenous peoples.* London, England: Zed Books, p. 140.

17. Bates, R. H., Mudimbe, V. Y., & O'Bar, J. (1993). Introduction. In R. H. Bates, V. Y. Mudimbe, & J. O'Bar (Eds.), *Africa and the disciplines: The contributions of research in Africa and to the social sciences and humanities* (pp. xi–xxiii). Chicago, IL: The University of Chicago Press, p. xxi (my italics).

18. Moore, S. F. (1993). Changing perspectives on a changing Africa: The work of anthropology. In R. H. Bates, V. Y. Mudimbe, & J. O'Bar (Eds.), *Africa and the disciplines: The contributions of research in Africa and to the social sciences and humanities* (pp. 3–57). Chicago, IL: The University of Chicago Press.

19. Zeleza, P. T. (2006). Introduction: The internationalisation of African knowledges. In P. T. Zeleza (Ed.), *The study of Africa: Disciplinary and interdisciplinary encounters* [Vol 1] (pp. 1–24). Dakar, Senegal: CODESRIA Books, p. 1.

20. Gordon, p. 200.

21. Ibid.

22. Ibid., p. 202.
23. Smith.
24. Porsanger, J. (2004). An essay about indigenous methodology. Retrieved from http://www.ub.uit.no/munin/handle/10037/906.
25. Vaughan, O. (1994). Political science and the study of African politics: A view from the grassroots. In A. K. Bangura (Ed.), *Research methodology and African studies* [Vol 1] (pp. 147–163). Lanham, MD: University Press of America.
26. Ibid., p. 149.
27. Smith, p. 43.
28. Porsanger, p. 2.
29. Louis.
30. Comaroff & Comaroff, p. 79.
31. Ibid.
32. Sexton, J., & Copeland, H. (2003). Raw life: An introduction. *Qui Parle, 13*(2), 53–62, p. 53.
33. Mignolo, Epistemic disobedience and the decolonial option.
34. Mignolo, W. D. (2007). Introduction: Coloniality of power and de-colonial thinking. *Cultural Studies, 21* (2–3), 155–165.
35. Walsh, C. (2007). Shifting the politics of critical knowledge. *Cultural Studies, 21*(2–3), 224–239. p. 234.
36. Mignolo, W. D. (2009). Epistemic disobedience, independent thought and de-colonial freedom. *Theory, Culture and Society, 26*(7–8), 1–23.
37. Ibid.
38. Grosfoguel, R. (2007). The epistemic decolonial turn: Beyond the political-economy paradigms. *Cultural Studies, 21*(2–3), 211–223.
39. Walsh, C. (2002). The (re)articulation of political subjectivity and colonial difference in Ecuador: Reflections on capitalism and the geopolitics of knowledge. *Nepantla, 3*(1), 61–97.
40. Walsh, Shifting the politics of critical knowledge.
41. Mignolo, Epistemic disobedience and the decolonial option, p. 275.
42. Grosfoguel, The epistemic decolonial turn, p. 213.
43. Ibid.
44. Walsh, Shifting the politics of critical knowledge, p. 22.
45. Lander, E. (2002). Eurocentrism, modern knowledges and the "natural" order of capital. *Nepantla, 3*(2): 245–268, p. 257.
46. Grosfoguel, The epistemic decolonial turn, p. 257.
47. Mignolo, Epistemic disobedience, independent thought and de-colonial freedom.
48. Ibid., p.18.
49. Walsh, Shifting the politics of critical knowledge.
50. Mignolo, Introduction: Coloniality of power and de-colonial thinking, p. 162.
51. Maldonado-Torres, N. (2004). The topology of being and geo-politics of knowledge: Modernity, empire and coloniality. *City, 8*(1), 29–56.
52. Neill, C. (2008). Severality: Beyond the compression of the cogito. *Subjectivity, 24*, 325–339.
53. Houseley, W. (2009). Interaction, discourse and the subject. *Subjectivity, 26,* 96–86.
54. Fanon, F. [1952] 2008. *Black skin, white masks*(Trans. Charles Lam Markmann). London, England: Pluto.

55. Layton, L. (2008). What divides the subject? Psychoanalytic reflections on subjectivity, subjection and resistance. *Subjectivity, 22*, 20–72.

56. Neill.

57. Ibid.

58. Said, E. W. (1989). Representing the colonised: Anthropologies interloculators. *Critical Inquiry, 15*(2), 205–225.

59. Dunst, A. (2011). Guest editorial: Collective subjects, emancipatory cultures and political transformation. *Subjectivity, 4*, 1–8.

60. Said, p. 207.

61. Zizek, S. (2005, July–August). Against human rights. *New Left Review, 34*, 115–131.

62. Ibid., p. 212.

63. Said.

64. Fanon, F. (1961) 1990. *The wretched of the earth* (Trans. by Constance Farrington). London, England: Penguin.

65. Zizek, p. 123.

66. Mouffe, C. (1993). *The return of the political.* London, England: Verso.

67. Zizek.

68. Ibid., p. 123.

69. Mouffe.

70. Ibid., p. 4.

71. Ibid., p. 6.

72. Ibid.

73. Thomas, D. (2007). *Black France: Colonialism, immigration, and transnationalism.* Bloomington, IN: Indiana University Press, p. 42.

74. Smith.

75. Porsanger.

76. Ibid., p. 13.

77. Louis.

78. Comaroff & Comaroff, p. 82.

79. Ibid., p. 85.

80. Mustapha, A. R. (2006). Rethinking Africanist political science. In P. T. Zeleza (Ed.), *The study of Africa: Disciplinary and interdisciplinary encounters* [Vol 1] (pp. 187–202). Dakar, Senegal: CODESRIA Books, p. 200.

81. Zeleza, p. 1.

82. Ibid.

83. Mignolo, Epistemic disobedience and the decolonial option.

84. Ibid, p. 48.

85. Comaroff & Comaroff, p. 91.

86. Smith, p. 4.

87. Mignolo, Epistemic disobedience and the decolonial option, p. 44.

88. Smith.

89. Sklar, p. 103.

90. Calvo, L. (2003). Book review. *Signs, 29*(1), 1–4.

91. Smith, p. 47.

92. Comaroff & Comaroff.

93. Smith, p. 39.

94. Porsanger, p. 1.

95. Vaughan, p. 148.
96. Mignolo, Epistemic disobedience and the decolonial option, p. 48.
97. Ibid., p. 50.
98. Ibid., p. 51.
99. Ibid., p. 45.
100. Ibid., p. 46.
101. Comaroff & Comaroff, p. 82.

Chapter 13

Decolonial Turn and the Case for an Afrocentric Analysis of African Integration

Siphamandla Zondi

Introduction

> *If we are adequately Afrocentric the international implications will not be lost on the others.*
> —Kwesi Prah quoted in Mafeje, 2011, p. 33

> *A Union of African states will project more effectively the African personality. It will command respect from a world that has regard only for size and influence.*
> —Kwame Nkrumah, 1961, ix

The possibility of emancipatory thinking and novel insights into Africa's quest for unity and integration as central to its assuming its rightful place in the community of nations is huge, but this must wait until decolonial Afrocentric paradigms founded on true epistemic plurality are applied to reinterpret this phenomenon. This begins by accepting, at least, that the prisms commonly used to understand African integration, mainly functionalist and neo-functionalist theories born out of the European integration experience, can be prisons of thought that limit our ability to understand the rationale and locomotives of this from within.

This is not a case for valorisation of every thought, philosophy or theory with African origin, but a demand for recentering Africa by de-centering Europe in the study of Africa. It is a call for Afrocentric methodologies in the in-

239

terpretation of African affairs. There cannot be a further advance in our understanding of Africa as a geopolitical phenomenon and the African integration theme born out of the struggle to free Africa from the shackles of Western colonialism, without scholars making a serious endeavour to understand it for what it is rather than as a site to test Eurocentric theories. This is made all the more necessary by the fact that Eurocentric paradigms in their various forms are premised, even if not openly stated, on the assumption that the European experience is not just applicable in all situations including African phenomena, but that it is the only experience worth using to understand phenomena, including integration of political systems, the world over. On this basis, the basis must be Europe's experience as a standard against which other experiences are measured.

This assumption forces African scholars into options of methods within one mega-method, namely: Eurocentrism. Thus scholars of Africa are transformed into stooges in the silencing of epistemic lenses whose locus of enunciation is Africa, Africans, and their experiences. They are thus enlisted in an epistemicide against epistemic pluralism in order to maintain the imperialism of social science as it pertains to African integration studies. The fact that the integration idea is born out of efforts at decolonisation of African political geography and that Eurocentric analysis seeks to understand this from of geography of reason that is Western-centric makes this one of the worst forms of cognitive injustice. Practically speaking, colonisation involved piercing into the African's mind, soul and his land in order to create colonies in his mind, his soul and his land.

Nowhere is the need for Afrocentric decolonial thinking more pertinent than in the study of African regional and continental integration since the 1960s because this was the main frame in which African continental politics has been understood and discussed. The participation of Africa at the Berlin Conference in 1884–5 in order to transform it into a collection of colonies in the form of nation-states was one of the worst forms of wounds inflicted on the geopolitics and body politics of Africa. These wounds manifest in the failure of development, sovereignty and security in these invented enclaves. Continental integration was conceived as a form of healing the bruises evident on the African map in the hope of killing the infection of underdevelopment, poverty and despair that continue to haunt Africa in the community of nations. The integration story is thus an attempt to reverse the curse of Berlin, re-center Africa in its politics and development, re-humanise Africans, and enable it to associate with the blessings of common prosperity, peace and justice. The unity endeavour is an epitome of Africa's search for an authentic voice and position in the world. Continental unity and regional integration have over the period become the central tenets of Africa's battle to undo the vagaries of being balkanised and of having been brought onto the periphery of the world system by the project of colonisation. Thus the concept of integration was born out of the age-old dream of African renaissance, from slavery through colonialism to the globalisation era. This cannot be understood from the perspective of the empire that colonised in the first place and cannot be adequately understood from the Euro-American locus of enunciation. We thus have a precious opportunity to test the utility of Afrocentric methodologies in helping scholars gain deeper insights into the prospects and limits of the African renaissance as has been pursued in the past half century.

This chapter, therefore, moves from the premise that the subject of African continental politics and the theme of unity in particular are inadequately understood until there has been an epistemic break with Eurocentric illusions and negations masquerading as universal truths and objectivity. This is because a discourse about Africa that centers Europe's experience, theories and imaginaries can only lead to alienated narratives. Central to a decolonial turn in the analysis of African continental politics is to accept the fact that the construction of the African continental reality remains dictated from outside, so that Africa comes to represent a problem in a pathological sense. It comes to be presented and represented as a problem of existence. Thus Africa is represented as negations and Africans as the damned. Because African politics and international relations are disciplines within Westernised social science, Africa and Africans suffer epistemological invisibility and exclusion. The chapter proposes to contribute to epistemic justice and an end to paradigmatic domination by taking a decolonial turn to a liberating and authentic discourse on African continental politics and integration in the form of an Afrocentric methodology because it promotes the study of Africa from inside, the re-centering of Africa in the discourse about its experience. It thus makes it possible to see, understand, interpret and debate the African agency in continental integration endeavours. On this basis also, Africa's aspiration to help fashion an equal, just and fairer world order makes sense. As the quote from Nkrumah above suggests, the integration process can be linked to the processes of decolonisation of Africa, and this extended to the efforts to decolonise thinking about Africa, as suggested by his constant reference to the theory of African personality when discussing this.

Fragmentation and Subjection:
The Eurocentric Prism on African Affairs

The limiting effects of pervasive Eurocentrism on our ability to grasp the creative interface between various cultures, civilisation, knowledges, epistemology is now well known. It is not a mere alternative perspective in the free interface of epistemes on Africa, but it is a hegemonic epistemology and methodology thriving on the silencing and the foreclosing of space for other ways of knowing and explaining African phenomena. It tends to homogenise everything under its ethnocentric perspective, rendered as the only logical point of view. It thrives on the erasure of epistemic plurality and closure of the kaleidoscope of universes of knowing. It thus blocks our understanding of these phenomena from within.

The theories and methodologies used to understand the European integration process which dominate scholarship on African integration are obviously not adequate for the purpose, for they are almost completely deduced from the liberal economic theories and ideologies born out of European experience. It is assumed, for instance, that "[t]he impetus for regional integration draws its rationale from the standard trade theory, which states that free trade is superior to all other trade policies," which comes from the European experience applied to Africa.[1] Thus the space for exploring the primary impetus for integration on the basis of the thinking of those who have driven the process since the 1960s is foreclosed. There is no possibility of finding it in the fact that colonial rule was premised on the fragmentation of statehood and economy, and therefore integration was effectively a process of decolonising African political geography. Thus, it has been common for studies to refer to political statements of key African drivers of unity and integration, such Nkrumah's above, as a mere statement of the fact of integration and look for the reasoning for this statement from Eurocentric theory even though the statement includes an indication of how they arrived at this determination that Africans must unite. In this sense, it is like making the point that a united Africa "will project more effectively the African personality" is merely an emphasis of the point rather than a profound statement of purpose and end. It may be that even the idea of African personality is assumed to mean Africa as a whole geographically. This is a refusal to give this Afrocentric theory space to be heard and explored in understanding this very statement, for many that quote it do not explore the implications of the suggestion that integration is a manifestation of this particular Afrocentric thought, even in occasions where scholars acknowledge that Nkrumah was referring to a theory, but described as his theory it is left at that. It does not seem to dawn on scholars that this is an invocation of this and related Afrocentric theories. To do so would have translated to effectively loosening the stranglehold of functionalist and neofunctionalist interpretations, forcing them to compete for insights with Afrocentric thought.

For this reason, the explanations do not sufficiently locate the analysis in a struggle to free Africa from a global system that the Pan-Africanists of the early independence period saw as neo-colonial and imperial in nature. This is why it has been a dominant underlying assumption that Africa has to be integrated internally in order to integrate with the world. Even slightly radical analyses premised their analysis on the idea that the integration was a response to marginalisation in the global economy and, therefore, its intent was to prepare Africa to integrate into this global village, for it is assumed that such integration is beneficial. The idea that even if this were true, Africa may be integrating into a periphery of this world system, as aptly described by Immanuel Wallerstein, is not even considered.[2] Anyway, Samir Amin makes the point that the error of dominant analyses is the assumption that Africa was marginalised from globalisation, suggesting that it was not integrated enough. Instead, he shows, Africa was integrated into the periphery by the imperial centre during the process of colonisation. For this reason, it was for a long time before the end of colonial rule the supplier of raw materials to Western societies and profits for Western corporations.[3] Thus, Africa was the basis on which the core-periphery dynamic in the world system functioned, for this dynamic operated on the basis of super profits and the availability of cheap labour and raw material.[4]

Nkrumah's proposition that in fact the African integration story is part of Africa's historical responsibility to the world, the duty to help decolonise the world by relocating Africa from the bottom of the hierarchy of power, as determined by imperial designs, to a respectable place, a position of influence, is not explored. This is the meaning of the phrase: "It will command respect from a world that has regard only for size and influence." This is an intention to correct the positioning of Africa in the world system, where it is in the periphery, to a respectable place, which is what the centre is currently, and thus effectively transform the world. This transformative evocation and challenge to the colonial order of things in the statement and the whole discourse of the time is lost in a rush to apply Eurocentric theories straight-jacketed by the assumption of an integration that happened in the centre of the system and thus required no decolonisation in order to happen. This is what is meant by the possibility of new insights emerging from the use of lenses from within in the study of integration. The implication from the above reflection is that it is not sufficient to have African sources such as speeches of African leaders and the materials that they wrote in integration studies, for if seen through the Eurocentric lenses the juicy stuff that lends itself to the decolonial paradigm is sifted out.

Conceived within the dominant paradigm, the logic of integration was about creating incentives for market forces to create economies of scale, change the terms of trade, improve business efficiency and promote the specialisation that underpins various theories of economic change. In this sense, dominant customs union theories and trade theories are premised on assumptions that market dynamics that enabled progress in European integration exist in Africa and are necessarily catalytic in the integration process. This is a crude importation of experiences and their motive forces rather than an attempt to understand Africa's dynamics in their own right and allow for divergence or convergence of trends to emerge from such study. There is thus no space for the possibility that the dynamics considered may not prevail in the African experience and may not even be desirable or necessary. These theories function on the basis that promised benefits (economic growth, efficiency, leveraging of commodity prices, etc.) have to be found for the motivation to integrate. The integration thus conceived mirrors a selfish business transaction where each actor is drawn into it by the extent to which it can maximise its profit position as a result. If this was the European model born out of its being a locomotive for global capitalism in which the business of selfish transactions is in vogue, it is also expected to be invariably Africa's; it is the only way to learn how to be part of global capitalism, going by the name globalisation.

The fundamental objective of integration in this variety of Eurocentric theories is the liberalisation of markets, including through further weakening of the state. It is not possible within a state-led development model, which Africa may have preferred. Thus it is part of the logic of the neoliberal agenda, especially the Washington Consensus, whose key message is to shrink the state into a lean and managerial instrument for creating an enabling environment for markets. In this paradigm both as policy ideology and a theory of study, the idea that African states would be devoted to stimulating human development by intervening to change the structure of the economy from one dictated by colonial logic to one dictated by the historical responsibility to ensure a better life for people is out of question; it is silenced. A huge body of literature is marshalled by scholars that do not question Eurocentrism in the mainstream thinking on regional integration and by the usual instruments of the Washington Consensus like the IMF and World Bank, in favour of the idea of creating bigger transnational spaces for market forces to make profit presumably for the good of all.[5]

The range of factors offered to explain the failure of integration is often useful but insufficient in that it fails to integrate reasons related to the coloniality of economic logic and geography as well as decolonial Afrocentric aspirations. For instance, the matter of weak infrastructure linkages is correctly noted as one of the inhibiting factors without relating this to the inherited and maintained economic logic of the colony, which was to build infrastructure for extraction and exploitation rather than national and regional development.

When the impact of donor dependency and donor choices in influencing national investment patterns are not factored in, then Africans only are to blame for this and are responsible for fixing it.[6] It is assumed the size of national investment markets discourage investors of significance. Thus, integration is first and foremost a creation of economies of scale, not to enable Africans to attain a respectable position in the global economy, as Nkrumah's statement intimates, but to make it easy for market forces to maraud larger areas with much more natural resources, commodities and cheap labour than national spaces. Market forces are seen as motives of virtue, while African states, which remain the only institutions of power under African control, are viewed as stumbling blocks. They are considered good only if they accelerate integration, not to strengthen this newly gained political authority, but to create an enabling environment for market forces to flourish in the hope of some trickle-down effect in the long run.

The factor of currency non-convertibility is not always linked to particular choices that African governments have had to make in regard to how monetary policies could shield them from the vagaries of an unequal global economy. Instead, it is seen as part of enabling market diffusion from country to country in a process generally described as causing national borders to disappear, and with them nation states. Whereas currency integration such as the one of the Franc in Central and West Africa, of course done under French tutelage, might have offered opportunities to avoid a complete collapse of many weak economies in these regions if understood from within, it is assumed in the dominant paradigms only as part of enabling capital interests to flourish.[7] This is a subtle argument for conformity to the global neoliberal prescripts.

Studies using dominant paradigms have also suggested that African economies have intrinsic features that militate against stronger growth in intra-African economic activity and regional integration. These include factors like narrow production bases, insularity, and so forth.[8] Often this is linked to mistakes by dominant forces like the IMF and the World Bank as well as policy choices by the national elite. The studies do not see this as necessarily a part of a global ideological endeavour and therefore its inherent weakness. They fail to contextualise these features in the history of a post-colony in which colonial economic logic of extraction and the supply of raw material for the development of the centre has not been undone for the purposes of creating space for integration, cooperation.

The Bretton Woods institutions have produced a number of studies since the early 1990s promoting approaches to regional integration that conform to its ideology, Western neoliberalism. This is part of their unwillingness to be overtaken by paradigms promoted by the UN Economic Commission for Africa (UNECA) and the UN Commission on Trade and Development (UNCTAD), which viewed regional integration as an outcome of and a stimulus for endogenous development, as a means of collective self-reliance in response to the fragmenting effects of globalisation. IMF and Work Bank reports remind readers that fundamentally what stops Africa from economic integration is failure to liberalise. This results, in this logic, in distorted trade regimes. This is often nothing but an indirect push for neoliberal economic reforms, especially the liberalisation of key economic sectors, privatisation of key industries, relaxation of exchange controls and inflation control, among other things.[9]

Routinely, analysts employed by Bretton Woods institutions churn out research marshalling mountains of data collected on the basis of hegemonic theoretical models to demonstrate that high transaction costs caused by inadequate communication infrastructure and transport as well as restrictive trade regimes in the form of tariff and non-tariff barriers explain Africa's failed economic integration. Therefore, they suggest, the answer to Africa's integration aspirations is voluntary end to protection of essential industries and jobs, and putting hope for investments before the protection of national sovereignty.

What is even more baffling is the peddling of theoretical assumptions linked to neoliberal economic ideology even when it contradicts the very evidence that these institutions produce. For instance, one of the often-mentioned hypotheses for weak economic integration in Africa is that poor growth performance leads to protectionism, while trade liberation is made easier by strong growth performance.[10] The Bretton Woods institutions have also had a hand in popularising such deterministic theoretical assumptions in a manner that is akin to causing objective realities to fit assumptions derived from specific research fields.[11] On this basis, economists speculate that the reason for poor economic integration in Africa must have to do with poor growth performance triggering protectionism.[12] Yet, the same economists and international economic agencies have been churning out evidence to show that Africa has consistently registered superior economic growth rates in the post-Cold War era.[13] There is one plausible explanation for this: it is likely that scholars succumb to the attractiveness of clever theoretical postulations of the dominant economic ideology to the point that glaring contradictions in the objective reality go unnoticed.

The problem of a weak political will is a common factor in dominant explanations of slow progress in economic integration, but on closer examination it emerges that by this is meant a poor commitment by governments and the political elite to champion neoliberal economic dogma. It is said they are reluctant to liberalise economies and surrender sovereignty over macro-economic policymaking to regional authorities.[14] This latter point about ceding sovereignty seems to be in complete agreement with the Pan-Africanist explanations of the integration conundrum, but the divergence is that for the latter this is linked to creating strong supranational states that would drive strong industrial development and strengthen Africa's voice and choice in international relations. In the dominant paradigm, by sovereignty it is meant economic policy sovereignty, for other elements of sovereignty relating to strengthening political authority are frowned up. So, the agenda is to take away from states control over economic policy and thus de-link it from this strong sense of national sovereignty.

The slow progress in negotiations on tariffs in some regional economic communities in Africa is said to be "probably indicative of a lack of political commitment to liberalization."[15] Weak developmental outcomes coming out of otherwise stable integration schemes like the Southern African Development Community and East African Community are also ascribed to the absence of strong and sustained political will to take hard decisions regarding tariffs, customs and non-tariff barriers. But it is not explained what their fears are. It is not made clear what trade-offs are inevitable in the process of taking the difficult decisions envisaged and what bearing these undertakings would have on economically weak countries in the context of globalisation. There is generally very little attempt to understand the reasoning or fears that these governments and political leaders have, but their reluctance comes across as irrational.

The reasons proffered for the renewed focus and momentum in regional integration in the 1990s and 2000s are based on the assumption that neoliberal economic models now hold sway and are the only successful response to globalisation. It is argued quite leisurely that African countries are increasingly showing greater political will to overcome the above-mentioned constraining factors and to accelerate integration as a direct consequence of the spread of the Washington Consensus in Africa. In keeping with the teachings of neoliberal theory, it is said that economies that open up their markets with the assistance of Western-dominated Bretton Wood Institutions create a conducive environment for economic cooperation with each other. It is assumed that outward-looking economic policies that form part of the package of neoliberal economic reforms imposed by these institutions promote openness, which in this view is the overriding reason for integration. Trade liberalization is seen as particularly catalytic motivation for the new-found interest in integration in Africa.[16]

In this sense, the succession of major African decisions regarding integration, from the Lagos Plan of Action of 1980 through the Abuja Treaty on the Establishment of the African Economic Community in 1991 to the New Partnership for Africa's Development in 2002, relate solely to Africa's embrace of neoliberalism and nothing else. Thus, these initiatives are divorced from two very crucial processes and ideas that influenced decisions about them: South-South cooperation and Pan-Africanism. The reason is that these ideas may have a disruptive effect on the narrative of liberalisation and neoliberalism because the alternative ideas are founded on the logic of a search for decoloniality of existence and development in which must be included the African pursuit for continental self-reliance and the Global South's search for collective self-reliance.

Neoliberal Turns in the Global Coloniality Project

We argue here that predominantly the perspectives on regional integration and African unity invite the reader to see neoliberal economics as the only way to development. And this is not an accidental trait of this type of thinking, but is part of the very DNA of the global designs that neoliberalism provides a paradigm for, exported as a universally applicable ideology on economy and development.

Neoliberalism was born out of the broader Western pursuit of dominance, as were global capitalism and colonialism. Before one is accused of using the term 'neoliberalism' loosely, it is crucial to explain the context that gives the concept its contours, useful for understanding the challenges of integration and unity in Africa. The concept signifies a sort of a revival of old liberalism, an ideology it shares roots and its essential vocabulary with, but it is somewhat distinct.[17] Of course, the distinction is not significant except within the broad liberalism school of thought where the difference between 'pure' liberalism and neoliberalism matters. In critical studies in Africa and other parts of the developing world, the concept is used to refer to economic liberalism, the belief that states should not intervene in the economy, but should leave the economy to free and self-regulated markets.

The ideology for global capitalism is an inextricable part of the colonial/modern and Euro-centred project. In this sense, globalisation has a specific historical context that gives it two key features: one is the spread and deepening of a capitalist system of economy and the other is non-economic, being the homogenisation of plurality of thought and diversity of cultures and civilisations under Western modernity.[18] In this sense, globalisation is not a post-imperialist era, but a phase in the evolution of imperialism because like earlier phases its locomotive is the spread and deepening of capitalism and the growing distinction between the affluent centre, mostly in the West, and the poor periphery in the former colonial territories. Technological revolutions, transformations of capital, transformations of labour, financialisation of the global economy, and a neoliberal model of economic development all represent key features of this process.[19] In this sense, the neoliberal project shares its roots with the liberal project before it, and both sprang out of the same process, sometimes called imperialism and sometimes termed modernity.[20]

As a project of Western modernity, neoliberal globalisation has a darker and a lighter side. The lighter side refers to the positive outcomes or economic and material benefits for some, derived from the faster movement of goods and factors of production, the uses of technology and innovations, accumulation of capital and so forth. The darker side is what Anibal Quijano terms *coloniality*,[21] which is the colonial matrix of power in which non-Western peripheries are responsible for propping up the affluent Western centre, what Walter Mignolo calls 'the hidden agenda' of Western modernity.[22]

As Mignolo shows, in the post-war economic realm the matrix of power manifested itself in unidirectional orders from the International Monetary Fund, the World Bank, the White House, the Elysee Palace, or Number 10 Downing Street, and so forth.[23] What binds these institutions together is a neoliberal paradigm of development, which is a component of the civilising mission of Western modernity. This finds expression in a set of measures uniformly imposed on debt-stricken poor countries looking for capital from international financial institutions to help them cope with balance of payment challenges or to stimulate their economies. These measures form part of the Washington Consensus, whose purpose is to support neoliberal globalisation.[24] For instance, debt-stricken countries were required to undertake painful austerity measures, cutting back on state funding for social goals, privatising state enterprises and key services like water and energy, and decentralising government as part of what was called economic structural adjustment programmes.

The neoliberal measures continue to be directed at former colonial territories and countries elsewhere whose economic difficulties qualify them for a place in the global periphery. Professor Williamson, who developed the Washington Consensus in the first place, recalls that the consensus meant that the big wigs in Washington, and to some extent in London, agreed that "there are no longer two competing economic development paradigms" and the hegemonic paradigm was the message that the Bretton Wood institutions needed to promote. There was, therefore, also consensus "on what the developing countries should do."[25] Of course, as late as 2004, when he explains this, he did not see it as anomalous that Western powers were having a consensus about development in the developing world without their input or consent. This assumption was not an isolated behaviour of a small group of ignorant economists, but was very much embedded in the West's view of itself in relation to others (the non-

West). This self-view is an integral part of coloniality or supremacist Western modernity. Quijano explains how this came about like this:

> The success of Western Europe in becoming the center of the modern world-system […] developed within the Europeans a trait common to all colonial dominators and imperialists, ethnocentrism. But in the case of Western Europe, that trait had […] the racial classification of the world population after the colonization of America. The association of colonial ethnocentrism and universal racial classification helps to explain why Europeans came to feel not only superior to all the other peoples of the world, but, in particular, naturally superior. That perspective imagined modernity and rationality as exclusively European products and experiences.

These neoliberal measures designed to serve the darker side of Western modernity, as far as the periphery is concerned, combined with the weaknesses of African politics and leadership to further weaken the power and capacity of the state to protect and promote endogenous development policies. Elite politics and states converge easily with an ideological-cum-policy consensus designed without participation of non-Western societies.[26] Often times, weaker countries succumbed to the pressures and adopted neoliberal measures in the hopes of stronger macro-economic conditions and a reduction in poverty and inequality, but only saw stabilisation of macro-economics lead to even deeper poverty.

African and non-African civic formations have been involved in efforts to resist and subvert this imposition of the Western paradigm of development and economics on debt-stricken African countries. They have been part of transnational social movements opposed to the tendency of globalisation to reproduce the coloniality of power by which an affluent centre and poor peripheries are perpetuated. This de-linking from the idea that Western modernity is the only single way to develop is what Mignolo has called decolonial cosmopolitanism.[27] The dominant paradigm of cosmopolitanism drawn from Immanuel Kant's philosophy and made universal through imperialism promotes global diversity based on a hierarchy of power and culture where the imperial centre has a pride of place. Decolonial or reflexive cosmopolitanism is in nature a dialogical and pluralist paradigm of cosmopolitanism, advocating an end to the imperial version and in its place a diversity of cultures, loci of power and knowledge.

The integration theories we use to understand and interpret African integration do not promote this reflexive form of cosmopolitan thinking, but seek to impose a cosmopolitanism of Western ways and views of life, as other ways and views do not have the right to exist. They allow diversity of data sources without a diversity of lenses through which such sources are interpreted. They multiply within alterity and keep the subaltern and decolonial perspectives and ways silent. There has not been a break between dominant integration theories and methodologies and the paradigm formed out of the analysis of the making of the German empire in the 19th century. The framework borrows heavily from the lessons learned from the unification process that created a hegemonic super-state, replicated in the 20th century by Germany and France in the initiation of the integration of Europe. As theories of economic liberalism began to imagine advanced levels of global capitalism, they interpreted the integration as following the rules of science and politics followed by the Germans and Europeans. The following quote illustrates this:

> The technical stages of the process (the progressive customs union, the emergence of a common market and of a dominant, then of a single currency, the diversification and specialization of the economic geography) have been severed from their political stages (the rise of Prussia, the exclusion of Austria, the defeat of France) and offered up as preconditions for integration, and not as consequences of a politics of integration. Yet if truth be said, the German integration process was more a function of political necessity than of economic requirements.[28]

In this sense, the dominant frameworks of analysis are joined together by this European experience interlaced with economic liberalism, and propagated directly and indirectly in the global periphery as part of imperial cosmopolitanism, or the homogenisation of the world after the Western way of things. In this sense, integration is conceived of as being in furtherance of globalisation rather than as a form of coping against it or delinking in order to create space for endogenous economic development, as originally envisaged in Pan-Africanist thought.

Thus, even the scholarship on African integration within Africa still affirms Western modernity as the only legitimate prism for understanding life and how it progresses while marginalising others.[29] Bernard Magubane makes no distinction between the current state of scholarship in the social and human sciences and the "intellectual cannibalism" that accompanied imperialism and colonialism.[30] Race underpinned the latter more openly than is the case today. In this sense, he says, concepts and categories invented to understand Africa were to social scientists what roads, railroads and harbours were to colonial administrators charged with establishing the imperial hegemony. On this question, Quijano suggests, "The racial axis has a colonial origin and character, but it has proven to be more durable and stable than the colonialism in whose matrix it was established."[31]

Thus, traditions of scholarships emanating from imperial designs continue to deny Africans their voice and choices, including in regard to what we mean and do to pursue regional integration. Magubane argues that because race was central to the construction of the imperial hegemony and the very making of South African and African scholarship in general, there is no possibility of epistemic emancipation without deconstructing this in whatever disguise it comes.

Of course, many fail to see this hierarchy of knowledge and cosmopolitanisation of Western modernity in scholarship on African affairs because this is a hidden agenda camouflaged as common sense and rationality. Thus, we easily accept the automatic view that the political will of African leaders and their failure to implement 'recommended' policies are mainly responsible for the slow progress in regional integration, for weak intra-African trade, and for the peripheral role of Africa in a globalised world. In this sense, African agency in the creation of these problems is emphasised to the point of absolving the world system and external imposition of their role in frustrating African integration. The assumption is that because the origin of problems is internal, the solutions that work must come from Western historical experiences, and this is called "international best practice." Thus, we African scholars assume that the concepts and categories we use are valueless signifiers of phenomena we analyse and are designed to help us to genuinely understand the African integration conundrum.

But as Archie Mafeje shows, we ought to be conscious of the impact of categories and concepts as epistemic lenses in themselves. He says,

> The fashionable 'free-floating signifier' is an illusion in a double sense. First, nobody can think and act outside historically determined circumstances and still hope to be a social signifier of any kind. In other words, while we are free to choose the role in which we cast ourselves as active agents of history, we do not put on the agenda social issues to which we respond. These are imposed on us by history. For example, we would not talk freedom, if there was no prior condition in which this was denied; we would not be anti-racism if we had not been its victims.[32]

Africa-Centredness: Methodological Possibilities

It is for this reason that it is of necessity for students of African integration to view the process from below or from within Africa, while being open to the applicability of insights generated elsewhere on that basis. This is because the process and concepts used to conceptualise and operationalize integration in Africa are born out of historically determined circumstances that need reinterpreting from the point of view of Africa if we are to fully understand why the integration process remains in limbo and why the analyses of it are less than illuminating about this. These analyses, we propose, would be more illuminating if they were not founded on what Jinmi Adesina calls "the erasure of memory and closure of history" that define dominant scholarly perspectives on African phenomena,[33] the denial of space to perspectives informed by Afrocentric epistemic lenses. Indeed, the challenge is bigger than concepts and categories used in the analysis of integration in Africa, for it relates to the very rubric of dominant paradigms in social science scholarship out of which analyses of integration are born. Adesina's point about sociology, like Magubane on anthropology, and Paulin Hountodji on philosophy, applies to international relations and African politics: At some point, "[s]cholarship became little more than proselytising and regurgitating received discourses — left or bourgeois — no matter how poorly they explain our lived experiences."[34] This has been the crisis of the analysis of African integration and unity for decades now.

The point that Mafeje makes repeatedly is that we would not proclaim Africanity, if it was not denied or degraded as an ontological centre, and we would not insist on Afrocentric methodologies, if not for Eurocentric negations. So, it is the historical juncture, which defines us socially and intellectually, that makes it imperative for us to be Afrocentric in our analysis. Unless and until we understand this, he contends, there cannot be an emancipatory methodological approach to the study of African phenomena.

On this, Mafeje further avers there can be no African renaissance without "a conscious rejection of past transgressions, a determined negation of negations." So, Afrocentricity or what he prefers to call endogeneity is a methodological "antidote to Eurocentricism through which all knowledge about Africa has been filtered."[35] In this sense, Africanity "is nothing more than a legitimate demand that African scholars study their society from inside and cease to be purveyors of alienated intellectual discourse." In his view, "It is logical to suppose that when Africans speak for themselves and about themselves the world will hear the authentic voice, and will be forced to come to terms with it in the long run."[36] This is nothing but to accept that Africans can speak for themselves in ways that are authentically their own, even if they choose to appropriate fitting pieces of their thinking from elsewhere as necessary.

The various Afrocentric methodological options are joined together by a few theoretical constructs that they share among them, concepts that offer possibilities for better understanding the integration phenomenon.

Unmasking Coloniality

This is about the need to unmask the deleterious, constraining, distorting and obfuscating effects of received or imposed perspectives. This is generally called the epistemology of alterity from which are born methodological options that treat Africans as subordinate others, that erase their historical memory, negate their cultural context and ontological density, and subsumes their thought patterns to Western modernity. We have already described the implications of this in the review of literature on integration above. The point we made was simple: the dominant paradigms fit African lived experiences and objective realities into epistemic or methodological straightjackets designed for the Western experience. As a result, they limit our ability to explain deviations from received theories that are evident in the story of African integration. So, the first step towards epistemic plurality and giving space for Afrocentric voice in the analysis is to conduct what Walter Mignolo calls "an analytic of the limits of Eurocentrism (as a hegemonic structure of knowledge and beliefs)," which he contends is a necessary first step to decolonial thought.[37]

Delinking from or Unthinking Eurocentrism

This is what Mafeje aptly describes as the Afrocentric negation of Eurocentric negations without replication of the hegemonic tendencies of Eurocentrism. The distinction between this and unmasking is not self-evident, but is necessary for purposes of explanation. It is possible to unmask coloniality without engaging necessarily in a decolonial combat with it. There are many Eurocentric theories that unmask many distortions in Eurocentric thinking without challenging the whole of Eurocentrism, for instance, theories that decry the neglect of class analysis or individuals' ability to construct their own social reality or environmental or political economic questions, but do not extend to questioning the foundational motifs in the Eurocentric story, including Western modernity and the Manichean subject. These critical theories are critical within rather than outside Eurocentrism simply because Eurocentrism must be seen as a heterogeneous phenomenon with many layers in the hierarchy within itself. Therefore, Afrocentric methodological options offer possibilities to conduct negation on negations, the corrective exercise, without at the same time defending by omission or commission the foundational myths of Western modernity. Describing this, Walter Mignolo says, "'De-linking' is then necessary because there is no way out of the coloniality of power from within Western (Greek and Latin) categories of thought."[38] This is not a turn to nativism that harks back to some pure and glorious past, or anachronistic nationalism that tends reproduce coloniality through notions of nationhood and national sovereignty that preserve colonial territorial logics or fundamentalism that replicates the binary propositions of Eurocentricism. Rather the intention is to appropriate, subsume and redefine the emancipatory rhetoric of modernity in order to understand citizenship, democracy, economic relations, human rights and humanity beyond the narrow definitions of European modernity. This makes it possible to study Africa from inside and to generate endogenous intellectual discourses and thus enable Africans to speak for themselves about themselves in a non-hegemonic conversation with the world. In this sense, delinking or unthinking alterity offers opportunities for a decolonial turn in African scholarship.[39]

The Agency of the African Centre

Another pillar of Afrocentric methodology is the affirmation of the agency of Africans who have lived experiences of the phenomena we study. If the above pillar is a challenge to alterity, the latter pillar is a demand for African phenomena to be understood inside out. It is an expectation that the analyses are based on a good understanding of the ability of Africans and African institutions to be actors, subjects in the making of their history, rather than objects of Western history and culture. Of course, they do so in contexts that are historically determined and circumstances that are not always of their choosing. So, this is not to suggest that they are not constrained; in fact, even the story of structural limitations and determinism is better told from their vantage point and relationship with what they do or do not do about it. For this reason, the idea is not to allow subtle spaces for Eurocentric negations under the idea that Africans, too, are guilty of problems and therefore responsible for solutions, as the idea of African solutions for African problems can sometimes imply. Instead, it is to recognise that Africans have authentic voices that can speak through our analyses when we are attentive enough. Such speaking is not just in quotes from interviews or discovery of untouched indigenous material or some pure precolonial or recorded voices, but it is in the manner in which we do the reading and the approach to the redeeming in our studies. It is about affirming Africa and Africanness as a frame of reference capable of offering deeper insights on complex phenomena playing out in Africa. It is about accepting the ability of Africans to self-write without extending this to uncritical adulation.

African Integration and Agency

The rationale, challenges and advances of the African integration agenda are best understood on the basis of unmasking the veil of Eurocentrism that foregrounds the European experience as a framework of reference on key variables from the model and phases of integration to the relationship between and sequence of political and economic integration. We have already presented examples of how Eurocentric theories of integration that dominate the study of African integration represent incomplete insights into the rationale and approach to integration in Africa.

The assumptions that the African integration process relates squarely, positively or negatively, to various phases of functionalist theories of institutions and integration erase an important part of the African historical memory: the imaginations of Pan-Africanists at various stages in the 20th century. The point is that it is often argued or assumed that the push by leaders like Nyerere in the 1970s or Qadaffi and Museveni in the 2000s for continental or regional political integration were ill-advised because they violated the rules formulated by functionalist and neofunctionalist theories of integration. This dominant thinking is derived from work of David Mitrany and Ernst Haas that showed, on the basis of the EU experience, that the key drivers of regional integration are exogenous factors, especially the technical nature of the problem being solved—usually matters related to the movement of goods and services or demand for integrated services—rather than internal dynamics within a region. In this sense, integration is seen as a quasi-automatic process. So, as the demand for integrated services increases and as associated activities spill over to linked sectors not yet integrated, the impetus for integration also increases.[40] Economic integration then leads to political integration in a sequence of phases, when political actors at the national level are persuaded to shift their loyalties and expectations towards the already existing new centre, which needs jurisdiction over the pre-existing nation states.[41]

The Pan-Africanist paradigms on integration see an inextricable link between political and economic integration rather than a sequence of phases that must follow each other. Kwame Nkrumah, the first president of independent Ghana, put it this way:

> Never before have a people had within their grasp so great an opportunity for developing a continent endowed with so much wealth. Individually, the independent states of Africa, some of them potentially rich, others poor, can do little for their people. Together, by mutual help, they can achieve much. But the economic development of the continent must be planned and pursued as a whole. A loose confederation designed only for economic co-operation would not provide the necessary unity of purpose. Only a strong political union can bring about full and effective development of our natural resources for the benefit of our people.[42]

In this sense, African unity was viewed as strategic in and of itself. It was considered a necessary undoing of a colonial legacy of fragmentation in which very little could be achieved for the good of Africa. The economic benefits of this and economic integration were some of the outcomes expected to flow from political unity. The argument made, which remains a strong element of the Afrocentric proposition on integration, was that the statehood inherited from colonialism was simply inappropriate for the process of decolonisation and development. Key African leaders were not in agreement about the route to take towards such political integration, with the Nkrumah-led group arguing for an immediate proclamation for a unitary state and Mwalimu Julius Nyerere in the group for a gradual process of integration, but not on whether political unity per se was paramount or not.[43]

As is evident in the quotation above and quite common in exchanges on Pan-Africanism among early independence African leaders, political unity would foster mutual help among new African countries. Key to this is the ability of the continent to devise continent-wide plans for its development because its underdevelopment was partly seen as an artefact of a nationalistic approach to development. For this reason, Nkrumah rejects the idea of mere economic cooperation among newly independent countries because he considered it to be a deviation from the fundamental imperative for political integration in its own right.

The view is that political integration is imperative for purposes of correcting the positioning of Africa in a changing world. For this reason, in the same piece, Nkrumah argued, "The emergence of such a mighty stabilising force in this strife-worn world should be regarded not as the shadowy dream of a visionary, but as a practical proposition, which the peoples of Africa can, and should, translate into reality."[44] This is a fundamentally significant impetus for integration, for in this it becomes a form of agency by Africa in shaping the international system and order with a view to position Africa together with others at a centre that is without a periphery. In this sense, it is in contrast to the Eurocentric paradigm mainly propagated by the ubiquitous functionalist theories, where integration is conceptualised as a mechanism to ease and accelerate the insertion of the marginalised into the global periphery in order to reinforce the centre-periphery dynamic undergirding global capitalism in its current form.

The fact that there had then not been a birth of a post-colonial world (and it is yet to emerge to this day) justified the need to maintain a focus on decolonising the global order by undoing global hierarchies and heterarchies that have been built over centuries of the darker side of Western modernity, which is imperialism and colonialism. Even before exposure to dependency theories that flourished in the 1970s and 80s, Pan-Africanists like Nkrumah had understood that, seen over the *longue durée,* the global economy and politics constitute a system with a centre and a periphery, the latter being mainly former colonial territories, meaning also the whole of Africa. This system is a product of the West having been able to take advantage of its control over the world economy to establish the hegemony of its culture, ideas/knowledge and political institutions, thus directly contributing to structural inequality between them and others and inequalities within countries.[45]

For this reason, to paraphrase Nkrumah, the main focus of African affairs for decades was on seeking first the political kingdom. The economic ramifications of this are self-evident, but are not the primary and overriding motivation. The strengthening of the OAU was not an end in itself because the OAU itself was not the end, but a compromise *en route* to a full union, and also because a strong OAU would enhance unity of purpose and action for the benefit of its members. In this sense, the criticism that the OAU years failed to focus on economic integration should also include an explanation that the agenda was to undo fragmentation as the basis for such integration. In fact, the criticism misses the point that actually the OAU had blueprints for acceleration of continental development founded on self-reliance and integration through sub-regions—the Lagos Plan of Action and the Abuja Treaty, but these failed partly because the global and continental environment was not propitious and partly because of the anachronism of African nationalism that flourished in the independence period. The climate of the Cold War with the tendency of powers to scaffold states that joined their camps weakened commitment and the effect of intra-African consensus. Neoliberal structural adjustment programmes worked directly opposite the Pan-Africanist ideals. The anachronistic character of African nationalisms became a key defence for the colonial heritage of unviable states, arbitrary borders and insularity, and thus helped frustrate African unity and regional integration efforts. Jean-Francois Bayart reminds us that "Africans here were active agents in *mise en dépendence* of their societies, sometimes opposing and at other times joining in it."[46]

The African Union, which succeeded the OAU, does not represent a full jettisoning of the idea that political integration is needed as the basis for fruitful and beneficial economic integration. Instead, it is a consolidation of the work of the OAU on political unity and integration by building deeper consensus on the continent in the hope of bringing about full unity and self-reliance. There is better integration of economic development, rights and democracy issues in the AU following reflections on the next phase of the integration process after the OAU achieved its mandate on independence with the freedom of South Africa in 1994. This takes the form of a more prominent mentioning of socio-economic matters in the founding document, a continental development plan in the New Partnership for Africa's Development (NEPAD) and a stronger institutional structure at the heart of the AU for social and economic development, including commissioners responsible for coordinating policy implementation in these sectors.

Conclusion

The process of integration in Africa remains in progress, and the hope remains that as Africa unites politically, the economic integration will find real meaning. The strengthening of the AU, the Regional Economic Communities and the relationship between them remains the key focus of the Pan-Africanist agenda. This can be easily misunderstood or inadequately understood if studied through a Eurocentric lens because such a vantage point is founded on the homogenising of perspectives, which prevents the emergence of epistemic plurality. It is part of the coloniality of knowledge by which the possibility of voices from below and views from within is made difficult. Thus, dominant perspectives on integration in Africa seek to validate Eurocentric theories by fitting the integration story into a rigid framework born out of the successful, but European experience, without much regard to differences in context, conditions and cultures.

Therefore, a decolonial turn is needed in the study of African politics in general, and in the integration story in particular. Such a turn involves de-linking from Eurocentrism in order to enable the flourishing of perspectives that seek to understand African phenomena from within and to give Africans an authentic voice among the world's voices on integration and development. We sought to show how Afrocentric methodologies in their variety offer useful opportunities for such a decolonial turn by affirming the locatedness, centredness and agency of Africans in their experiences, while unmasking the orientalising Eurocentric perspectives.

Indeed, whereas the fundamental logic in the Eurocentric prism is economic, in elements of Afrocentric decolonial thought it has wider implications for the broader struggle for the full emancipation of Africa and Africans from all forms of coloniality so that Africa could contribute to transforming the world, with a view to realising the possibility of decolonial cosmopolitanism of nations. In this sense, it is part of the healing of Africa and Africa healing the world.

Notes and References

1. Geda, A. and Kibret, H., 2002. Regional Economic Integration in Africa: A Review of Problems and Prospects with a Case Study of COMESA,' SOAS Working Paper, June. Available at http://www.soas.ac.uk/economics/research/workingpapers/file28853.pdf (accessed on 12 February 2013).

2. Wallerstein, I. (1989). *The Modern World—System III*, San Diego: Academic Press.

3. Amin, S. (2002). 'Africa: Living of the Fringes,' *Monthly Review*, March.

4. Wallerstein, *The Modern World-System III*, p. 3.

5. Some of the major literature is reviewed in glowing terms by Lyakurwa, et. al., 1997. 'Regional Integration in Sub-Saharan Africa: A Review of Experiences and Issues' in Oyejide, Ademola, Ibrahim Elbadawi and Collier, P. (eds.) Regional Integration and Trade Liberalization in Sub-Saharan Africa, Volume I: Framework, Issues and Methodological Perspectives. London: Macmillan.

6. See, for instance, the slant of the perspective on this in an influential OECD research paper published in 2001. Longo, R. and Sekkat, K., 2001. 'Obstacles to Expanding Intra-African Trade', OECD Technical Paper No. 169, Paris: OECD.

7. Geda and Kibret, 'Regional Economic Integration,' p. 19.

8. Foroutan, F. and Pritchett, L., 1993. 'Intra-Sub-Saharan African Trade: is it too Little?', *Journal of African Economies*, 2(1), pp. 74–105.

9. See, for instance, Khandelwal, P. (2004). 'COMESA and SADC: Prospects and Challenges for Regional Trade Integration,' IMF Working Paper 04/227, Washington: IMF; and Iqbal, Z., and Khan, M. (eds.), (1997). *Trade Reform and Regional Integration in Africa*, Washington: International Monetary Fund.

10. This theoretical postulation is borrowed rather too literally from Baldwin's assessment of very specific conditions in the West. See Baldwin, R., 2003. 'Openness and Growth: What's the Empirical Relationship,' NBER Working Paper No. 9578, Cambridge, Mass.: National Bureau of Economic Research.

11. See, for example, how the World Bank popularizes the low growth-protection thesis in World Bank, (2004). *Global Economic Prospects 2005: Trade, Regionalism and Development*, Washington: World Bank.

12. Subramanian, A., Gelbard, E., Harmsen, R., Elborgh-Woytek, K. and P. Nagy, (2000). 'Trade and Trade Policies in Eastern and Southern Africa,' IMF Occasional Paper No.196, Washington: International Monetary Fund.

13. 'IMF Reports Strong Economic Growth in Sub-Saharan Africa,' http://www.voanews.com/english/archive/2006-04/2006-04-22-voa1.cfm?CFID=9018 5405&CFTOKEN=56930731 (accessed on 3 April 2008).

14. Lyakurwa *et al.*, 'Regional Integration,' p. 176.

15. Geda and Kibret, 'Regional Economic Integration,' p. 12.

16. See, for instance, Geda and Kibret, 'Regional Economic Integration,' pp. 2–3.

17. For a fuller discussion of the difficulties presented by the term for those concerned with the continuum of ideas that define the West's relations with the world, see Thorsen, D.E. and Lie, A. 'What is neoliberalism.' Available at http://folk.uio.no/daget/What%20 is%20Neo-Liberalism%20FINAL.pdf. (accessed on 23 March 2013).

18. I borrow this characterization from Amin, S. (1996). 'The Challenge of Globalisation,' *International Review of Political Economy*, 3 (2), ps. 216.

19. This is a condensed summation of Amin, S. 'The Alternative to the neoliberal system of globalization and militarism Imperialism Today and the Hegemonic Offensive of the United States,' Unpublished Paper Presented at Cubasiglo XXI Congress, 25 February 2003.

20. The concept of coloniality was first introduced by Anibal Quijano through a chapter of the same title in a 1992 book on entitled, *Los Conquistados*'.

21. Quijano, A. (2007). 'Coloniality and Modernity/Rationality', *Cultural Studies*, 21 (2–3), pp. 155–67.

22. Mignolo, W. undated. 'Coloniality: the darker side of modernity.' Available at http://www.macba.cat/PDFs/walter_mignolo_modernologies_eng.pdf (accessed on 6 April 2011).

23. Mignolo, W.D., (2009). 'Cosmopolitanism and the De-Colonial Option', *Studies in Philosophy and Education.* 29(2), p. 112.

24. Rodrik, D., (2006). 'Goodbye Washington Consensus, Hello Washington Confusion?,' Unpublished Paper, Harvard University, January.

25. Williamson, J. (2004). 'A Short History of the Washington Consensus', Paper commissioned by Fundación CIDOB for a conference "From the Washington Consensus towards a new Global Governance," Barcelona, September 24–25.

26. See, for instance, Olukoshi, A.O., (2011). Democratic Governance and Accountability in Africa in Search of a Workable Framework, Discussion Paper 64, Nordiska Afrikainstitutet, Uppsala, pp. 9–10.

27. Mignolo, W.D., (2009). 'Cosmopolitanism and the De-Colonial Option', *Studies in Philosophy and Education.* 29(2), p. 111.

28. Idrissa, A. Divided Commitment: UEMOA, the Franc Zone, and ECOWAS, Unpublished Research Paper. Available at www.princeton.edu/-pcglobal/conferences/GLF/Idrissa_glf.doc (accessed on 23 April 2013).

29. Magubane, B.M. (2007). *Race and the Construction of the Indispensable Other,* Pretoria: HSRC.

30. Magubane, *Race and the Construction of the Indispensable Other,* p. 5.

31. Quijano, A., (2000). "Coloniality of Power, Eurocentrism and Latin America." *Nepantla: Views from South* 1 (3), pp. 533–580.

32. Mafeje, A. (2011). 'A Combative Ontology,' in Devisch, R. and Nyamnjoh, F.B. (eds.). *Postcolonial Turn: Imagining Anthropology and Africa,* Bamenda and Leiden: Langaa, p. 32.

33. Adesina, O.O., (2006). 'Sociology, Endogeneity and the Challenge of Transformation,' *African Sociological Review,* 10, (2), p.137.

34. Adesina, 'Sociology,' p. 138.

35. Mafeje, 'A Combative Ontology,' p. 33.

36. *Ibid,* p. 32.

37. Mignolo, W., (2011). 'Epistemic Disobedience and the De-Colonial Option: A Manifesto,' *Transmodernity,* Fall, p. 45.

38. *Ibid.*

39. This is what Walter Mignolo describes as the value of epistemic disobedience. See Mignolo, 'Epistemic Disobedience,' p. 46.

40. Haas, E.B., (1991). 'Does constructivism subsume neo-functionalism?', in T. Christiansen, K.E. Jorgensen and A. Wiener (eds.), *The Social Construction of Europe,* Thousand Oaks: Sage Publications, p. 23.

41. Farrell, H. and Heritier, A., (2005). 'Rationalist-institutionalist explanation of endogenous regional integration, *Journal of European Public Policy,* 12 (2), April, pp. 273–90.

42. Nkrumah, K. (1961). *I Speak of Freedom: A Statement of African Ideology,* London: William Heinemann Ltd., p. xii.

43. Professor Issa Shivji makes this point aptly in his analysis of Nkrumah-Nyerere dynamic in Pan-Africanism. See Shivji, I., (2009). 'Pan-Africanism in Nyerere Thought,' *Third World Resurgence,* Dakar: Third World Network.

44. *Ibid.*

45. Immanuel Wallerstein has consistently argued the point that there is a world system and the logic of its organization gives rise to a core-periphery dynamic. See, for instance, Wallerstein, *The Modern World-System III*.

46. Bayart, J.F., (1993). *The State in Africa: The Politics of the Belly*, Harlow: Longman, p. 22.

Index

T

tariffs, 246–7
Teboho, xii, 45, 47
teleological suspension, 118–20, 123–5, 234
tendencies, 18, 114, 138, 151–2, 161
testimonial injustice, 196–7
    pre-emptive, 196–8
testimonies, giving, 202, 212
Thabo Mbeki African Leadership Institute (TMALI), xii
theodicy, 122–5
theories, 24, 44–5, 57–8, 123, 125–6, 133–4, 148–9, 163–6, 169–70, 172, 176–8, 183–4, 191–3, 232–5, 241–2
theorists, 132–3, 170
theorizing, 19, 167–8, 171–5, 177
Theory, Culture & Society, 163–4, 178
thinking subject, 140
Thiong'o, Ngugi wa, 5, 22, 24, 32, 34, 44, 85, 86–7, 90–2, 94, 95–6, 98, 101–3, 105
Third World, 23, 61, 65, 69, 73, 89, 108, 151–4, 158–63, 184, 188, 200
Third World approach, 81
Third World Approaches to International Law *see* TWAIL
Third World Quarterly, 23, 44
Third World states, 71, 74, 77
TMALI (Thabo Mbeki African Leadership Institute), xii
tourism, 18, 151–4, 156–7, 159, 161–3
    discipline of, 159, 162

    practice of, 151–2, 159, 161
    subject of, 151–2, 156
tourism industry, 161
tourism knowledge production, 154, 162
tourism research, 163–4
tourism studies, 18, 151–64
trade, slave, 7, 32–3, 41–2
traditions, oral, 200–1
train, 27, 203–4
trajectories, 14, 35, 200
transdisciplinarity, 12, 23, 107
transformation, 15, 21, 59, 62, 161, 192, 218, 248, 261
    disciplinary, 39, 146
transforming education in South Africa, 61
transmodernity, 23, 43, 104–5, 129, 164, 234, 261
treaties, 16, 66–7, 70, 79
Treaty of Westphalia, 32, 66, 69
tribes, 41, 100, 142, 148, 152, 156, 163–4
TWAIL (Third World Approaches to International Law), 15, 65, 74–5, 77–8

U

UCT (University of Cape Town), 4, 62
UN (United Nations), 16, 30, 66, 69, 71, 75–9, 81
UN Charter, 67–8, 70–1, 75, 78–80
UN Commission on Trade and Development (UNCTAD), 245
UN Economic Commission for Africa (UNECA), 245

Kwame Nkrumah.
Ngugi wa Thiong'o

William DuBois

Jean Paul Satre
Kizito Muchemwa → Chimurenga aristocracy
Albert Memi

Claude Ake → Africa!
Kwasi Wiredu → Know thyself.